CO-LABORERS, CO-HEIRS

A FAMILY CONVERSATION

BRITTANY SMITH

DOUG SERVEN

The proceeds generated from this book will benefit women in ministry in the Presbyterian Church in America.

Book profits will be donated to the Reformed University Fellowship fund that provides matching grants for female Campus Staff working on college campuses in vocational ministry.

See ruf.org for more information.

"Where Are the Women?" by Caroline West was adapted from "Feminism and Women's Leadership in the Church." *The Dialectic*, vol. 1, no. 3, 2017. Used with permission.

"Jesus Loves All the Women" by Emily Hubbard was adapted from two previously published essays. Used with permission.

"Complementarians, Egalitarians, and a Third Way" by Scott Sauls was adapted from chapter 6 in *Jesus Outside the Lines, Revised and Expanded Edition* (Tyndale House Publishers). Used with permission.

Published by White Blackbird Books, an imprint of Storied Publishing

Permission requests and other questions may be directed to the Contact page at www.storied.pub.

Unless otherwise indicated, Scripture quotations are from the ESV Bible (The Holy Bible, English Standard Version), copyright 2001 by Crossway, a publishing ministry of Good News Publishers. 2011 Text Edition. All rights reserved.

Printed in the United States of America

ISBN-13:978-1-7335921-5-4

Cover design by Caroline Clark

Edited by Claire Berger, Paige Britton, Julie Serven

This is a wonderful, much-needed book. The story of Emma and the movement acknowledging women should be in ministry is worth far more than the price of the book. It is a book every pastor and elder should have to read before taking up their office and before making any decisions about whether or not women should serve in ministry. Of course they should! They are indeed fellow-laborers in God's kingdom and are needed in every church in the world.

Jerram Barrs, Professor, Covenant Theological Seminary, St. Louis, Missouri

This is a necessary and valid discussion that won't go away simply because it's uncomfortable. We are all members of one body and as such, need to continue to attend to each other with care and genuine concern. This book asks the question, "How can we do this better?" One of the authors encourages us to do so by being intentional, humble, and charitable. Since those are three of my favorite words, that seems like a great place to start and return to over and over.

Elizabeth Miller Hayes, Author, *Ever Light and Dark: Telling Secrets, Telling the Truth*

Every word here resounds with love for the Body of Christ and with a desire to see men and women working together in the ways God intends. Anyone who hopes for the PCA to flourish in the future ought to listen closely to these voices.

Amy Peterson, Author, *Dangerous Territory: My Misguided Quest to Save the World*

If we say we love the women in our churches, then we must listen to them. This collection of essays is an invaluable opportunity to do just that. The authors, who come from a range of backgrounds and life experiences, do not represent every Christian woman, but they likely represent some in your own congregation. Their words are theological, practical, and most of all, deeply personal—powerfully so. Lord willing, these stories will ignite a much needed public conversation about the

experience of women in theologically conservative churches. As a pastor seeking to honor our sisters and to empower them to serve and lead in my local church, I found *Co-Laborers, Co-Heirs* to be humbling, instructive, and a rich source of insight.
Duke Kwon, Pastor, Grace Meridian Hill, Washington, DC

It's hard for me to express how enthusiastically I'm recommending this book. As I read it, there were times that I took a screenshot and sent it with a *yes!!! this!!!* There were other times when it touched a deep hurt, and I realized how so much of what these sisters and brothers are saying about gender relationships in the church must be said. Women, you are not alone. Men, please hear our voices and don't give into an easy knee-jerk reaction by calling this liberalism or feminism. It's not. It's a call to do the hard work of finding ways to honor the imago Dei in us and utilize the gifts the Spirit has given us—all to the church's benefit.
Elyse Fitzpatrick, Author, *Finding the Love of Jesus from Genesis to Revelation*

While this book is largely written by women, its words are instructive for everyone. While the context of this book is the PCA, its message is immensely valuable to those in other denominations. Indeed, as a man serving in the Anglican Communion, I found myself challenged, heartened, and edified by the essays which comprise this beautifully written book. It deserves a wide, careful reading—I hope it gets just that.
Dustin Messer, Author, *Sacred Sacraments: Finding Grace in the World and Sin in the Church*

A great part of humility is listening. Here is a book from sisters and brothers in the Church telling their stories—stories of frustration, stories of service, and stories of grace. I have strong views based on Scripture about reserving church office to qualified men. However, in upholding that view, I have not always listened to or honored women in the Church as well as I could have. I am trying to do better. The biblical word for that is repentance, and this book is a valuable aid toward that end. While one does not have to agree with every conclusion reached, we are required by our Lord to listen, and to listen well, so that we do not miss out on the full breadth of gifts and wisdom that Christ gives to his Church. We are to remember King David, who submitted to Abigail, because she was right and he was wrong. In this book, we have a host of Abigails and their supporting brothers. May we listen well.

Christopher A. Hutchinson, Author, *Rediscovering Humility*

This book is timely, bold, and greatly needed for those of us ministering in the PCA. I was deeply moved by the stories of real women in our churches, and I cannot wait to read it with my own elders. I hope that conversations around these chapters will challenge us to consider ways the Gospel calls us to faithfully value women and their giftedness.

Scott Brown, Pastor, New Valley Church, Phoenix, Arizona

When I watched Clint Eastwood's great movie *Gran Torino*, I felt deeply thankful that someone held out love and hope for redemption for men like my father, instead of just scolding them. I felt something similar when I read *Co-Laborers, Co-Heirs*, but this time for me. I am basically the reason such a book needs to be written. I appreciate these authors and friends speaking with love and hope for redemption for me and for my beloved, dysfunctional church family. Reading these chapters gives me optimism about becoming a better co-laborer and co-heir of Jesus' grace.

Charles Garland, Pastor, Midtown Pres, Tucson, Arizona

Our culture is so incredibly confused about gender and family. How can our churches grow in Gospel impact in this culture, while continually living under the authority of Scripture? This book provides deep help in the form of a mirror on these issues. Each unique chapter reflects back to us how we are doing as the family of God. How can our church polity and practices help us more fully know, affirm, and honor our women as the gifted sisters in Christ that they are? We gain wise perspective by hearing well these gracious stories, written by women and men from different parts of the country, different ethnicities, and different stages of life. We all, men and women both, will do well to read it with courage, pushing past our fear of change. By seeing more clearly, we can act with compassion and serve more fully as Jesus' family.

Tasha Chapman, Professor, Educational Ministries, Covenant Theological Seminary, St. Louis, Missouri

The telling of Emma's story is compelling, insightful, and powerful. The plea is humble yet very convincing and lays out the essential need for change. This work represents my experience with countless women and presents a solid case for change. I cried as I read it for the many women who have been utterly alone and without a safe voice with men in leadership. This presentation is not likely to make men defensive or shut them down. May we go forward in the spirit of these writers.

Stephene Vanden Brink, MA, LPC, St. Louis, Missouri

As the broader culture is increasingly polarized and vitriolic, *Co-Laborers, Co-Heirs* serves the church well by giving voice to women to whom we need to listen and from whom we have much to learn.

Josh Hahne, Pastor, King of Kings, Goodyear, Arizona

As a complementarian, I find it easy for myself and others of my ilk to slip into a tacit paternalism. So, it is important for me to hear the voices of my sisters and brothers, allowing them to challenge my attitude and mindset. You will be enriched if you ponder these essays and reflect on the implications of their message.

Bob Burns, Pastor, Spiritual Formation, Church of the Good Shepherd, Durham, North Carolina; Co-author, *Resilient Ministry*

My sisters in Christ have called for a denominational family meeting to discuss some critical questions in our churches that have long gone unanswered. The voices of these complementarian co-heirs and co-laborers are a call to listen. Their stories are worthy of our attention and reflection. In order to value women in our denomination, we must first seek to understand, and this collection of essays will help. This book is helpful in offering both breadth and depth regarding our sisters' experiences across the PCA.

Alexander Jun, Professor, Azusa Pacific University; Moderator, 45th General Assembly, Presbyterian Church in America

An insightful work that captures a wide variety of voices in the church that are honestly and faithfully seeking wisdom in how women can serve and be served in the church. If you are in the PCA, wherever you stand on women's roles in the church, you will come away with a new perspective.

Alan Noble, Professor, Oklahoma Baptist University; Editor-in-Chief of Christ and Pop Culture; Author, *Disruptive Witness*

Though written from a PCA perspective for a PCA audience, this collection offers valuable reading for those of every denomination. In it, we find the personal reflections of our sisters as they share their hurts, questions, desires, and frustrations. Our Savior not only teaches and leads his people, he listens to, knows, and sympathizes with them. To be Christlike shepherds, merely teaching and leading our sisters is insufficient. We must understand their hearts and hear their stories. *Co-Laborers, Co-Heirs* helps us do that and forms a starting point for conversations in the local church.

Eric Schumacher, Pastor, Grand Avenue Baptist Church, Ames, Iowa; Author, Songwriter

This anthology is a plea not only for ecclesial clarity, but a cultural change in how our churches treat women. The focus and fear spent on what women can and can't do in ministry seems to have wiped out our capacity for our more fundamental responsibility: loving, serving, and equipping women in our life together. This collection of real-life experiences provides essential data for removing that handicap. By sharing their heartbreaking and humbling stories, these committed PCA members teach us and lead us to repentance. This book is going in my elder training manual.

Reyn Cabinte, Church Planter, Uptown Community Church, New York City

The importance of this book could not be overstated and should be required reading for anyone in leadership in the church. As a father of three daughters and husband of thirty-eight years, I find this discussion refreshing and long overdue. I both wept and rejoiced for these gentle and powerful voices. Why are our sisters having to strain so to be heard and noticed? No matter what your approach or where you come down on the issue of women in ministry, there is much here to be prayed and repented over.

David Wilcher, Pastor, Grace Presbyterian Church, The Woodlands, Texas

This work will enable you to live from a place of confidence and not fear as you collaborate with brothers and sisters in Christ. Too often as we attempt to navigate gender roles and relationships in the church, we stumble blindly forward. This book comes from the hearts of real men and women who share their experiences and biblical truths. There is a place in Christ's body for each of us to thrive as we use our gifts for his glory and others' encouragement.

Dana Anderson, Healthcare Professional; Pastor's Wife, Roseville, California.

Co-Laborers, Co-Heirs is an important book. Its many voices, like a diamond's many facets, are joined together to produce a work of art that deserves your attention. As you study it, what you will discover is a force of argument that is simultaneously adamant and sensitive, beautiful and clear. Pick it up and read.

John Meinen, RUF Campus Minister, University of Vermont

As a young open-minded pastor in the PCA, I thought I was ready to read this book. I have grown up around and been greatly influenced by strong, gifted women. I thought I knew their plight, understood their pains and identified with their struggle. I was wrong. The authors of this book deeply blessed me with their biblical insights, challenged me with their stories, and brought me to a place of humble repentance. If you are a pastor or leader of a church, please read this book. You will be challenged, you will cry for your sisters, and you will gain a much needed perspective on the experience of over half of your congregation. Hear what they have to say. It is so important.

Joel Fitzpatrick, Pastor, Conference speaker, and Author.

ABOUT WHITE BLACKBIRD BOOKS

White blackbirds are extremely rare, but they are real. They are blackbirds that have turned white over the years as their feathers have come in and out over and over again. They are a redemptive picture of something you would never expect to see but that has slowly come into existence over time.

There is plenty of hurt and brokenness in the world. There is the hopelessness that comes in the midst of lost jobs, lost health, lost homes, lost marriages, lost children, lost parents, lost dreams, loss.

But there also are many white blackbirds. There are healed marriages, children who come home, friends who are reconciled. There are hurts healed, children fostered and adopted, communities restored. Some would call these events entirely natural, but really they are unexpected miracles.

The books in this series are not commentaries, nor are they meant to be the final word. Rather, they are a collage of biblical truth applied to current times and places. The authors share their poverty and trust the Lord to use their words to strengthen and encourage his people. Consider these books as entries into the discussion.

May this series help you in your quest to know Christ as he is found in the Gospel through the Scriptures. May you look for and even expect the rare white blackbirds of God's redemption through Christ in your midst. May you be thankful when you look down and see your feathers have turned. May you also rejoice when you see that others have been unexpectedly transformed by Jesus.

Follow whiteblackbirdbooks.pub for titles and releases.

Brittany:
For Claire and Sarah, my dear friends
For Dan, who supports me unceasingly
For Penelope and Jonah

Doug:
For my mother, Donna, and my sister, Denise
For my wife, Julie
For my daughters, Ruth and Anna, and for Mady, my newest daughter
For my sons Cal and Drew, and my newest son Adam
For the women who mentor me, partners together for good
For the women in my church
For the girls growing up
For the boys, men, and pastors
For the church

CONTENTS

INTRODUCTION

Brittany Smith

Attending the 2017 General Assembly of the Presbyterian Church in America (PCA) was a strange experience. I've been in the PCA since 2003. Though I didn't grow up in the PCA, I joined the denomination in college and haven't looked back. All of my adult life has been shaped and formed by the ministry of PCA churches and pastors. I'm used to male-only eldership and pastors. And yet, experiencing a 1500+ assembly of almost only men was strange and disorienting. Particularly in the 2016 and 2017 General Assemblies, where issues about women in ministry were hotly debated.

In 2016 a proposal was made to create a formal study on the issue of women ministering in the church. Just the proposal alone was considered a huge issue. And these long debates and public speeches about women serving in the church were only spoken between men. There were women who served on the committee that composed the study report, and we did get to hear from them at a panel presentation at the 2017 General Assembly, but public debate at GA was only available to commissioners, who are all men. So I had this experience, dare I say a bizarre one, of a bunch of pastors and church elders (all men) debating about women. Surely I wasn't the only one wondering what all the women watching and listening (present in the room or with the live feed online) were thinking or feeling.

Now just because something is uncomfortable or strange doesn't mean it isn't perfectly good or appropriate within its context. I do understand what the General Assembly is (a court), how it is formed (delegates of elders and pastors sent from presbyteries), and what its purpose is (governing of the church, particularly denomination-wide issues). But as someone with a decent familiarity with our denomination (both its glories and warts), if I felt unsettled by this experience, I could only imagine what outsiders were feeling. In my experience, male-only ordination is often shocking to those coming from outside an orthodox Christian tradition. Our faithfulness to the Scriptures on the qualifications for ordained pastors and elders needs a strong apologetic to distinguish such boundaries from oppressive forms of gender roles, which are rightly being rapidly eradicated in the broader culture.

And if we want to have a strong apologetic for why we consider it biblical to continue to have male-only eldership, we need not only the willingness to attempt to thoughtfully articulate our beliefs (as was done in the Ad Interim Study Report on Women in the Ministry of the Church), but also a willingness to root out latent misogyny in the church. We must be above reproach in this area if we hope to have a faithful witness to biblical sexuality and church leadership.

Another result of contemplating the strangeness of General Assembly was the realization that while that event is not a time when we would hear from women, the need to hear women articulate their experiences in our churches was necessary for the growth and health of the future of the PCA. In this feeling I was not alone.

Doug Serven, co-editor of this volume and editor of a similar compilation on race in the PCA, *Heal Us, Emmanuel*, also began to wonder how he could seek out the voices of women in our denomination. We talked about compiling a book of essays, started asking around about contributors, and brainstormed the message we hoped might arise. A growing group of men and women, ministry leaders, pastors, and laypeople encouraged us to pursue this work. Pastors passed along names of women in their congregations who might be interested in writing. Several pastors and elders committed to write in support of amplifying women voices.

Early in the project, we had women who joined us with an interest in writing. Some submitted drafts right away, as if their stories had been just waiting for a place to be heard. Others came in later, after contemplating what they might write.

There is also a significant group of women who considered writing and chose to decline. One woman cried with me about the difficulty of revisiting the grief of her experience trying to work in ministry in the PCA—and felt she couldn't do it. One woman self-selected out of writing, knowing her tone could not yet be gentle and kind. Another retracted her story out of fear of pushback from her local church leadership. Some stories and laments are still ongoing and waiting on the outcomes of those situations.

The women who did write also experienced God at work in them and through them in this project. One woman had conversations with a family member that opened up new areas in their relationship to know and be known by one another. Some of them are taking risks in opening up about painful stories or experiences. All of them wonder how their words will be heard.

I commend to you these brave sisters and brothers who have soberly decided to open their hearts and minds to you in the following pages. Heed their words of lament and hope for our dear denomination, for the broader church, and for Jesus Christ himself, whom they love and cling to fiercely as they step forward to speak to you here. I also commend to you all the women who did not write for us, but whose voices echo between the lines and are cherished by Jesus all the more.

WORDS FROM OUR
SISTERS: LISTEN

~

EMMA'S STORY
JESSICA RIBERA

Jessica Ribera began attending a Presbyterian Church in America (PCA) church in Seattle when she moved there for professional ballet training. She later graduated from the University of Washington Foster School of Business (BA). Her artistic attention is now directed toward raising her children and developing as a writer. Her husband is an elder at their church where they met, fell in love as teenagers, and now attend as a family of six. She blogs at jeskybera.com about art, faith, and motherhood.

I had heard many times about the oyster farm where Emma grew up, but this was my first visit in our fourteen years of friendship. Snuggled on lawn chairs under fleece blankets, we looked up through the chilly, summer night air and counted shooting stars. We have walked many phases together from first days of college classes to marriage, motherhood, and first days of kindergarten for our children. Now, I had finally come to her childhood home to visit her and her children. They were hiding out there while lawyers worked to establish protective orders and temporary parenting plans.

I changed my opinion about how the Church needs the ministry of women because of Emma, her friendship, and my involvement in her story. It took something big to make the issues plain to me. I've always believed that God created men and women to have partnership in accomplishing his work, but my vision of how he can and does do this in our churches has expanded. I will walk you through my learning process, but first I'll explain my former posture toward women (and toward myself).

I never expected to be an advocate for women in ministry. To me, this difficult term simply means: women entrusted, sanctioned, trained, but not ordained with diaconal and shepherding roles for the good of the congregation. But I haven't always allowed myself to want these roles for women. For years, I have been happy to explain away every complaint or request for this kind of female leadership.

A few months before the lawn chair scene, I worried, "If I start working toward fuller inclusion of women in ministry, will I arrive at 'believing in' women's ordination?" I was afraid of having my mind changed. I knew worse things could certainly happen, but I feared that change would explode my relationship with my husband and my church leaders. I realized that this fear of man (literally, though, I'm sure there would be plenty of women disappointed in me too!) prevented me from listening to the Lord's call to understand Scripture myself and to work to protect the unprotected. Then God invited me to be a part of Emma's story, and I saw how things could work, how men and women could actually be complements for each other in the context of ministry.

Emma's story is one of salvation from an abusive relationship with a Christian man. For years, many knew of her husband's sex addiction and their contentious relationship, but I did not know he was abusive. When I asked, she'd always say her marriage was miserable. They separated once under the supervision of the session. I thought it was because of the sex addiction, and I tried to give her space because of the sensitive, personal nature of it all. I assumed the men were looking out for her. And they thought they were, though with hindsight we see signs that required more attention. There were harder questions we could have asked.

When they got back together, I assumed that was what she wanted, and three years passed during which I marveled over her commitment, her obedience to God and to her marriage vows. "I just have to accept," she once said, "that I will probably never have a happy, healthy marriage in which I feel safe and loved." She was, to me, a woman showing a largesse of grace from God to her husband embroiled in sin and mental health issues. This was the extreme end of "in sickness and in health," and she was ready to trust God with her comfort and hopes for the long haul.

Eventually, my intuition began telling me that something was really wrong with my friend. I began praying more and more for the two of them and their children. A couple weeks in, I got a call from another close friend. "I'm worried about Emma," she said. "She told me some things, and I'm just not sure that she should still be married." That really scared me. I knew adultery or abuse was in play. All the stories I had ever heard from Emma started to come back to me, and they all took on a much more sinister tone than I had given them before. The last thing I wanted was to be a busy-body inserting myself where I presumed the elders were already deeply involved.

Thankfully, my friendship and concern for Emma pushed me to get the story for myself. One night, we had plans, and a third friend had to back out. I found myself with private space and time to finally talk to Emma.

"Don't feel like you have to talk to me," I began. "But I'm worried about you."

"Oh, I want to tell you. I know I need to, actually, but it's all so hard to talk about because I just wish it wasn't happening."

"Well, just tell me whatever."

And then, she slowly revealed the most recent incident and how after the last separation she had told herself that if it ever happened again, she was gone. Faced with it now, she was in denial and obvious fear. There is no need to include details here, but, because I'm certain many will wonder, I will say that multiple lawyers, pastors, friends, and domestic violence advocates agree that what transpired was nothing short of abuse.

I cried and clutched her to myself. "I'm so, so sorry," I said. "No one can treat you like this. You are a daughter of God, and no one should ever, ever treat you like this." She sobbed as I held and rocked her the way I hold my children.

I don't remember all that was said. I do know that some of her tears were relief to have me reflect with words and emotion that what was happening was absolutely terrible, impermissible. I carefully asked if she wanted to get divorced but felt like she wasn't supposed to want that. "Yes," she cried, "but I'm afraid it's dishonoring to God. I think everyone just wants me to stay with him."

I then had a terrible war in my heart. Could *I* tell her she could get divorced? Was I allowed to make that kind of a statement? Everything in me wanted to drive immediately to her house, pack her things and her children, and keep them all with me. Part of me was inside an after-school special in which I knew exactly what to do when finding out that a friend is being abused. The other part of me felt helpless. I had no authority to tell her she could get divorced. What if I told her she could, but the leaders and pastors (the session) disagreed? Would she then be in a worse position than before? Wouldn't she then just have to leave the church?

I prayed, screaming in my heart, "Groan, Spirit! I don't know what to say! Give me wisdom!"

"No one wants you to be in danger," I said. "Do the guys understand that *this* is what has been going on?"

"I haven't told them about this latest thing."

"But, last time?"

"Well, last time everyone just kept asking me if I was ready for him to come back, so I just felt like they didn't think it was that bad."

"Huh. OK. Well, do you think you could talk to my husband? I'll be with you. I just think you have to talk to a man about it. And since he's on the session, maybe he could actually help you."

It was nearly midnight. As we walked out of my bedroom to wake up my poor husband who had just fallen asleep in an armchair, I felt an iron ball of resolve form in my heart: I have got to protect her and help her get out. I anxiously prayed for my husband to respond like I thought he would with the same sadness and shock that I felt. I hoped he, a ruling elder, would give her the assurance that I couldn't.

Things did not start out well. He was exhausted and confused. He could barely keep his eyes open, so I interrupted Emma to tell him to go take his contacts out. He came back a little perkier, and she calmly, meekly gave him the story. He did give her an, "Ohh, I'm so sorry. I had no idea. He did say that something had happened, but I didn't think this." Then, my husband did something I did not expect. He launched into musing over the providence of the fact that he had just that morning stumbled upon a Presbyterian Church in America (PCA) committee report that referenced "The Westminster Divines on Divorce for Physical Abuse." I could tell that he thought this was very fascinating and important. He and the rest of the guys were going to need to figure out if she was "allowed" or not to get divorced. That would be an important way for them to support them both. But, there in my dark living room next to my broken friend, I was really frustrated that we were even talking about all that yet.

After she left that night, he said to me, "How'd I do?"

"Well, I wish you had been way more empathetic about it all. That was impossibly hard for her to do, and you went off about Westminster!"

"I know, but we have to think about all that. I'm the newest guy on the session, and I felt like I had to be really careful about what I said."

"Yeah. I know. I get it. I felt like that too. I just wish that you could have given her more sympathy."

I'll pause the narrative here to point out what I see as two of the major lessons from this situation.

First, my response of empathy and desire to empower her to speak further was vital to helping Emma that night, but the logical thinking my husband and the pastor had to do were just as important. Without both, she may still be stuck, and her husband may still be under the delusion that his treatment of her is somehow within his husbandly rights and simply open to interpretation. Of course, all glory goes to God for his rescue of this family, and God did it by guiding Emma to make the hard decisions. The rest of us are just support.

Second, the opportunity to speak one-on-one with a woman who could help her should have come much, much earlier in this story. It should have happened years earlier, at least at the time they were separated. While men were busy keeping tabs on a rampant pornography addiction in her husband, she still felt trapped in a terrible gray zone, wondering if she was truly expected to put up with the kind of abuse she endured. She hadn't given complete details of the incidents leading up to their prior separation. She was too embarrassed. It was too uncomfortable as a woman speaking to only men. And her abuser/husband fed her lies to keep her separated from those who could be her best advocates.

Emma says that she was asked, "Are you wanting a divorce?" But she felt it came across as, "We hope you don't want a divorce." At the time, she didn't know what she wanted. She was a trauma victim in disbelief over her situation and was doing her best to honor her husband and preserve his reputation. After all, if they made it through all this, she hoped her friends would still be willing to let her husband into their lives!

For years it seems, Emma and her husband existed in separate silos of care. Women like me empathized and commiserated with her over her cross to bear. We should have asked harder questions, and I kick myself for not doing so. We didn't know to ask, and we assumed that the leaders had all the information they needed and were monitoring Emma's spiritual and physical safety. As a woman in the church, I had collected an impression that my view was not needed.

Meanwhile, her husband controlled the story his friends heard as he regularly painted Emma the way he wanted them to see her: a shallow, worldly woman obsessed with career and unwilling to participate in his fight for their marriage. Had there been more crossover between our gender-based friend groups, maybe we would have heard that he described her these ways, and we could have challenged it. We could have told our husbands something was fishy. But there was not much meaningful overlap between the male and female groups.

The night that I dragged Emma out to talk and tried to telepathically splash water in my husband's face, the intersection finally occurred, and the ball began to roll in the right direction. (I must, again, acknowledge that Emma herself was ready to get out, and God guided her every step of the way.) We ask ourselves now: "How can we get that overlap happening sooner? What are the right questions to ask? What should be the procedure?" My personal feeling is there should be feminine perspective on every case of marital disruption. This leads me to ask if, perhaps, there should be the opportunity and expectation to get feminine perspective on all kinds of things.

Over the next couple of months, Emma and I continued to have big, difficult conversations. All manner of challenging circumstances came up including their landlord deciding to move back into the house they were renting. On Holy Saturday, two close friends and I received a text that Emma had told her husband that he could not move into the new house with her and the girls, and we were invited to come help her clean the new place. Naturally, we bee-lined over there. We dusted an old chandelier hanging in the small dining room as she described his aggressive behavior of the last few days, and she burst one of the hot lightbulbs in her hand. After that, we sat in the corner of the bare, cold room and talked. She knew she needed God to give her peace to leave her husband once and for all. We pointed out all the circumstances and the work God was clearly already doing. I simply don't have space here to write of all the remarkable ways God made himself plain over those months. Finally, she asked for the first and last time: "Do you all think I should get divorced?"

"We can't tell you what to do. It has to be your choice."

"I *do* think you should get divorced," said one friend. "What he has done to you is illegal. You and the children are not safe."

"I'm worried that I won't have support," Emma said.

"The minute you make the decision, we are all immediately behind you. But if you decide to stay, we will be there too."

The talk went on like that for a while, and in the end, all three friends had in one way or another said divorce was a completely reasonable option and that we would help her no matter what. Then we laid our hands on her, and we prayed for a long time. She prayed through the night, and in the morning, she announced her decision to pursue divorce. It was a strange Easter Sunday worshiping and rejoicing in Christ's ultimate victory even as we quietly cried for our friends. We hosted an incredibly awkward Easter lunch for twenty-three people, her family included. From that time on, she has marched steadily through the painful process of divorce, all while praying for her husband and telling everyone that she hopes someday to be at the marriage supper of the Lamb with this man she loves even though he causes her so much pain.

Here is what keeps me awake at night: What is happening to women in my church, or in the PCA, or anywhere, who do not happen to be best friends with three session wives? The kind of pastoral care we provided to Emma for months, that night, and in the months since could not have been done by a man. During those months leading up to her divorce decision, she envisioned herself deep down in a murky, cold sea tangled with kelp. There was no clear area of light shining for her to see and swim toward, and so she held her breath, waiting for God to point her in the right direction. To be with a person in a spiritual (and physical) place of entrapment like this requires intimacy and time. It would, of course, not have been appropriate for any session member to dwell in the dark sea with Emma like I did. We spent long hours, late nights together, and I'm convinced that every hour was necessary.

One of the most spiritually intimate experiences of my life occurred when Emma and I flopped down on her couch after an exhausting day of moving all her things into the new house and setting up her girls' room. It only took about five minutes of stillness for Emma to curl into the fetal position and begin to shake with sobs. There was nothing to say, nothing to do but weep with her. Slowly, the other two friends there, still vacuuming and unpacking, noticed us there crying and just came to sit. No one dared break into this grief with words. In our communion there, we all understood that only the Holy Spirit could speak for her now. I knew we were all silently praying together as our tears rolled down. Music was playing, and I prayed, "God, give us a song we can all pray to you together." The next track was "Your Hands" by J. J. Heller. Part of that song says, "I have unanswered prayers. I have trouble I wish wasn't there, and I have asked a thousand ways that you would take my pain away." My heart was breaking, as was hers. This song spoke to this exact moment.

I pray that I never forget the sensation that the veil between here and eternity thinned to a membrane, and we women were as united in soul as I have ever known. The only word that comes close to describing that time together is "holy." A group of male pastors, elders, or deacons could not have had this kind of experience with a woman. One would hope that any church member has a friend with whom she could spend time like this, someone to receive hard, humbling confession, someone who could cry and hug and stroke her hair. But we all know that so many members of our congregations do not have this, and how likely it is that even if there are bosom friendships, there may not be the biblical knowledge or spiritual maturity to guide one another in right paths.

Subtle messaging within our churches comes to us through every piece of communication, every decision, and every policy. In churches, like mine, where no woman ever goes through the kind of vetting or training that deacons and elders undergo, women (and men!) automatically assume that women are not qualified to provide reliable spiritual counsel.

There is a woman at my church who is widely respected by all as a godly leader. She has spent her life providing rich, Christian education materials for children. I often ask her for advice or opinion, and she always follows it up with, "But be sure to ask Pastor." On one hand, I respect this woman's humility and deference; on the other, I wonder, "Is any woman ever able to speak real truth with confidence?"

More subtle messaging comes across every time someone in front of the congregation says, "If you have any questions or needs, please always feel free to speak to one of the pastors, elders, or deacons." The implication: there aren't any women you can talk to. For many, I'm convinced, this is a major barrier to women receiving help and spiritual care. Some things are just too hard to say to a man, especially a man you don't know very well, no matter how much you love his preaching or the way he really moderates the heck out of those congregational meetings.

While Emma's story indicates that some things did not go well or right, I believe that the tandem male/female pastoral care she received was essential for the rescue of not just her but her children and husband from a reign of sin in their home. I'm very proud to have worked alongside the men of my session, especially my husband and our senior pastor.

My hope is that we can equip more women in some kind of "official" capacity to do the same. Emma is not as much of an outlier as we all wish she were. Even now, I have other women for whom I am concerned. Some I am close with; others I worry over from afar. For now, I pray for them, answer their texts and calls, and do my best to make them feel safe and comfortable in sharing with me. I encourage them to talk to the session or pastors and offer to be with them if they need a companion. That is all I can do, and I believe that all people would be better served by more women being commissioned somehow for this kind of work. I don't mind just doing what I'm doing, but I am limited in the impact I could have if I had more information, more empowerment and authorization to pursue and serve people, more training, and public advertisement that my care is available and good. I use the example of myself, but I would never insist on being included in a group of deaconesses or women advisors. I believe that women should be nominated, vetted, and voted the way that men are. A girl can dream!

In the Genesis creation account we read that both men and women have been made in God's image. Our church bodies are made of many parts, and the feminine intelligence is one of those vital parts. I often use this little analogy: when a male doctor performs a sensitive procedure on a woman, that woman is offered the presence of a female nurse. While we as churches could at least offer an equivalent, I hope that the PCA's male leaders can see this as a bare minimum. Women have more to offer via their unique experiences, skills, and perspectives than just a soothing or reassuring presence.

In our churches, if men don't really believe women have more to offer the Church than just care for other women and children, if women have no opportunity for training and deputization, if men care more about "the appearance of evil" than the actual evil of neglecting full-spectrum care and regard for women, then situations like Emma's will absolutely continue to occur. We will waste the skills and resources found in the fairer half of Christ's body. I do thank and praise God that I can tell ten stories of love, grace, instruction, and consideration for every one story of hurt, neglect, embarrassment, or marginalization from the men who have shepherded me in the church context. Is there a system that is perfect? I think not. No salvation is to be found in the systems of this world. But we are called, friends, to be stewards, and I can no longer deny that the PCA could do better.

UNCIVILIZED FRUIT

PAIGE BRITTON

Paige Britton earned a BA in English from Haverford College and an MA in Special Education from Millersville University. Her writing has appeared in Modern Reformation Magazine *and on the World Reformed Fellowship website. Paige writes and speaks on the subject of biblical and theological literacy, which can be found at @GrassRootsTheo. Paige serves as a volunteer legal advocate at her county courthouse, assisting plaintiffs in protection from abuse cases. She lives with her husband, son, and daughter in rural Pennsylvania.*

~

When I first became captivated by the Reformed expression of the faith, I was the only Reformed person I knew in town. An encounter with Romans 4:4 had left me reeling—a Martin Luther moment that precipitated adult-onset Calvinism, all because I'd caught a glimpse of unadulterated grace as the vehicle of salvation.[1] Once it had my attention, I couldn't look away.

So in my late twenties, striking out alone, I began to relearn my theology from the ground up, replacing "God does 99 percent of the work, but you have to add that last little 1 percent to accept him" with "It's God's initiative, from first to last." Soteriology, I learned much later, is a common entry point for new Calvinists, and it's a predictable sticking point for conversations with their non-Calvinist brethren. In the moment, though, I only knew that I saw something profound in the Scriptures that the believers around me either couldn't recognize or didn't seem to care about. If I was going to deepen in this strange new theology, I was entirely on my own.

An apple tree that takes root in the forest, isolated and untended, is apt to develop its own distinctly flavored fruit on its uncivilized branches. In the same way, I was developing during those years into a Reformed theologian without the benefit of an appropriate church, let alone seminary, and the fruit of my studies would always retain the individual flavor of those isolated beginnings. All of this I realized a decade later, after I had been transplanted into a Presbyterian Church in America (PCA) orchard and found myself beginning to think about things that had been only peripheral to my initial theological dive. Sacramental theology, church polity, confessions, and ecclesiology were new emphases for me in this new setting, as was the very personally relevant matter of women in the Church. In all of these things, especially the last, I found I was the person in my PCA church most apt to ask questions, sometimes troublesome ones. Some of the answers I received were biblically or at least logically satisfying; some seemed arbitrary. Sometimes, no answers were available.

In what follows, I want to trace for you the experience of an "uncivilized" female Reformed theologian finding her way in a very conservative PCA space. What happens to that unconfined apple tree when it's subjected to the expectations of systematic cultivation? What is gained, what lost? In what ways have these past dozen years in the PCA shaped me, for good and for ill, as a woman and as a Christian? What do I wish for my intellectually astute younger sisters who might follow on this path themselves? These reflections are at least the beginnings of answers, or perhaps the beginnings of more questions. In any case, they are the fruit I bring to the table.

～

Notwithstanding my affinity for Reformed thought, it was not theology that drew our family to the PCA church up the street, but the sudden need to find a new church home. And even a decade of theological study didn't make this transition a smooth one for me. Joining this new church required a degree of personal sacrifice from both my husband and me, as he graciously agreed to bear with a theology, worship style, and polity that felt foreign, and as I faced the reality that becoming a member would mean giving up the teaching role I'd enjoyed in our previous nondenominational congregation.

This wasn't the first time I had encountered the idea of restrictions on women's roles in ministry, but it was the first time that I had ever faced accepting those limitations for myself. Words like "egalitarian" (which described our old church) and "complementarian" had already entered my vocabulary, and I was beginning to familiarize myself with the writings of both camps. In our previous church, I had been *the* Sunday school teacher for adults, most of whom were at least forty years older than I was, and I'd loved it. But from conversations with the pastors of this PCA church, I knew that with the exception of educational emergencies in missionary settings, women in this congregation would only be permitted to teach children, teen girls, and other women. I also knew that in joining an elder-led church I would want to be at peace with these limits, and not rock the boat.

Why would anyone voluntarily submit to limitations when she doesn't have to? My answer at the time was that it probably wouldn't kill me not to get my way for a while; and there were so many other obvious benefits to being part of this church that I thought I could set aside one thing I loved in exchange for the blessings of proximity, age-mates, strong biblical instruction, and attractive opportunities for our son and daughter. Besides, there were not a lot of compatible churches to choose from in our neighborhood. I reasoned that if I couldn't teach, I could always write. So I took a deep breath, and the apple tree from the forest was transplanted into the orchard.

It wasn't long before I began to experience the sobering implications of my decision. The first signs I was in alien territory came early on, as I sat under an elder's teaching in a Sunday school class. Thinking I'd add something to the discussion that would be familiar to these Presbyterians, I offered as a relevant illustration Augustine's four states of man, in Latin.[2] But our instructor didn't recognize the phrases, and an older woman commented sternly, "I don't think we need to get so *theological* about it." Abashed, I began to wonder: How can I follow the rule about women not teaching mixed groups, if when I open my mouth in Sunday school I'm likely to be teaching *somebody*—perhaps even the teacher?

Posing this question to the men in leadership proved fruitless. Of course I could speak up in Sunday school, they said; I just couldn't *teach*. No one, however, was able or willing to define "teach" for me in a satisfactory way. Did it mean (as it seemed to), *explain something that someone didn't know before?* If so, then I shouldn't speak up in Sunday school—or anywhere, for that matter—in case learning inadvertently occurred. Did it mean *stand in front of a class while explaining something?* This would be rarer, but sometimes the senior pastor invited me to handle a five-minute stretch of a Bible lesson. Would "teaching" have occurred after the five-minute mark, and up to that point was I doing something else? I soon became so entangled by this knotty puzzle that I went mute. Silence in that setting was just safer.

Meanwhile, my theological bent drove me to look more closely at the relevant passages about women's roles in the Church, now that I was actively subject to them. I had begun to hear rumors of other PCA churches that had adopted a more lenient policy regarding women teaching, and I wondered how they squared their practices with the text.[3] Even if our session supported a different conclusion, I could at least make up my own mind about it.

Many commentaries and articles later, I decided that nobody really knew anything for certain. Paul's words were just too ambiguous, coming to us from so long ago and far away. He *probably* didn't have the modern adult Sunday school arrangement in mind when he wrote 1 Timothy 2:12, but the safest bet for a Scripture-led session was to put a hedge around that ministry too.[4] So my local PCA elders weren't crazy, just extremely cautious; and the more permissive PCA people elsewhere weren't crazy either, just more willing to take a risk. I certainly knew in which direction I'd prefer the interpretation to go; but I also knew better than to stake an exegetical argument on my personal preferences.

～

There was more to this transition than just navigating church policy and wrestling with hermeneutics, though. I had thought I was merely resigning myself to the loss of a teaching role, but as time went on I found I had signed up for a whole *culture*, regulated by a minefield of unwritten rules and deeply held beliefs about men and women. Some of these expectations governed the contours of friendships, conversations, and cooperation with the opposite sex; the rest translated into presuppositions about the gender-specific ways men and women would contribute to the life of the Church.

At first it surprised me that both men and women in this church assumed I would find satisfaction in attending and teaching women-only groups, and I floundered in my attempts to explain to them why I didn't. It would take years before I could articulate that the deep divide between their expectations and my aversions had to do with the relative *emphasis* in women's and mixed groups. In a women's Bible study or class, the emphasis traditionally falls on relationship over content; but in a mixed group, this emphasis is reversed. As it happens, I breathe easy when I get to deal with cognitive things; small talk makes me panic. Thus giving up mixed-group teaching was, as far as I could see, the same thing as giving up teaching, period.

In fact I instinctively avoided associating myself much with women's or children's ministries, suspecting that once situated in one of these traditional roles I'd be forgotten by the leadership. I had observed that a church's women's ministry typically happens on an island where few male elders visit. If I went in that direction, I reasoned, I'd become Somebody Else's Problem, invisible to the elders and other teaching brothers who might otherwise think up interesting things for me to do, if they saw I was still hanging around.[5]

Figuring out interesting things for me to do was nobody's priority, as it turned out. I found this discouraging, because there were very few interesting things that I *could* do without an invitation from one of my brothers. Some invitations came: I wrote curriculum for leader training, edited some writing, co-chaired a search committee. I kept my expectations low, but waiting for more was hard.

I don't recall which one of us came up with the idea, but at some point a band of brothers and I worked out a deal. I would write Sunday school lesson plans, and they would take turns using them to teach a group of adults who needed the foundations of the faith. It was an unexpectedly pleasant partnership, so long as I ignored the pangs of homesickness for that teaching role: a creative combination of my abilities and limitations, and their abilities and freedom. The safe space we created for these older beginners became a safe space for me too—it was the one room in the building where I would voluntarily speak up, just a little, about the things I knew.

As the years wound along, this room started to collect everything else that was waiting, unspoken, inside me. The life of my mind began to blossom out onto the walls in huge painted maps: cities and rivers and mountains and sea (with a dragon!); the places where Jesus walked, and Paul, and Abraham. Chronologies branched above it all, keeping track of centuries and empires and ordinary people. Every brushstroke was a conversation I couldn't have, a lesson I couldn't teach—but the bitter was made somewhat sweeter when I saw how well the visible expressions of my mind complemented the lively teaching of my brothers. Once more, it was an unexpectedly pleasant partnership.

Over time I was finding my voice again, too, and even taking my place at the front of that room sometimes. A wise friend understood that if I was ever going to teach women, she'd have to handle the small talk; other women showed up, hungry for Hebrews, and came back for more. Even a hardship assignment has its oases.

~

You can take the apple tree out of the forest, but in the end it's still an apple tree from the forest. Though I voluntarily submitted myself to the leadership of elders and the rules of the house, and although that submission has left its marks, I remain at the end of a dozen years in a PCA church more a part of the culture I came from than the culture I joined. It's as if I've been an embedded journalist, an ethnographer studying what's foreign to me. It's true that the experience hasn't killed me: in fact I am more myself than I was before, and bold enough now (*old* enough now!) to share the uncivilized fruit of my perspective.

Why tell my outsider-insider story here, in a book by and about women in the PCA? I have sisters, many of them younger, some of them theologically trained, who out of necessity or choice will spend at least some of their adulthood in a PCA orchard. Some of them will feel deeply out of place, as I have, especially if geography constrains them to a very conservative setting. I want them to know they can survive it, with managed expectations and creativity and unexpected partnerships and a whole lot of heartfelt prayer. A flexible sense of humor doesn't hurt, either.

Also I have brothers who will encounter these gifted women, and I want to encourage these men to look at these, their sisters, and really *see* them. Don't let them fade into Somebody Else's Problem, absorbed by the women's and children's ministries so you don't have to take responsibility for their well-being. Find them suitable work to do; honor their unusual gifts; leverage your freedom while they submit to the restrictions. *Treat them as sisters*, as Paul writes—a cheerful command, to my mind, because it holds out hope that my brothers will be proactive in befriending me rather than avoid me because I'm inherently problematic or threatening.[6]

Is my experience truly representative of the PCA? Both men and women have told me that maybe I'm in "the wrong church," that my gifts would have flourished in a different PCA setting where women are allowed more opportunities as teachers. But those churches are not nearby. This has been the "right church" for this time and place and chapter in my life. And so long as this denomination includes *both* conservative and more permissive expressions of church policy, any individual congregation is, indeed, representative of the whole PCA, no matter how much its detractors would like to disown it. For better or worse, we still belong to one another.

Ultimately, in *any* male-elder-led church, even adopting a more permissive policy won't in itself overcome the indifference and unawareness of the decision-makers. No matter how the practical details play out, it's part of the territory that more effort will be required of the male leaders to encourage and care for the gifted women in their midst, even just to remember that they are there. The bare fact that women may teach mixed groups in some PCA churches doesn't guarantee that those women who teach will feel they are known, affirmed, and honored by their shepherds. Neither do the specific boundaries set by my PCA church mean that individual brothers haven't looked out for me and seen to opportunities for my flourishing.

You can take the apple tree out of the forest: but even in the orchard, the gifts of rain and wind and sun are the same. My three constants have been my husband Josh, the Scriptures, and my Trinitarian God—Josh, who built me an office space and bookshelves, who protected my time as a young mother so I could dive deep in uninterrupted study, and who continually affirms and honors me in my "uncivilized" individuality; the Word of God, shallow enough here for the lamb to play, deep enough there for the elephant to swim;[7] and Father, Son, and Spirit, who arrange my path, walk before me on it, and make the journey sweet.

In all my life, I have never felt so conscious of and discouraged about being embodied *female* than in these last dozen years. I have not been won over by this civilization, and although I love my church, I do not find its underlying culture winsome. But whether in the PCA or out of it, whether flourishing or frustrated as a theologically minded woman in the Church, whether planted in the orchard or in the forest, the truth is that I have continued to be nurtured and nourished.

I am planted by streams of living water, and so I yield my uncivilized fruit in due season.

---

1. Romans 4:4 reads: *"Now to the one who works, his wages are not counted as a gift but as his due."* This simple statement, applied by analogy to the narrative of conversion, turned on its head the notion I had always heard, that we must meet God partway by *deciding* to believe. Rather, Paul says that anything less than complete grace would be *wages*, something owed to us by God. If there is no diluting of saving grace, then there can be no "deciding" to believe independent of God's initiative.

2. Augustine's four states of man are as follows: *posse peccare, posse non peccare* (able to sin, able not to sin); *non posse non peccare* (not able not to sin); *posse non peccare* (able not to sin); and *non posse peccare* (not able to sin).

3. The gist of the policy in the more permissive PCA congregations is that a woman may do anything that a nonordained man may do. This preserves the male-elder-led nature of the Church but opens the possibility of mixed adult or youth class instruction to women as well.

4. 1 Timothy 2:12 reads: *"I do not permit a woman to teach or to exercise authority over a man; rather, she is to remain quiet."*

5. After Douglas Adams, Life, the Universe, and Everything (New York: Crown, 1982). "'An S.E.P.,' Ford said, 'is something that we can't see, or don't see, or our brain doesn't let us see, because we think that it's somebody else's problem. That's what S.E.P. means. Somebody Else's Problem. The brain just edits it out; it's like a blind spot. If you look at it directly you won't see it unless you know precisely what it is. Your only hope is to catch it by surprise out of the corner of your eye.'" (28)

6. From 1 Timothy 5:1b–2, which reads: *"Treat younger men like brothers, older women like mothers, younger women like sisters, in all purity."*

7. After Gregory the Great, d. 604 AD.

THREE STRIKES AND I'M OUT?

ASHLEY WILLIAMS

On Being a Single, Black Female in Our Church

Ashley Williams earned a BA in English from Southeastern Louisiana University and is working toward an MA in Biblical Studies at Reformed Theological Seminary. She has previously worked for Reformed University Fellowship at Jackson State University and is currently ministry coordinator at Grace Mosaic Church in Washington, DC. If she's not in her office, Ashley can be found roaming the local record store or with her headphones in at a third-wave coffee shop around town.

∾

In 2016 I attended the Presbyterian Church in America's (PCA) 44th General Assembly in Mobile, Alabama. I went with a couple of girl-friends who were also serving at the time as interns with Reformed University Fellowship (RUF), the college ministry of the PCA.

We thought it'd be fun to rub elbows with the big wigs in the denomination and hear the towering presence of Tim Keller preach. I lost a small fortune on books alone, jumped in and out of interesting seminars, and enjoyed roaming the town with my girls. When it came time to gather as an assembly for Keller's sermon, we sat left of stage, second row in the convention center. While waiting for the program to begin, we struck up a conversation about race and the PCA with an older White man sitting in front of us, appropriate considering the resolution on racial reconciliation that would be passed in the following days.

What at first was a light and informative dialogue suddenly became serious when I noticed the man's eyes growing red and watery. In slow motion, it seemed, he looked at the three of us and said, "I am so glad you are here. Please don't give up on us." In the heightened emotions of that moment, I only wanted to console him, so I offered a naïve and thoughtless but resolute, "We won't." I knew the man's intentions, but in the poeticism of that moment I didn't discern the gravity of his plea. This was a home run of a figure: a White, married man, asking a bunch of Black, single women who had struck out on every one of those tosses to keep swinging.

It's usually those fixed characteristics about ourselves that are the same ones used to wall us off or protect us, depending on how you look at it. The sovereignty of God through the coding of DNA determined I'd be a woman. The sovereignty of God through generations upon generations of darker-skinned folk in my ancestry determined I'd be Black.

It's the sovereignty of God too that determines my singleness, though I'd often attribute it more to my overt selfishness and paralyzing fear of commitment. None of these aspects of myself are sinful. I am not lacking any good thing. I don't wish I were male. I love being Black. And despite what my worrisome married friends think or superimpose on me, I love being single. But I'd be silly to think these descriptors do not carry massive assumptions, weight, advantages, and disadvantages in life generally and in the PCA specifically. I joke often with friends and strangers alike that I went and jumped into the denomination most diametrically different from me. According to a 2014 survey, the Presbyterian Church in America is majority male, at 52 percent, majority White, at 80 percent, and mostly made up of married couples, at 57 percent.[1]

I knew exactly what I was joining when I became Presbyterian. Initially I joined the PCA by necessity as an RUF intern at Jackson State University. Then in my first year of seminary at Reformed Theological Seminary in Jackson, Ligon Duncan's class on covenant theology absolutely wrecked me and changed the way I read Scripture. My convictions changed and confirmed my commitment to the PCA's theological confession.

But it gets old being the only African American in most of the spaces I fill. And the pitiful eyes of well-meaning men and women who see singleness as sickness grow harder to ignore as I trip toward my thirties. It's also glaringly clear that seminary professors have no idea how to talk to their female students without needing limitless layers of accountability, as if single women are attending seminary either to grab an MRS or a professor's virtue and reputation. I haven't quite figured out which strike is more damning.

Right Theology, Wrong Color

The hot topic in evangelical circles, as confirmed by that General Assembly meeting I attended, is race and racial reconciliation. I imagine when I walk into a room, it is my Blackness that is noticed first. Thankfully, I'm used to being the only Black person around. Being a minority is nothing new for me. I was separated early in elementary school when my first-grade teacher decided my habit of walking around and chatting up other students was not due to deficit in attention. Moving into the magnet-track in the East Baton Rouge school system essentially meant removing me from a majority-Black environment and displacing me into a White one. At age twelve, my parents joined a Reformed Baptist church and we remained, till I left in 2015 for seminary, the only Black family in the congregation. Outside of extended time with relatives, my world was completely and unequivocally White. As such, I swim in White streams seamlessly.

This can often be a gift. I don't find myself easily frustrated by missteps and slightly offensive words, phrases, and ideas shared with me by White brothers and sisters who are honestly trying to learn. I can talk confidently and comfortably in all-White spaces. I never noticed this benefit of the gift until I was scheduled to meet with over a dozen White men in Oxford, Mississippi, to talk about my work at RUF at JSU. One of the interns who I was on staff with, upon hearing about this meeting of mine, quipped, "Girl, I don't know how you can talk to White men like that. I couldn't do it." From her and many other Black friends who haven't grown up in the experiences I have, I learned quickly how unique my comfort among White people was. It's not all gift though.

One consequence of this ability is how I tend to assuage instead of challenge White discomfort.

An example of this happened about a year ago. An older pastor friend had asked me to do something for him, and while his errand was on my agenda, I hadn't gotten to it yet. The next time we ran into each other, I told him I had not gotten to his request yet and he jokingly responded, "I'm gonna have to get the whip out for you!" Another older woman who was in our company laughed, and I sheepishly smiled and went about my normal business. In my head, I thought, "Ashley, he's older, and it's just a saying. He would have said it just as easily to a White person. It's a common phrase." And I still believe those thoughts are true.

But in the moment, instead of pointing out how those words could be offensive to another Black person, I put my comfort and conflict aversion over lovingly correcting an oversight of a fellow brother and sister in Christ. I imagine many African Americans in the PCA are doing this often. It's a part of survival Black people in White spaces learn quickly. What then happens is these White brothers and sisters think they are doing "racial reconciliation" when they are in some form of a relationship with me. They aren't though. In this way, I am an easy Black. I am speaking their language, using their metaphors and colloquialisms, watching their movies, reading their books, and listening to their sermons. I have dinner at their houses, teach their White children, and essentially render myself colorless.

As a result, a war rages within me between how I feel at church and work, and how I feel with extended family or serving at a Black RUF. I feel displaced everywhere. In White spaces, I feel traitorous. In Black spaces, I feel inauthentic. Often I am angry—slighted by parents who joined a White church, embarrassed at Black girls who are loud in coffee shops, annoyed at White kids who listen and appropriate hip-hop culture, and I am ashamed they are comfortable to do so around me. I am no challenge to anyone. And that is really the crux of the matter: the ease with which White people move around me.

What does it mean? Often, I believe it means what I have feared for years is true—that everything those elementary and middle school kids said was right. I am an Oreo. I talk White. I act White. I know these are the playground insults of immature children fueled by chocolate milk and chicken nuggets, but those accusations still take up residence in my mind. What else am I supposed to think when every book studied, every sermon recommended, and every conference promoted lacks anyone who looks remotely like me? The absence of darkness is quite illuminating, implying a preference, a superiority, and an ideal to which I must assimilate. After years of this assimilation, every interaction with a White congregant or communicant at the church I serve provokes thought in me. My internal accusations scream, "See! They like you because you're like them."

This would already be enough. If I were a Black, married man, this is a doozy to navigate. Besides, on some level, Blackness is "chic" in Reformed circles. Even without a completed seminary degree, I've had no problem in the job opportunity market. Offers abound because Black Reformed men and women, while becoming more common, are still relatively few. What I've found to never be chic is my devastating-to-everyone-else singleness.

Why Are All the Women Sitting Together in the Kitchen?

Being a single woman in a congregation made primarily of nuclear families can often feel like walking around with no clothes. Everyone sees and often points out this supposed vulnerability. Single women don't have a husband to cover them emotionally, physically, and materially. They don't have any children to carry them through asinine small talk during the fellowship time of the service. These married brothers and sisters often have a hard time categorizing their single counterparts. At one event, I was in a conversation with two married women and one of their kids asked her for a sip of her wine. The mother responded, "Oh no! This is a drink for adults," to which the child curiously inquired, "Well what's an adult?" Without hesitation, my friend responded, "Adults are mommies and daddies." Where did that definition of adult leave me? It seemed innocent enough, but it implied people without children (and in our circles, despite the very present reality of single mothers and fathers, this automatically implies marriage) have not arrived. We are left in a perpetual state of waiting to be made whole, complete, and adult.

In such company, I do struggle to see myself as a woman. At twenty-seven, I'm older than many of the married mothers in my congregation, and yet I don't think of myself as on par with them. I feel younger, less mature, and unworthy to be listened to or regarded. After all, what advice could I possibly give when I haven't bagged my Boaz yet? Sure, this may all be the internal banter of an overly sensitive millennial, but when considering the culture surrounding most of our congregations, these silent musings are only confirmed. Often what we celebrate proves what we admire and value most. In my church, we celebrate births and infant baptisms and throw tearful going away parties for covenant families that move away. No such parties are thrown for singles who leave for new and exciting job opportunities, or even as they are sent to the mission field! One of my closest girlfriends here defeated an insane amount of college debt in two years and invited others to celebrate her victory. Only one other single friend came. What we celebrate reveals what we value. These friends were shown that what is most valuable is having a family. We mourn their leaving because we feel they have more to contribute and we lose more in their absence. Not so with our single friends. We can make it without them.

I have been attending a Bible study recently where the women of our church work through the book of Ephesians. I already struggle being there as the one single woman in the group, regardless of how wonderful the lesson is. However, in one particular study, we got to the passage I dread where Paul talks about living out the implications of the Gospel in the realm of the family. Paul spends the first four chapters of the book expositing the riches of God's grace through Christ's death and resurrection. He champions the Gospel's implication of oneness (not sameness, mind you) among all kinds of believers. Yet, ironically, this particular Thursday the oneness permeating the entire epistle was completely ignored when we came to chapter five, as if Paul's words to husbands, wives, and children had absolutely nothing to do with the rest of what he said. As if being one in Christ required marriage and procreation. Instead of making much of God's fatherly love and our role as his beloved children, an hour was spent venting about various failures to be patient moms and respectful wives. Hear me out—there is a place to confess, repent, and be encouraged to new areas of holiness. But we missed the entire forest for one tree about being a mom and a wife.

A warning sign for missing the forest for a singular tree is exclusion. For instance, if I taught a lesson on 1 Corinthians 7 and focused solely on Paul's preference for singleness and made that my tree so much so that my married sisters felt excluded and isolated (or even judged), then I missed the greater picture of serving God wisely and sacrificially whether married or single. The point is not for me to make a case that being single is better. This wasn't Paul's point either. He's saying all our faithfulness may look different, but we are all called to be faithful. Everyone can take a seat at that kind of table. At this Thursday study, instead of showing how respect of a husband, parent, or boss are some earthly examples of how we are to respect God, or how a husband loving his wife is an imperfect picture of God's perfect love for his church, or how exasperation of children is sinful because it does not exhibit to children how our heavenly Father deals patiently and kindly with us, we truncate Paul's larger message and exclude by making much of the symbols and little about the God to whom all these pictures point.

When Woman and Wife Are Synonyms

This is no surprise when the terms "Christian woman," "wife," and "mother" are treated as interchangeable. I was recently asked to be on a panel at a women's conference to talk about practicing the Gospel in daily living. There were five other women and the first order of business was to introduce ourselves. Down the line, these incredible women explained why they were asked to be on the panel, what kind of kingdom work they were involved in, but all of that followed the initial preamble of, "I am wife to... and mother to..." When it got to my turn, fourth in line, I jokingly quipped, "I'm Ashley, and I'm married to Jesus." In full disclosure, I am one of those people who absolutely loathe the "Jesus is my husband" vibe of Christian singleness. Something in that moment, though, prompted me to say it. Perhaps it was a biting remark of frustration, but I'm not that clever. If I'm honest, I felt like if part of my identity didn't include who I was married to, then my purpose there wasn't valuable or necessary.

I had similar inklings in seminary. The women who were attached to male students seemed to walk around with a confidence I didn't have. I even noticed how other men behaved differently around them. They were safe. Professors were disarmed at the sight of their occupied ring fingers. With my fingers bare and hands unheld, I was a threat to be avoided. It's already hard being a woman in seminary. I was one of a handful of women in most of my classes. The added factor of being single only intensified very implicit marginalization. I survived, of course, but often our churches aren't much better in welcoming and honoring women (single and even married) in their midst.

There is a fear in the underbelly of the Reformed, evangelical beast. Many men, especially in church leadership, are afraid of women. Jen

Wilkin wrote an article a few years ago that so eloquently articulated this fear.[2] She described three caricatures of women that "haunt" the Church and its male leaders. These ghosts, she wrote, "strike fear into the hearts of both men and women, and worse, they breathe fear into the interactions between them. Their every intent is to cripple the ability of men and women to minister to and with one another."

First, there is the usurper, and being haunted here looks like fearing that every woman with strong opinions or leadership qualities are out to steal the authority of male leadership. Second is the temptress, and a male leader haunted by this ghost will see women as seductresses out to wreck homes and churches alike. Last, the child ghost influences male leadership to see women as inferior emotionally, intellectually, and certainly not equals in any significant way.

What is often so appealing and scandalous about Jesus is how he clearly was not controlled by any of these fears. Being removed from first-century Israel often means we miss the earth-shattering things Jesus did. Talking to that Samaritan woman at the well, a woman clearly promiscuous enough to prefer burning in the noonday sun to draw water than be subject to heated gossip during the cool of the morning from women looking upon her with judgment and contempt, was a shocking sight to witness. Such encounters did not happen, at least not in the light of day. And yet, casting culture, people-pleasing, and ghosts aside, Jesus talks to an unmarried woman alone, and an entire town is saved because of it! Female disciples were co-learners and co-laborers. Though this behavior of Jesus was likely considered radical, as apparent by the reactions of the disciples who walked up during this meeting, it is behavior nothing short of understanding and honoring the imago Dei in women.

How I long for the men in our congregations to be like Jesus, lead like Jesus, and love like Jesus in this way! Or even like Paul, who in a letter denouncing ethnic superiority and affirming the equality of all peoples under the blood of Christ wrote these words:

> In Christ Jesus you are all sons of God, through faith. For as many of you as were baptized into Christ have put on Christ. There is neither Jew nor Greek, there is neither slave nor free, there is no male and female, for you are all one in Christ Jesus. Gal. 3:26–28

A celebration of my femininity in all its holiest forms is nothing short of a celebration of God. The implications of a paradigm like this are huge! Men, like Jesus, would view women as co-laborers, co-teachers, co-disciples, equal in worth and dignity and equipped to do great work for the Kingdom of God. Pastors would teach women like Jesus taught Mary at his feet (Luke 10:38–42). Women would be championed in their efforts to raise godly men and women, sons and daughters, both biological and spiritual (as I consider myself a spiritual mother to the abundance of children in my congregation), as Paul did Lois and Eunice (2 Tim. 1:3–5). The unity of men and women in Christ would reflect the diversity within the very Godhead. Those roles, equally important, meeting different needs, accomplish the fullness of our salvation. The kingdom work we are left on this earth to participate in requires nothing less than to celebrate our differences and value what both men and women bring to the table.

Until those dreams are reality, I continue to wrestle with the reality of being single, female, Black, and Reformed, with all the nuances and challenges. As I do so, I stumble and trip with vigor. All the while I am trying to find the balance of celebrating my imago Dei, while also believing Paul when he appeals to our oneness in Christ, an identity that must trump all the others that I'm outwardly defined by. I don't know the path forward. I am praying and hoping our denomination will go past resolutions and seminars and make seminal strides to reflect the manifold vision of God articulated from the very beginning. A vision where, long after the tears of sexism, racism, and hatred of the human heart are wiped away, all men and women of every tribe, nation, and tongue will be one bride, without spot or blemish, dressed for her presentation to our Lord and Savior, Jesus Christ. Oh! How beautiful she will be!

---

1. Pew Research Center. "Members of the Presbyterian Church in America." Pew Research Forum. http://www.pewforum.org/religious-landscape-study/religious-denomination/presbyterian-church-in-america/#beliefs-and-practices.
2. Jen Wilkin, "Three Female Ghosts that Haunt the Church." The Gospel Coalition. https://www.thegospelcoalition.org/article/3-female-ghosts-that-haunt-the-church/.

WORSHIP TOGETHER

KATIE RIBERA

Katie Ribera has served as an intern with Reformed University Fellowship and has worked with various nonprofit agencies in case management and volunteer coordination. She has served churches in the Northwest and Midwest, most notably as a musician and worship leader, and is the co-producer of the Seattle Hymn Project. Her education background includes the University of Oklahoma (BA) and the University of Washington (Certificate in Nonprofit Management). Katie lives with her husband in St. Louis, Missouri, and is a student at Covenant Theological Seminary. She also enjoys hearing and making good music, learning about and exploring new places, and playing complicated board games.

My life at this point has a level of symmetry and balance that, as a Myers-Briggs ESFJ personality type, feels very comfortable to me. When I walk across the seminary campus each morning, a quick glance to the horizon gives me a view of the hospital where I was born, less than a mile from where I now attend classes. I will graduate from Covenant Seminary exactly thirty years after my father graduated from the same institution. I have been a member of the same denomination since the day I was born, and my husband's church story mirrors mine in many ways.

I love the simplicity and consistency of my personal faith story that is contained within these few lines. I love being a part of God's church and being committed to the place where he has planted me. I have come to care deeply for our denomination and for its particular churches. Yet, what is not obvious here is that it has not always felt simple, and it has not always been consistent. While at times I have felt at home within my faith, my church, and my denomination, there are also times when I have wondered, "What am I doing here?" and "Is there a place for my gifts in the church?" I have wrestled with these questions personally, but they are also questions I have heard often from fellow sisters in churches and communities of faith I have been a part of.

I have faced the practical implications of what it means to be a woman with ministry gifts within the Presbyterian Church in America (PCA). I wonder about the answers to questions like: What does it mean for a woman to practice and profess her faith within our denomination? What does it look like, feel like, and sound like?

It can begin to be easy to assume a malicious intent from those who may have contributed to that feeling of marginalization, but I remain committed to being a part of this conversation because I *do not* believe malice is the only cause to blame. Sometimes there is a misunderstanding. There is often miscommunication. Things can be missed or overlooked. And there is often a general, not willful ignorance.

None of these possible reasons for the feelings of marginalization are malicious. However, there are women in our churches who are asking these questions, and it is tragic, both for the hearer and for the asker. If we believe these questions are problematic, then it is critical we begin to explore together the reasons why they are being asked. This is what I hope we can consider together as I share my story and experiences from the last decade and a half.

~

Music has delighted me from a very young age. Whether I was dancing enthusiastically along to my parents' John Denver eight-tracks as a child, performing for friends and family at a piano recital or musical theater production, or singing alone in my room as a teenager, I felt the same deep joy each time I participated in the experience of music. As early as elementary school, I connected this joy and feeling directly with God himself and his common grace to us in the music of creation. I could easily relate to the imagery of Tolkien, who describes the Creator as singing creation into existence in the beginning of all things. As a highly emotive person, it was often difficult for me to articulate my feelings. Music became a language that allowed me to express myself beyond words.

I attended a small Christian private school beginning in elementary school, and though I played the piano at the time, it became fashionable in that setting for me to learn to play the guitar. I remember being deeply inspired by one of the senior girls who played the guitar, sang, and often joined in leading small groups of worship music after school or at Bible studies hosted in her home. Something inside me clicked as I saw two things I loved happening at once: I saw this woman capably and sincerely worshiping God through the music she made, and I watched as others were drawn to participate with her. She was a musical evangelist, and it was beautiful to behold.

My parents bought me a guitar for my twelfth birthday, and my sole purpose in learning to play was to serve with the music team for my school's chapel services. The first songs I learned to play were "More Precious Than Silver" and "All in All," and I practiced these simple songs incessantly and labored to sing along while I played. Once I got the hang of it, I started playing with the music team in chapel services each week, delighted to be able to serve God and his people in worship through song.

Once I entered middle and high school, I found many opportunities to use my musical gifts for worship among my peers. On a domestic mission trip with my church's youth group, I was the only one who had brought a guitar, and I was asked to lead the group in a few worship songs each night. This became an ongoing request once we returned home from the trip, and it wasn't long before I was asked to lead music each week for the youth group during Sunday school. Not only did this role require my musical abilities, but it also utilized my administrative gifts. I selected songs each week, printed and prepared chord charts and transparency sheets, and led rehearsals. If you had asked me at the time, I would have borrowed the words of Eric Liddell to say that when I was singing, I felt the Lord's pleasure.[1] It became an absolutely essential part of how I came to know and experience the Lord in a personal way and how I came to understand myself and my identity as a daughter of God. I was earnestly thankful to be growing these skills while serving the Lord and his church.

At the same time, I had become one of the primary leaders in the chapel band at school. There were chapel services three times each week, and many students were involved in the rotation of musicians who helped serve the student body through music. During my sophomore year, I was one of the only female students who could sing and play the guitar, and one of only about three students who felt confident to lead the band and to lead the singing. In a sort of organic development, I began to fill this role on a more regular basis. It was only when an authority figure approached me about this that it occurred to me it could be a problem.

My father, who happened to be the school chaplain, approached me one day after chapel had ended. As I remember it, he wanted to express his concern that my leading in chapel might be usurping authority from the male musicians who participated in leading music, and that it would probably be best to allow the males to lead in more of the visible roles. While he admitted that the male students currently participating as musicians may have been lacking in leadership gifts or even in vocal quality, my primary takeaway was that even a tone-deaf, timid male would lead more effectively than me, a woman.

It is difficult to climb back into my sixteen-year-old skin and imagine exactly what I felt in that moment. Although my father has loved and supported me in other ministry efforts over the years, he and I had not revisited this encounter until very recently. While there may have been other factors and intentions at play behind what he said, the message I received that morning left its mark on my heart in ways I continue to sense in adulthood.

As far as I could discern, this was an authority figure I both loved and respected telling me I was using my gifts in a way that was inappropriate, even sinful. The sin, as I understood it, was that I was not to lead or direct any aspect of corporate worship due to my gender. I was heartbroken first and foremost because my sole intent had been to honor God, not to disobey him! My understanding of what it meant to return my first fruits to the Lord was deeply affected, and I began to wrestle through what it meant to offer my gifts to the Lord if it didn't look the way I had imagined. Even though my intentions had been honorable, a seed of doubt was planted and my heart became full of questions. "What *did* Scripture say about women serving in the Church?"

In the midst of these questions, I stepped back from leadership in the chapel band as requested. I would play in the band or sing in the choir, but I wouldn't lead the songs or prayers. When I did sing, I would hear from people how blessed they were by it and how valuable my leadership was. I received regular affirmation of my gifts, and at the same time I felt completely paralyzed in knowing how and when to exercise them in ways that would honor God and not violate his commands. I began to think it would be best for me to use my talents outside the Church, and I began to focus my time and energy on writing songs for myself rather than for worship. It was just about this time that I packed up my ambivalence and confusion and moved away to college.

Despite my intentions, it took about thirty-six hours at the university before I was asked to lead worship music again. On the very same day I moved into my dorm on the campus of the University of Oklahoma, the Reformed University Fellowship campus minister and intern came to meet me and welcome me to campus. One (or both) of them spotted the CD of recorded songs I had made over the summer, and before the weekend was over, the word had spread to the RUF worship leader who invited me to play at the first RUF worship service the following week.

I couldn't believe it! Of course I wanted to participate, but I had such uncertainty about what my role within the worshiping community was even allowed to be. In the end, I showed up for rehearsal and played with the band at my first ever RUF. I played nearly every week for the next four years.

My experience as a student in RUF was incredibly formative for me. I was invited to play with the band, and then later was asked to serve as leader and co-leader of the band during my later years on campus. I continued to receive consistently positive affirmation for my gifts in music as well as my gifts in leadership. I was invited to join the RUF student leadership team, where I learned more about discipleship and service to the larger community. I experienced personal pastoral care for the first time in my life, as I had regular access to meet with my RUF campus minister and work through spiritual, life, and identity issues with his help. I was learning more about the Gospel than I had ever realized before, even as a born-and-bred PCA woman.

What was, perhaps, one of the most significant discoveries during this time was the affirmation of my value as a member of the body of Christ and an affirmation that my gifts, along with those of my believing brothers and sisters, were valuable to the Church at large. A primary message within RUF is that the ministry serves the Church by growing and equipping future church members to serve in their local communities. This message did not go unnoticed, and I began to truly take it to heart as I moved toward adulthood and committed church membership.

After college, I moved to Seattle to work on staff with RUF. This brought up additional questions for me in regards to my service to God's people and to the local church, but I tried to simply be faithful in the places that I could be and to grow in my knowledge of God and his Word. One of the questions I had at this time was shared by several of the women in my majority-female RUF intern cohort. On at least one occasion, we asked it aloud to an RUF staff person, but I have no doubt that a similar sentiment has been expressed many times since then. Essentially, we were asking something like, "This opportunity to receive ministry training in RUF is wonderful, but what ministry jobs are available to us that we can put this training toward?" Perhaps if we had known as much then as we do now, we might have additionally asked "What ministry opportunities will be available for us in the Church *at all?*" Though I cannot recall his precise words, the response we received was essentially an apologetic shrug. Even as RUF was "equipping [us] to serve," there were no guarantees that our local churches would have or make space for us to serve there. Once again, I was left with unanswered questions and unresolved ambivalence.

Early on in my relationship with my now-husband, Mark, we recognized there was an opportunity to collaborate on a music project for the Church. Mark was serving at the time as the worship director at a PCA church in the city where we lived while I was working with RUF and attending church at a sister congregation across town. Mark and I would both tell you now that working together on this project was formative in our relationship with one another primarily because of the way we were able to contribute our strengths to a common goal and create something better in the process than either of us could have created on our own. Mark is incredibly creative and musically talented. He has strong interpersonal connections and a warmth that draws people to him. He is not, however, organized with detailed plans or the logistics of coordinating people. I enjoy songwriting but often struggle to create music that is original and singable. I can create plans for accomplishing tasks and easily communicate with people to get the work done and reach a vision. Mark is great at getting people excited about that vision.

In working together, Mark and I were each contributing different skills and gifts, supplying our individual strengths in places where the other was weaker. I wrote the lyrics and Mark set them to music. I created a schedule and Mark got people on board. Together, we created a song, and then an album, and then a second album. We collaborated with more than sixty different musicians from six different PCA churches in our region. We gave away more than 1,000 copies of the album so that these songs and hymns could be a gift to the worshiping congregations in our city and across the country. This is a personal and practical example of the way I see the Church being called to embrace men and women working together as brothers and sisters in the ministry of the Church. As each of us offered our gifts to this project, we saw our work be used by God for the purpose of flourishing and blessing our congregation and the Church at large through our partnership with one another.

It was experiences like this one that made me continue to pray and to hope that the Lord had indeed prepared a place for me within the ministry of his church. I continued to play music regularly at my local church and was asked to lead music during the worship service on several occasions at PCA churches around the city. Throughout this season, I was prayerfully discerning whether the Lord was calling me to vocational ministry and to seminary study. This decision was not made lightly or impulsively. Rather, it required years of consideration and prayer, seeking counsel, and receiving affirmation from pastors, friends, and family that it was a prudent choice and calling. It required financial sacrifice and uprooting my family to leave our community and resettle across the country.

Yet, even in the midst of the vocal support I received, there remained a whisper of doubt. No church was sending me off to be trained or offering to invest in my education so that I could return better equipped to serve in that community. I was not brought "under care" or added to prayer lists and newsletter updates. The lingering questions in my heart rose to the surface, asking whether a seminary degree might finally validate my service to the Lord and his church. My decision to pursue a counseling degree was, at least in part, informed by the question I had been asking since high school: "Is there a place for my gifts in the Church?" I still couldn't answer this with certainty. Just as I had once decided to pursue music outside of the Church, I found safety in the crossover that my counseling degree would allow me if I discovered the answer to be "no." I remained hesitant, yet hopeful, that I would someday hear the Church echo God's resounding *"Yes"* to women like me who love the Lord, love his church, and love to offer their best gifts to God in the churches of the PCA.

~

The conversation regarding women in the Church is not a new one. Many individuals, as well as denominations, have resisted and challenged the biblical constraints placed on women's roles within the Church. This resistance has caused suspicion and hypervigilance in denominations which have continued to hold to more conservative viewpoints. Conservative denominations have enacted policies and practices to preserve the wide margin between the "permissible" roles of women in the Church and the "slippery slope" leading to indiscriminate women's ordination. In many contexts, this has created an atmosphere in which ministry efforts are siloed by gender and can manifest a culture of not knowing, not seeing, and not hearing that women are struggling.

The reality is that there are many women who have wondered without challenging and who have submitted in obedience but whose gifts have been lost to the Church and the body of Christ. I add my voice to the chorus of others who have recognized this loss and have tried to identify ways in which women can serve in the Church alongside their brothers in ways that Scripture affirms and which greatly benefit the Church. I do not believe men and women must necessarily do all of the same things, but I propose we are called to be doing more things together with input from one another. Our collective identity as image-bearers does not mean we are the same; instead, *because* of our differences we need one another. Our partnership and collaboration with one another more completely and robustly reflect the image of God, for *"all the members of the body, though many, are one body"* (1 Cor. 12:12).

In many conservative denominations, the conversation about women's roles has been limited to a choice between allowing women to preach or requiring that women remain silent at all times in worship. It has been too convenient to quote a handful of verses in 1 Timothy and ignore the broader testimony of Scripture which affirms that women are indispensable to God's ministry and work in the world. Throughout Scripture we see women invited and involved in the ministry of the Church (Luke 2:6–7, Luke 10:38–42, John 4:39, Acts 18:26, Rom. 16:1,

3–5, 6–7, 12, 15, Phil. 4:2–3), in advisory roles (Judg. 4:4–9, 2 Kings 22:14–20), prophesying and praying (Acts 1:14, Acts 21:9, 1 Cor. 11:5), and having their words, prayers, and songs edify the Church by their inclusion in Scripture (Exod. 15:20–21, 1 Sam. 2:1–11, 1 Sam. 18:6–7, Luke 1:46–55), even while they are not permitted to hold the office of elder (1 Tim. 2:12). Covenant Theological Seminary professor Dan Doriani astutely comments that God "has distributed gifts to every believer, male and female alike. No Scripture suggests that the gifts are gender-specific."[2] However, many churches have adopted an interpretation of Scripture that prevents women from exercising many gifts which the Holy Spirit is said to give to all people. I echo the analysis of Kathy Keller, who says that "not only does this disenfranchise half the Church; it amputates the body of Christ... and many women have been crushed by being told that their gifts, gifts given by the Holy Spirit, are not allowed, not wanted, even nonexistent or imaginary."[3]

The polarized options regarding the roles of women in the Church have come to define the debate between complementarian and egalitarian viewpoints in many ways. For many in Reformed circles, it has been enough to reject women's ordination without taking the additional step of exploring the acceptable practices women may engage in service to the Church. It can indeed be difficult to determine what was customary in the practice of corporate worship in the Old and New Testaments because Scripture does not speak to this issue very extensively apart from the offices of elder and deacon. However, we receive hints about what corporate worship may have looked like in regards to lay men and women in several of Paul's letters. Paul indicates in 1 Corinthians 14:26 that everyone has a hymn, a word of instruction, or a revelation to be shared for the building up of the Church. Similarly, his exhortation in 1 Corinthians 11:4–5 indicates that men and women are praying and prophesying among the believers. It is from these select passages that our denomination has developed a varied set of practices in regards to public worship. As summarized by the "Report of the Ad Interim Committee on Women Serving in the Ministry of the Church," there are at least three approaches within the denomination in regards to women's roles in public worship:

> 1) Some churches have no leadership roles for the laity, and thus their women, in their worship services. 2) Some churches open some roles in their public worship service to laity, and thus their women,

including leading the congregation in singing, taking up offerings, reading Scripture, distributing elements in the Lord's Supper, leading in prayers, making announcements, et cetera. 3) Some churches open roles for women in their worship services by restricting the preaching, and sometimes the reading of the Scriptures, to ordained men and then stating that all other roles in public worship are open to the church's qualified men and women members.[4]

I have been a member of churches in our denomination who fall into each of these categories. The first category, which restricts all corporate worship roles to ordained roles at the exclusion of the laity, is the category that has given me the most pause and concern. Paul exhorts the Church in Ephesus by stating that the body of Christ grows in Christ as *"every joint with which it is equipped... is working properly"* (Eph. 4:15–16). This is the way in which the body of Christ is able to grow and build itself up in love. The roles of the laypersons within the body of Christ are essential joints which enable the body to work and to grow. Neglecting these members of the body is detrimental to the body's functioning and flourishing. There are many roles in which a lay man or woman may participate in corporate worship outside of the role of elder, and it would greatly benefit the church to develop a more robust theology and practice in this regard.

In more modern church history, Reformed churches have been significantly blessed by the work of female hymn writers such as Fanny Crosby, Anne Steele, and Sandra McCracken. It has been of great benefit to me, personally, to receive training and oversight from my church session as a participant in some of the roles within the worship service, including leading in music. One church I attended developed a liturgist training that our pastors used to equip laypersons in the congregation to participate in Scripture reading, collecting the offering, serving communion, giving the welcome and announcements, praying the prayers of the people, and leading congregational singing and music. Other churches within our denomination have intentionally hired women in nonordained church staff positions and invited those women to attend meetings of the session and deacons in the same way as male members of the staff. Some have created time and space within the worship service for occasional testimonies that highlight the work of God in the Church both in the lives of individual members as well as in its various ministries.[5] I believe by implementing some or all of these practices into our church life, we will more fully reflect the gifts of God in our congregations and in the world.

~

I challenge those reading to consider that there may be more than one possible intention in a woman's heart when she asks, "What can I do?" Many women have received (whether implicitly or explicitly) a message from church leadership and culture that their service to the Lord is restricted to domestic tasks and their spirituality to their private life. Furthermore, many have faced the assumption that if they take issue with that reality, it is a result of the sin of Eve and the sin in their own hearts which has prompted them to question God and the Church about it. The boys in my high school were not ordained and had no greater authority than I did to lead music in worship in that context. Yet they were taught all that they could do, while I learned all that I could not. I wonder how my understanding of myself and my place in the body of Christ would have developed differently if we had been encouraged to learn how to work and serve more effectively in partnership alongside one another, and how it may be impacting the way that we serve in our local church contexts even now. I also wonder what else I could have spent my time and energy on if I had not needed to spend so much of it worrying what parts of me God didn't want.

It is essential for us to consider together the reality that many women desire to more faithfully serve their churches, and their sincere intention is to serve God to the greatest possible degree without the ulterior motive of "usurping power." Language like this is unhelpful and has created a culture of fear and suspicion of women that the Lord does not require and which actually grieves him. My hope is that the pastors and elders in our denomination would more and more see and believe in the value of the godly women in their congregations, women who are "clothed with strength and dignity" (Prov. 31:25). I pray these leaders would consider it to be their shepherding duty to build women up in the Lord, to make room for gifted women who may already be equipped to serve, and to witness the ways the Church as a whole is built up in the process. This will not simply be a benefit to the women in their congregations, but a "more vigorous adherence to the apostolic deposit of truth"[6] bestowed to us in Scripture. I pray women in the PCA would see their gifts affirmed and valued by their churches, would come to believe there *is* a place for them in the Church, and believe the Lord delights in their service to him and to the people of God.

---

1. *Chariots of Fire, dir. Hugh Hudson, perf. Ian Charleson, Ben Cross, Nicholas Ferrell* (USA: Twentieth-Century Fox, Allied Stars Ltd., Enigma Productions, 1982), DVD.
2. Dan Doriani, Women and Ministry: What the Bible Teaches (Wheaton, IL: Crossway Books, 2003), 101.
3. Kathy Keller, Jesus, Justice, and Gender Roles (Grand Rapids, MI: Zondervan, 2012), 31.
4. "Report of the Ad Interim Committee on Women Serving in the Ministry of the Church to the 45th General Assembly of the Presbyterian Church in America (2017)," *www.pcac.org*, http://www.pcaac.org/wp-content/uploads/2017/06/Women-Serving-in-Min.-of-Ch.-Study-Committee-Report-with-admended-recommendations.pdf, 51–52.
5. See the full list of recommendations given by the "Report of the Ad Interim Committee on Women Serving in the Ministry of the Church to the 45th General Assembly of the Presbyterian Church in America (2017)," 58–63.
6. Kathy Keller, *Jesus, Justice, and Gender Roles*, 34.

SINGLE MOTHERS IN THE CHURCH
SARAH JOY HAYS

Sarah Joy Hays lives in Baton Rouge, Louisiana, where she works remotely as the Acting Executive Director for the Data Coalition managing staff, finances, programming, and strategic decisions. She owns a small bakery, CounterspaceBR, where she serves baked goods and distributes wholesale to five different restaurants and coffee shops in town. Sarah Joy has an adorable red-headed son named Henry and is active in her community through her local church, Foot Above Foundation, Moms on Campus, Red Stick Moms Blog, and Reformed University Fellowship at Louisiana State University.

In the fall of 2014, I was living in Washington, DC, and working for Data Coalition, a trade association that advocates for the modernization of the federal government through transforming financial documents to machine-readable data. I was actively involved in the downtown congregation of my church, Grace DC, and was approached to share a testimony of thanksgiving at our fall Day of Vision and Prayer. I was humbled to be asked and then began to rack my brain as to *what* to say or share. I knew I was going to attempt to not cry, and I knew my story was one that was very uncommon in the church. The past year had come with much speculation, loads of explanations, lots of shame and guilt, multiple counseling sessions, tears, joy, grief, and a baby. I am a single, never wed mother.

Now let's rewind a tad. I lived a seemingly "good" Christian life. I attended church, was committed to my community group, and formerly served as campus ministry staff. I believed Scripture and knew God's grace through Jesus was my salvation. I worked hard, although I had some career struggles, and I appeared to be without certain sin struggles.

Then, on a very emotionally dark day in October of 2013, I realized I was pregnant. My world came to a halt. I was in a new place, away from DC and the Church there that I knew and loved. I was between jobs. I was scared to tell both the father and my family.

After talking to a few close friends, I immediately called my former pastor at Grace Downtown. Glenn prayed with me. He comforted me. And he reminded me that I was forgiven. That reminder was one that I clung to in the months to come and still do in parenting (three-and-a-half-year-olds, amirite?!). I was and am forgiven.

Many emotions and conversations later, I found myself living back in DC with a great job in a lovely house on a lovely block! Toiling over how to move forward, I began doing all of my research. Do I parent? Do I put up my baby for adoption? Then I had to begin to consider what was next for me and this baby inside me. In an attempt to explore all options, I made an appointment to visit an adoption agency. Enter my first true realization that we, the Church, aren't prepared to walk alongside single women who are pregnant.

Now, can we quickly come to the aid of pregnant teens? Yes! Case in point, the literature I received from the local adoption agency in Northern Virginia included a questionnaire to help a woman discern whether she was ready to parent. I was expecting questions about income and insurance and living situations. Instead I was greeted with questions about my education goals, specifically whether I had finished high school or planned to attend college. What? Seriously? I immediately dismissed the questionnaire and went to a counselor and friends for guidance.

That should have been the clue that Christian resources surrounding unplanned pregnancy were maybe lacking.

I decided to parent. This decision didn't come easily. I knew I would be doing it on my own. I also truly believed that this was a calling on my life. Don't get me wrong, indulging in a sinful sexual relationship was *not* part of my calling. And, even if I hadn't been called to long-term parenting, I still had to make a very important parenting decision. It was a decision most pregnant women don't even have to make. I had to decide who *would* parent my son.

When I chose this, I shared with my pastor that I was going to parent, and I told him that I have such a great community and am ready to accept this call. That's when he said one of the most profound things I still remind myself of regularly: "You have community and a church that loves you now, but all you are guaranteed is Jesus. There could come a time when is it just you, Henry, and Jesus." Whoa. Now that rattled me. But it was true. It was biblical. It was good.

That summer Henry came into the world. He was perfect. Henry was an amazing baby. He slept well, he ate well, and he wasn't a screamer. And my church came running at me with food and friendship and babysitting and love and encouragement. In a congregation full of single people, Henry was the community group baby. He was the Wylie Street baby. He was the Data Coalition baby. He was the Peregrine Espresso (the best coffee shop in all the world) baby!

That fall I decided the best thing I could share with my congregation on our Day of Vision and Prayer was a passage from *The Jesus Storybook Bible* (if you don't own this, buy it now). This children's Bible so beautifully shares the truth of the Gospel and the grace of Jesus. It does it in a way that makes me weep. My son and I can begin to better understand Jesus, forgiveness, grace, and obedience.

I shared the passage and did cry. My tears were of joy and gratitude. I was so thankful my community came alongside me in Henry's first months. They were a group of people who selflessly showed up with dinner and groceries and coffee and friendship and community. God was surely good.

The spring before Henry's first birthday, things became harder and more expensive (childcare, y'all, *childcare!*). That's when I approached my boss about moving closer to home. I went house shopping. I decided to take my baby, my world, my job (praise the Lord), and move back to Louisiana. I was so excited. Now, was I sad to leave the friends and neighbors that had become like family? Yes! To this day, I daydream about what life in DC might look like again in the future. But home in Louisiana was where I needed to be for this time. So, I went.

I was welcomed back to Baton Rouge with open arms! The church I attended in college finally had its own building, and my regular Thursday happy hour friends still gathered at the local taco shop weekly at 6 p.m. without fail. Things were familiar and good. Sadly, I didn't understand that familiarity would not equal community.

I left Baton Rouge seven years prior, as friends were getting married and having their first and second babies. I would come back for visits and catch up with people and assumed I would fit right back in, now even more so because I shared in the understanding of parenting. So, how to connect with these old friends? Thursday morning Bible study seemed to be the way. They provided childcare, but that didn't matter much because Henry would be at daycare. It would be tricky because I would have work, travel, and miss occasionally for conference calls, but I was really committed to trying.

I tried fitting into the mold of female church member. If that meant taking an early lunch and ducking out early, I would attend the women's Bible study. When that became hard, a few people recommended the nighttime women's study. Sadly, that study started at bedtime and no childcare was provided. At this point I leaned on a few scattered one-on-one meetings with women in my church and my pastors. Then I quickly committed to a Sunday night community group.

A few months in, my pastor shared that he was interested in the parish model community group! *My heart burst!* I was so excited. Our community groups in DC had been that model, and I loved it. Parish model community groups encouraged you to get to know your neighbors better as well as form relationships with people in the Church that might not otherwise fall in your social circle. I faithfully attended all the planning meetings. I voiced excitement and concern. I listened as others became more excited, and then we finally broke up into what would be our neighborhood groups. We brainstormed. Who lives in our area that wasn't at the meeting? Who was on music team, excluding Thursdays? Who was involved in Reformed University Fellowship, excluding Tuesdays? We settled on Monday at 6:30 p.m. at my house.

I was elated. I was so excited to host and to actually interact with people during the week who weren't just my son or his daycare teachers. There were quite a few young kids in the group, and we were going to rotate childcare. Our group decided on monthly potlucks the first Monday of the month. All was great!

Then, other parents began to leave our Monday night gatherings early for bedtime. I got it, I regularly had to leave events to tend to Henry. Then it became a talking point. Then time change was brought up. Now, to be fair, I can be stubborn. I like getting my way. I worked hard at helping scientifically decide the best time and date for our community groups over weeks of planning meetings. Then, just a few weeks into our group forming, based on the 90/10 rule (what can 90 percent of the group do), the time was moved up. I was heartbroken. Not just because I wasn't getting my way, but because that meant attending was now in question and hosting was definitely off the table.

I explained to the group, tearfully in my own backyard, that I worked and had to get Henry fed and ready. Being someplace at 6 p.m. on a weeknight was nearly impossible. The extremely short-sighted solutions included, "You can just come late. You will only miss the fellowship time" or "I can help you get Henry in the car." I was sitting and sharing very plainly, "This doesn't work for me." I felt so selfish. Then I began to believe maybe I was going against the entire purpose of community groups. Was I just unwilling to be flexible?

As I tried to convince myself of this, I became more and more frustrated. I am the 10 percent in my church. Actually, I'm more like the .05 percent of my church. I'm the only single parent. The 90/10 rule excludes me 90 percent of the time. This ranges from women's Bible studies all the way down to women's cookie decorating nights complete with frosting but "after bedtime and no childcare provided," because of course most mothers have a husband at home to watch the kids. Then I became bitter.

Not just for me, but bitter because this was affecting my son. Bitter because he was the fatherless. We actually were a scriptural demographic to be served. He needs community just as much as I do. He needs to be around Christian men who are seeking the Lord. He needs to have godly examples in his life spanning more than two hours on Sunday morning.

I cried the night the time change was decided for our group. Surrounded by no less than fifteen people who I know well, I explained that I don't have an extra person. I said I can't host; I work alone from home and *need* that social time you say I can just miss. I sat talking and crying and explaining about how I'm the unseen. And I wasn't seen, even in my own yard.

Now, if you knew me well you might be thinking, "How could Sarah Joy be the unseen in her church? She is involved with RUF still and has a side baking business. She's bubbly and outgoing and talks so easily with everyone." This is tricky for a lot of reasons. First, it's true I'm very social. I'm also good at appearing to be without need. I faithfully attend church. I attend social events at the church that are church-wide and include childcare. Many single parents struggle with needing resources or a flexible, well-paying job. I don't need those things. I am blessed beyond belief and have an amazing job that pays me well and affords me a lot of flexibility.

But that doesn't mean I am without need. I need community. I have no full-time partner. I have all the constraints of parenting without the freedoms that come with sharing that responsibility. I do the cooking and the cleaning. I go to the store and put the groceries away. I do the laundry and fold it. I either have to mow my own lawn or pay someone to do it. It's all on me.

You know what I often need? Someone to help rake my lawn. Maybe someone to watch Henry so I can run Saturday errands. I need friends.

Single parents have deficits in areas that can be overlooked. We don't have a partner, a second income, someone to tap-in when we are exhausted and need a break. We don't have built-in childcare for a women's retreat or outing. We need emotional support and another adult to talk to. We need encouragement and to know we aren't alone. We miss out on a lot of social opportunities because we don't fit neatly into any category. Sometimes we fit in with singles, sometimes with mothers, but not fully either way.

When considering community groups and inability to access programming, I have been told more than once by more than one person that I need to be inconvenienced. But what might be inconvenient to one person could be logistically impossible to another. I was literally the only woman in our community group who had logistical barriers to every other gathering our church offers weekly. My community group was my chance for community. This is when the 90/10 rule breaks down even further. The 90 percent that wanted an earlier community group time or encouraged me to be inconvenienced are *always* the 90 percent. They are the vast majority. This leaves the minority excluded every time.

So, lest this sound like a bitter rant of solitude and hurt, I try to remember what my pastor in DC told me years ago. Sometimes it will be me and Henry and Jesus. I am not guaranteed community. I am not guaranteed access to women's retreats. I am guaranteed Jesus.

Does that give the Church a pass? By all means no! So, Church, here are some ways I would like to encourage you to serve the single parents in your church:

First, reflect on this verse:

Let us consider how to stir up one another to love and good works, not neglecting to meet together, as is the habit of some, but encouraging one another, and all the more as you see the Day drawing near. Heb. 10:24–25

Second, throw away the 90/10 rule! You are probably excluding the same group of people more regularly than you think, not just single moms. Forget asking what the majority of people can do, and rather ask this, "Who isn't coming to Bible study or community group? Should we consider a different day, time, or schedule to ensure everyone who *wants* to be in a small group can be? Should we ask the women who *aren't* present how to include and accommodate them?" Maybe sometimes the 90 could be inconvenienced and sacrifice for the 10.

Third, do for single mothers what you do for anyone who has a chronic need or deficit. We don't need constant meal help or childcare, but it is such a blessing and emotional encouragement to be served in this way. What about a single parent ministry that considers single parents and how they could be loved and cared for?

Come alongside women who are attempting to date as a single parent. Y'all, dating as an adult is hard! And weird and confusing. Dating as a Christian is hard and weird and confusing at times too. Invite that single mom and her boyfriend on a double date. Challenge that mom on boundaries. Offer to take the kids so she can go on a date and not have to pay a sitter! I've been on a lot of bad first dates as a single parent, and the sting of a bad date is doubled when you have to pay a sitter too.

Fourth, don't be scared of what you don't understand. There is a trope of the single mom who can do it all. She sure is trying, but most single parents are holding their lives together by prayers and coffee. They want to be known beyond just the idea of the brave situation they are handling.

If you don't have any single parents in your church, ask why. Do you know any single parents in your community? Is your church one that is welcoming for nontraditional demographics? Does your congregation espouse grace in all you say and do, maybe helping assuage whatever guilt or shame might come with the category of "single mom"?

When I first found out I was pregnant, I spent about three to four weeks telling people close to me what was going on. That usually included reliving the sin and decisions that had already been repented of and forgiven. Once my belly couldn't be denied any longer and more people knew I was pregnant, that ushered in a whole new round of people wanting to know. Here is the deal: repentance is what we are called to, but re-hashing the nitty gritty of a sin should not be expected. If a woman in your church becomes pregnant out of marriage, check on her heart and her relationship with the Lord. Give grace, and don't indulge shame.

I recall another nugget of wisdom my pastor in DC shared with me during my first trimester. That trimester, until most people knew I was pregnant, I felt like I was constantly reliving my now-past sinful decision as I explained my situation... again and again. Glenn lovingly said to me, "Being pregnant isn't a sin."

Whoa. My pregnancy might have been a result of sin, but *pregnancy itself is not*. Let's say that out loud: "Being single and pregnant isn't sinful." Keep that in mind if you ever have the opportunity to minister to someone who is unwed and pregnant, in or out of your church.

Consider that I know Jesus. I know I'm forgiven. I know God's grace is bigger than my sin. I am the squeaky wheel about access to programming. Now think about a woman who isn't quite as brash or outspoken as I am. How would she fare in your congregation? The woman who is a single parent and worn down. The woman who needs grace. The woman who needs access to community. Maybe this woman also needs more practical support. Would your church know how to minister to her? Would she visit more than two weeks in a row? Or would she fall silently away because she can't make Bible study or women's retreat or afford childcare to participate in the social activities that are designed without her family in mind?

I just finished reading an amazing book about singleness in the Church, and one of my big takeaways from the book is that our communities will only be as rich as they are diverse.[1] Is your community working to be inclusive? Or is it inclusive of one type of woman? Do you understand the barriers to the Gospel that women unlike you might have? Do you work to break down the barriers of access for those exact women?

As a denomination, we rightly love to espouse grace and salvation in Christ alone. We point to the work of the cross. If Christ is truly our salvation and the Gospel is our message, let your programming and your approach to women reflect that. The Gospel is for all and is accessible for all. All you need is your need. I hope that going forward you will consider the single mothers in your midst and their need for community and the sacrificial love of Jesus Christ displayed through his people.

---

1. Joy Beth Smith, Party of One: Truth, Longing, and the Subtle Art of Singleness (Nashville, TN: Harper Collins Christian Publishing, 2018).

STORIES FROM THE FRONT

MARIA GARRIOTT

Navigating the Majority-Male Church Leadership Space

Maria Garriott and her husband Craig moved in 1981 to urban Baltimore to plant Faith Christian Fellowship, a multiethnic, socioeconomically diverse PCA church. Maria worked at the Johns Hopkins University School of Education for twenty years before joining the staff of Parakaleo, a ministry to church planting spouses, in 2009. She is the author of A Thousand Resurrections, *a memoir of urban church planting, and her poetry and articles have been published in numerous magazines and online forums. Maria and Craig have five adult children and five grandchildren.*

~

For ten years I have worked for Parakaleo, a ministry that supports and trains pastors' wives and church planting wives. I have had the privilege of attending presbytery meetings, conferences for church planting leaders, and denominational assemblies. I have worn the nametags and logged the miles.

In this majority-male space, mine might be the only XX chromosomes in the room, except for the kitchen help. I will have the bathroom to myself. During the extended opportunity for networking, men will often smile or nod on their way to talk to someone else. I can attend the meet-and-greet and not be greeted. I wonder if this means they don't think I am relevant. That I don't bring anything to the table, other than, perhaps, dinner.

I am here to advocate for other women—often their own wives or the wives of men they oversee. But they don't see me unless I take the initiative, so I must overrule my introversion. I approach small clusters of men sipping coffee from paper cups. I ask questions: "Where are you from? What do you see God doing in your work?" I learn about what is going well in their settings. I ask if there is training or support for their ministry spouses. When I initiate, they are gracious. Yet I am not seen unless I initiate.

This sense of invisibility or exclusion has not been my experience outside of ministry. For twenty years, I worked in education reform where I also attended meetings and conferences. I was evaluated according to my contributions, not my gender. I was allowed to put my shoulder to the wheel and welcomed as part of a team to help solve pressing educational issues. I was even recognized for my contributions.

Ministry is different. I sometimes feel that as a group, men in church leadership struggle to know how to engage women or deploy our gifts. I fear that to some men, my gender and I are a mystery.

To be fair, sometimes I attend these events with my husband (who is usually off networking with someone else), so perhaps other attendees think I am just a wife. An add-on. I hasten to add that those who know me are affirming and engaging; this invisibility is with men I don't know.

I'm not unsympathetic to men; as a clergy wife, I know that pastors face a fusillade of criticism, especially when it comes to women. They haven't done enough. They didn't do it quickly enough, or didn't get buy-in from everyone on their way to getting things done. They are criticized for leading and berated for not leading. The Enemy loves to sack the quarterback, and sometimes, so do people on the home team. Many men at these conferences and meetings live in fellowship deserts; they are dispirited and hungry for encouragement or affirmation from their male peers. They have already composed their resignation letters in their heads. They want to hear tactics to succeed, and to outrun the voices that tell them to quit, just quit, and now. Perhaps they think my experience, if I have any, is not relevant to their own.

There are theological and historical reasons for men's confusion or reluctance. Women have historically been excluded from the Church leadership space, and Evangelicals disagree on the biblical boundaries for women's roles (for example, are ordained deaconesses biblical, or a banana peel to speed us down a slippery slope to egalitarianism?). Women's voices and contributions have often been ignored or erased from the historical account. (For example, consider Rebecca Protten, a formerly enslaved woman who evangelized hundreds of enslaved Africans in the West Indies and helped create early African Protestant congregations in the Atlantic world).

Though I accept a complementarian framework, the literal biblical interpretation that reserves the pastoral role for males, my church is on the progressive side of complementarian. Women serve on staff, teach adult Christian education classes, speak from the pulpit, counsel, lead our small groups, advise the elders and deacons, and pray during the service. Most of our committees are women-led. They attend leadership classes and retreats. Women do everything but preach. Even within complementarianism, men and women can work in partnership, and fly the plane on more than one engine.

By nature, we are sinners who disrespect or dominate or strike back. Or just don't see each other. But perhaps God established this complementarian framework to make us work harder at communicating, at listening, at honoring one another, at asking each other questions.

Look at the example of Jesus. He overturned multiple cultural taboos and legalistic injunctions by having a one-on-one conversation with a disreputable woman from a despised minority culture (John 4). He allowed women to minister to him (Matt. 27, Mark 14, Luke 7) and included them among his followers (Mark 15, Luke 8, Luke 23). He taught them (Luke 10). He lauded their faith (Matt. 9, Matt. 15, Mark 5, Mark 7, Luke 8). In short, he recognized and valued them.

I know many men who strive to include and value women's ministry contributions. I have advocated for women long enough in my presbytery that I have a good, working rapport with many brothers. Our church session and Women's Leadership Team has been jointly hammering out a corporate confession on women. When Shari Thomas, an experienced missionary and church planting spouse, shared her research about the crisis in unsupported, untrained ministry wives, the Presbyterian Church in America's (PCA) all-male Mission to North America denominational church planting committee listened to her. Some wept tears in repentance. "I've been meeting with a church planter for two years, and I don't even know his wife's *name*," one leader confessed. They recognized her leadership skills and asked her to start a ministry. She founded Parakaleo, and they provided financial and practical support. They invited her to speak at conferences. They asked her to take a seat at the table, and God built a flourishing ministry.

We can do more together. Whether we serve from a complementarian or egalitarian position, God's kingdom will advance more rapidly, more justice will be done, more mercy extended, and more believers brought to maturity if we teach, train, and value women—as Jesus did. Our Savior took the place of the voiceless, the disenfranchised, and the overlooked outsider—sinners all—on the cross so that we could be seated at the Father's table. He embraced us as beloved sons and daughters. This Gospel gives men and women courage to fight for his bride, the Church, and to keep advocating for women to be heard and given a place at our earthly tables.

WORDS FROM OUR SISTERS: LEARN

A CONVERSATION WITH METHOD

CLAIRE BERGER

Claire Berger grew up in Houston, Texas, and studied at Texas A&M (BA) and Denver Seminary (MA). She has worked as a children's director, high school humanities teacher, and a spiritual formation and community coordinator. Claire is an editor for White Blackbird Books. In her spare time she volunteers her editing skills to nonprofits and enjoys cooking and reading. Claire and her husband, Josh, have three children.

"Beauty will save the world," declares Dostoevsky's protagonist in *The Idiot*. The skeptical reader asks, is the character a prophet, or an idiot?

For the past forty years or so, Evangelical egalitarians and complementarians have engaged in a conflict over the nature of women and their role in church and at home. Egalitarians, those who hold that "the climax of redemptive history would bring about the restoration of male-female relationships as evidenced in creation, that patriarchalism seeks to prohibit women from doing the very things we see women doing in the Bible,"[1] and complementarians, who highlight "differences between men and women created equally in the image of God,"[2] have their defenses stocked high and claim heavy stakes in the application of these varied doctrines. Are we prophets or idiots? If the stakes sit as high as we claim, some complementarians arguing the Gospel itself is at stake, where does beauty fit in?

Complementarians give their lives to the perplexing and mesmerizing rhythm of God's grand narrative, but this cadence is often absent in our defense of complementarian theology. The story of God making a people to live as makers of culture in communion with him and each other, our fall, our rescue, and the Maker setting all things right ties uniquely into complementarian theology. However, false application and inconsistent language toward women feed the predator of forgetfulness.

This chapter will look at the beauty in complementarian narrative by examining theological method, interspersed with a personal narrative, to explore habit-shaping ways to live what we believe about God's design. However, the subject of women in Christ's church does not fall prey to indifference. The subject becomes a war of attrition—a fight not about land gained or lost, but about preservation of your side and the destruction of the other. Instead, let us first discuss the method of our complementarian theology from the Trinity, and humbly look at blind spots that lead to uncharitable hearts, unthinking minds, and the binding of feminine hands from the Lord's work. We examine this theology not because we want to "win" a "battle" with egalitarians, but because theology has drastic implications for daughters, sisters, wives, and the whole body of Christ as we pursue the knowledge of the glory of the Lord covering the earth as the waters cover the sea. We examine this theology because a Christian believes beauty will save the world.

The term "complementarian" surfaced in the '80s when a group of Evangelical leaders sought to speak to the feminist agenda, and what came forth called itself the Council for Biblical Manhood and Womanhood. They teach on how men and women are made equal and different "because these teachings are essential for obedience to Scripture and for the health of the family and the church."[3] Much of how they talk about women comes from an analogy with the Trinity, so with the Trinity we will begin.

Method

Augustine (354–430 AD) introduces the *method* our Western tradition uses to talk about the Trinity. The term "method" not only houses content, but how one goes about studying: where to start, how different doctrines relate to each other, influence of prevailing values, etc.[4] In truth, someone's method communicates far more about the nature of their outcomes than the words on a page. Actions speak louder than words, as they say.

Augustine has an intentional and specific starting place for his work on the Trinity. He starts his conversation on the Trinity by first talking about the Trinity as one unified nature. He could have started talking about the Trinity an infinite number of ways, like talking about roles or attributes or differences, but instead he started with their relationship, the divine nature itself.[5] How you start your theology builds an infrastructure for all to come. In his work *On the Trinity*, Augustine discusses how:

> In this Trinity, as we have said elsewhere, those names, which are predicated relatively, the one of the other, are properly spoken of as belonging to each person in particular, as Father and Son, and the Gift of both, the Holy Spirit.... These are the things that we have affirmed; and the more often we repeat and discuss them, then, of course, the more familiar the knowledge of them will become to us.[6]

The theological work that initiated how Western Christianity discusses the Trinity begins talking about how the members of the Trinity belong together, and then later talks about how they are three without division. To speak of the Trinity according to its nature means to discuss them relationally, discussing the unity they hold, before primarily discussing various functions. Augustine thought we should repeatedly have this conversation, and people have.

Gordon Lewis and Bruce Demarest, who wrote *Integrative Theology*, explain Augustine's primary focus on the unity of the three: "The distinction between persons is not substantial, but only relational.... For Augustine, oneness of essence implies equality of perfections, unity of will, and oneness of operations."[7] In Augustine's discussion of the triune God's holiness, godliness, and divinity, he starts with exploring their similarity. Lewis and Demarest note how the distinctions in the Godhead are not substantial, meaning independent and self-contained existence, and substantial distinctions stand in contrast to a relational difference. Augustine addresses first the unity of the triune

God, and then shows their differences primarily in relationship, not self-contained functions. Augustine's starting place shows how the familial relationship gives me the most information about the nature of the Trinity. Relationship communicates beauty. Isolated roles do not.

This starting place carries significance because if we say the Trinity is analogous to complementarian theology, then conversations about complementarianism should be analogous to our conversations about the Trinity. The complexities of the Trinity require all kinds of conversations about it. However, if we discuss the Trinity *primarily* in unified and relational terms instead of substantive ones, and if we use the Trinity as a metaphor for complementarian theology, then our conversations about complementarianism need to be had *primarily* in unified and relational terms. Keep in mind these terms, relational and substantive, as we turn briefly from churning analysis about method, to looking at doctrine in practice. We will look at a time when I was newly engaged years ago. There are four men in this narrative. I am thankful for all of them and owe some part of my development as a Christian to each one. Well-intentioned, some operated out of a substantial approach, and others a relational.

Man #1, Man #2

When I was staring down college graduation, my plan was to attend seminary. Then a seminary student proposed. As his knee hit the ground, the CD player in my head clicked on and began to play a traditional narrative: married women don't go to seminary. Married women don't sacrifice countless hours and too much money on a selfish hobby. This is how the playing narrative described seminary for married women—a hobby. Where did that narrative come from? What exactly was I believing about women? I sought wisdom from four male leaders in my life to explore whether I should still go. In light of that narrative, I am not sure why I still felt the need to seek counsel from men, but I did. A friend recently asked why I didn't ask any women. I didn't know any women who had been to seminary for theology. Sure, I knew some who had gone for children's ministry, but that wasn't my thing.

Let's call this first guy, Man #1.

I sat sipping lemonade next to my fiancé on the kid-worn couch of Man #1. His wife sat across from us, a coffee table away, while she stroked the family dog. Man #1, a pastor, was doing something in the kitchen. From there, he shouted, "You don't need to go to seminary if your husband is going. My wife is given all kinds of leadership roles because she is married to me." I spewed lemonade across the coffee table.

My husband-to-be studies counseling, and I wanted to study theology. Man #1 says I will get asked to lead Bible studies on the merit of my husband. Never mind that I will have no training to lead once I have these positions of leadership. I won't be in the classroom with my husband, won't be required to read the books, won't get feedback on papers or presentations, and husband-to-be does not even study theology. Personally, I don't think anyone should call me when they need a Licensed Professional Counselor. They should call my husband. He's the one trained to do that.

So I continue my journey to the couch of Man #2. Sitting next to my fiancé, a former mentor unpacked how a seminary degree was like a card to get into the ministry club, and I could get into the club on my husband's degree, so I did not need to go.

Maybe these men did not go to quality seminaries? It made me wonder how valuable they saw their educations, if they thought of them as Costco cards. In their defense, I'm sure their concerns were primarily financial. Women can't get many jobs in our churches so how would a degree pay for itself? But maybe the problem isn't women getting degrees; maybe the problem we should address is providing jobs for theologically trained women. I felt deflated, dejected, unnecessary, but compliant. I would get a job to pay the bills while my soon-to-be husband finished his degree.

If you had to guess, would you say this was a relational or substantive understanding of women in the Church?

Conversation

The common pastor picks up this substantive complementarian theology from somewhere. One theologian's look at Jesus' baptism provides an example of understanding the Trinity in self-contained categories (substantively) instead of relationally. Jesus' baptism gloriously puts on display the doctrine of the Trinity. In Jesus' baptism, signaling the start of his earthly ministry, he goes to the Jordan River to be baptized by John:

And when Jesus was baptized, immediately he went up from the water, and behold, the heavens were opened to him, and he saw the Spirit of God descending like a dove and coming to rest on him; and behold, a voice from heaven said, "This is my beloved Son, with whom I am well pleased." Matt. 3:16–17

Wayne Grudem highlights from this picture how the three are performing different activities, "God the Father is speaking from heaven; God the Son is being baptized and is then spoken to from heaven by God the Father; and God the Holy Spirit is descending from heaven to rest upon and empower Jesus for his ministry."[8] Grudem discusses the text this way because Grudem's text gives a systematic overview of various theological elements, and therefore he goes to great lengths to emphasize the substantive qualities of personhood. Of course Grudem writes true things of the Trinity, but we cannot primarily address independent members of the Trinity "doing" different "activities."[9]

Grudem's theological method has implications beyond his giant book, *Systematic Theology*. He helped found the Council of Biblical Manhood and Womanhood, and his articulation of the Trinity in primarily substantive terms comes across in the fruit of complementarian theology. We do not allow the complexities and mystery of the relationship of the Trinity to enter our conversations about male and female relationships because we do not talk about either relationally. The way we talk to people, the way we talk about a subject, shapes us.

The *Harvard Business Review* discusses the phenomenon of language shaping people in a management setting, which speaks even louder to our church culture. They argue:

When we face criticism, rejection or fear, when we feel marginalized or minimized, our bodies produce higher levels of cortisol, a hormone that shuts down the thinking center of our brains and activates a conflict aversion and protection behaviors. We become more reactive and sensitive. We often perceive even greater judgment and negativity than actually exist. And these effects can last for 26 hours or more, imprinting the interaction on our memories and magnifying the impact it has on our future behavior. Cortisol functions like a sustained-release tablet—the more we ruminate about our fear, the longer the impact.[10]

I am not saying we should avoid conflict with women. I am saying when conversations about anything related to women in the Church remain primarily in terms of what they can and can't do, or scoffing at what they want to do, or making them the butt of a joke, or loudly crying about feminists making inroads against traditionalists, these have lasting effects on the listeners, and the speakers. Imagine you are twenty-two-year-old woman called to ministry. When this woman opens Twitter in the morning to daily find someone she respects saying she doesn't belong, it hurts the Church. Our bad method says we can talk about women this way. But the Church will not receive the gifts the Spirit has given that twenty-two-year-old if she daily faces criticism, rejection, marginalization, and minimization.

The Council of Biblical Manhood and Womanhood argues that in complementarian theology the authority of Scripture is at stake, the health of the home is at stake, the health of the Church is at stake, Bible translations are at stake, and the advance of the Gospel is at stake.[11] I want to add and emphasize that it is substantial instead of relational rhetoric and *misapplied* complementarianism, by both men and women, that functionally gags, enslaves, and mistrusts women, hurts Scripture, hurts the home, hurts the Church, and disenfranchises the Gospel.

A Consistent Method, A Truer Conversation

Complementarian theology works best when it remains married to its narrative, its intent. In the beginning of all things, God made Adam and Eve and gave them work: the Cultural Mandate. Before the Fall comes the vision of the harmonious relationship between Adam and Eve. In unity, in trust, they make culture in service and love to their Creator. In his book *Center Church*, Timothy Keller quotes Henry Van Til defining culture as "any and all human effort and labor expended on the cosmos, to unearth its treasures and riches and bring them into... service... to something."[12] Taking the raw materials and having them submit to a form that serves the world God loves: this is culture making. God said increase and multiply, fill the earth, and subdue it. Create culture. Make my name great as you make a world.

Women are made to help in this endeavor in similar ways in which God helps us. In her book *No Little Women*, Aimee Byrd discusses John McKinley's interpretations of *ezer* as "necessary ally."[13] She continues to push the idea that God made woman to be an ally to man, and locate places where God uses that same term to describe himself, and "ally marks the man's dependence upon her contribution."[14] Men and women were created differently, and equally, and made to fill the earth and subdue it in communion with each other and with God. The Cultural Mandate is the original intent of complementarian theology. With the Fall the work gets harder. The relationship gets harder. The communion with a holy God is cut.

I believe in complementarian theology because I believe God ordered the world in such a way that before creation he knew he would fill an earth with his glory through the means of men and women working in unity and diversity, and it would be clear who is called to go and die.[15] It would be clear that men should lay down their lives for those in their care. And since Adam couldn't in Eden, Jesus did on the cross. Keller argues, "At the heart of all of the biblical writers' theology is redemption through substitution,"[16] and a complementarian theology stands as no exception. Someone laying down a life for another sure sounds familiar. Lived out of its intention, complementarianism can embody a habit that models our purpose (the Cultural Mandate and Great Commission) and reminds us of the good news that Jesus has laid down his life for his Church. Consistency within the Scripture narrative argues God built a design feature for who was to lay down life. If there was the laying down of a life, would we really be envious of their leadership? Who envies the dying? Redemption through substitution. This is the beauty of complementarian theology.

From the Garden we move on, and our calling to together fill the earth and subdue it continues, as we are re-called, and fail again, through Abraham, through Israel, until Jesus takes up the call to be human for us.[17] Complementarianism is fresh and sweet and healthy when men and women embody different strengths and qualities of the person of God, and together they take chaos and cultivate life for the flourishing of others, with men appointed to lay down their lives for those in their care. Using the Trinity to argue for specific limiting roles within complementarian theology operates out of an incomplete vision of the Trinity. Speaking first, or longest, or loudest about what women (or those of the Trinity) can or cannot do operates out of a substantial view of the Trinity. A substantive understanding of the Trinity, and subsequently of complementarian theology, says women do not primarily swim in theological waters, and so efficiency justifies functionally barring women from seminary or theological jobs. A relational view says, if men and women work together for human flourishing, to deprive them of theological education would be a detriment to the Church. Complementarian theology works best when it remains married to its narrative, its intent, its story. Men and women go and make and go and tell for the glory of God as one. Men and women do everything together, depend on each other, and share the very essence of love and unity together, like the Trinity.[18]

To talk to and about women consistent with the nature of the Trinity will have its own effect on our brains: "Positive comments and conversations produce a chemical reaction too. They spur the production of oxytocin, a feel-good hormone that elevates our ability to communicate, collaborate, and trust others by activating networks in our prefrontal cortex."[19] To practice a consistent analogy of the Trinity, first linger longest and speak loudest on the unified work of men and women. Sure this will require creative effort because we believe men and women are different, but there is a difference between conversations that close doors and those that explore possibility. There is a difference between conversations that grow from cultural adaptations and those that explore theological consistency. Look again to our complementarian passages.

Ephesians 5, a standard complementarian submission passage, speaks primarily of husbands laying down their lives for wives. Paul admonishes mutual submission, then talks to the wives, and then watch for any talk of leadership or decision making as he talks to husbands:

> *Husbands, love your wives, as Christ loved the church and gave himself up for her, that he might sanctify her, having cleansed her by the washing of water with the word, that he might present the church to himself in splendor, without spot or wrinkle or any such thing, that she might be holy and without blemish. In the same way husbands should love their wives as their own bodies. He who loves his wife loves himself. For no one ever hated his own flesh, but nourishes and cherishes it, just as Christ does the church, because we are members of his body. "Therefore a man shall leave his father and mother and hold fast to his wife, and the two shall become one flesh." This mystery is profound, and I am saying that it refers to Christ and the church. However, let each one of you love his wife as himself and let the wife see that she respects her husband. Eph. 5:25–33*

Somewhere we picked up complementarianism as declaring who is in charge. We need to lay that down. Conversation primarily in terms of "who makes decisions" is not the essence of complementarian theology, so cease and desist talking about it that way. It perpetuates a bad habit and bad theology. Those conversations are the conversations of Man #1 and #2.

Speaking of "head" as who is in charge forgets the grand narrative. Michelle Lee-Barnewall argues for a kingdom corrective in how we traditionally apply this text:

> The point is that it is the head, not any other member of the body, that is acting this way [sacrificing].... As with Christ, the head/husband sacrifices rather than expecting sacrifice from the other. As the head, he fulfills his duty through the application of kingdom values rather than exercising his worldly rights.[20]

She continues to unpack how this subverting of tradition, laying down one's life instead of seeking traditional male leadership, creates "intimate unity and harmony between husband and wife."[21] Her kingdom corrective reflects a relational nature and not substantive roles to apply. Enforcing stereotypes and fixating on substantive rhetoric is not helpful. Instead first linger on equipping toward good, beautiful, and true ways, laid out in the whole counsel of God, to equip women to *ezer* in the story. I have had these methodologically consistent conversations. Watch what happens. You could be a Man #3 or #4.

Man #3, Man #4

Man #3, my fiancé, called me on the cultural hooey I had been hearing and believing. He told me that if I wanted to, I was going to stick to my plan of going to seminary. I argued, practically looked at the finances, looked for jobs. These other men said I shouldn't go. These other men said it was a waste of money because there are no jobs for women. Fiancé, Man #3, continued to hold the seminary door open for me.

Man #3 and #4 have something in common. Man #3 was just as conservative in biblical interpretation as #1 and #2 and knew the woman in front of him well enough to know she and the Church would flourish with a little training. Man #4, even more conservative in biblical interpretation than the other three, and even more aware of the needs in ministry, gave the final answer. Do you know what my Reformed University Fellowship minister told me, Man #4? "We need women trained in ministry. We desperately need it." The commonality of the last two—men from the Presbyterian Church in America.

We have been treating each other poorly since the Fall. Men treat women poorly, women treat women poorly, women treat men poorly. May we play catch-up with our theology together. We, our small denomination, need renewed conversations, renewed habits, renewed liturgies for God to meet us in and transform our hearts, because as Rebekah Merkle put well in an article from *Desiring God*, "Women being treated with respect is fruit that grows on one kind of tree, and that tree is a cross."[22] We believe in the story of the cross—a sacrificial story so beautiful it will save the world. A consistent complementarian conversation proclaims that story.

---

1. Michael F. Bird, Bourgeois Babes, Bossy Wives, and Bobby Haircuts: A Case for Gender Equality in Ministry (Grand Rapids: Zondervan, 2014), Kindle edition, 53.
2. "Mission & Vision," CBMW. https://cbmw.org/about/mission-vision.
3. Council of Biblical Manhood and Womanhood "History," https://cbmw.org/about/history/.
4.
5. J. N. D. Kelly, Early Christian Doctrines (New York: Harper Collins Publishing, 1978).
6. Augustine, On the Trinity, Book 8, trans. Stephen McKenna (Cambridge: Cambridge University Press, 2002), 3–4.
7. Bruce A. Demarest and Gordon R. Lewis, Integrative Theology (Grand Rapids: Academie Books, 1987), 256.
8. Wayne Grudem, Systematic Theology: An Introduction to Biblical Doctrine (Grand Rapids: Zondervan, 1999), 230.
9. I am not trying to argue that Grudem departs from the Western tradition. I am simply challenging some modernist tendencies in his method.
10. Judith E. Glaser and Richard D. Glaser, "The Neurochemistry of Positive Conversations," Harvard Business Review (June 12, 2014), https://hbr.org/2014/06/the-neurochemistry-of-positive-conversations.
11. Council of Biblical Manhood and Womanhood "Mission & Vision," https://cbmw.org/about/mission-vision.
12. Timothy Keller, Center Church: Doing Balanced, Gospel-Centered Ministry in Your City (Grand Rapids: Zondervan, 2012), 110.
13. Aimee Byrd, No Little Women: Equipping All Women in the Household of God (Phillipsburg: P&R Publishing, 2016), Kindle edition, 25.
14. Ibid., 25.
15. N. D. Wilson, Death by Living (Nashville: Thomas Nelson, 2013), Kindle edition, 80.
16. Keller, 40.
17. James K. A. Smith, Desiring the Kingdom (Michigan: Baker Academic, 2009), 164.
18. Stanley G. Grenz, Theology for the Community of God (Michigan: William B. Eerdmans, 1994), 66.
19. Glaser and Glaser, "The Neurochemistry of Positive Conversations."

20. Michelle Lee-Barnewall, *Neither Complementarian nor Egalitarian* (Grand Rapids: Baker Academic, 2016), 162.

21. Ibid., 163.

22. Rebekah Merkle, "Throw Like a Girl: Why Feminism Insults Real Women," *Desiring God*, http://www.desiringgod.org/articles/throw-like-a-girl.

LATE TO THE PARTY
ALISON MCNEELY BUXTON

Why I Am a Feminist

Alison McNeely Buxton is a staff attorney at the Oklahoma House of Representatives. She is a former prosecutor and has taught history, literature, and theology. She has degrees from Oklahoma Christian University (BA), St. John's College (MA), and Oklahoma City University School of Law (JD). Alison and her husband, Jonathan, have four children.

I love the story of Paul at the Areopagus. The writer of Acts tells us in Chapter 17 that the apostle spent time in Athens, the cradle of democracy and philosophy, conversing with adherents of various schools of thought. As part of his apologetic, Paul quoted Epimenides of Crete and the poet Aratus, showing the Athenians the kernel of truth contained in their own literature. I confess that I am a lifelong Hellenophile, so I feel both impressed and somewhat justified in my affections by Paul's knowledge of Greek poetry. As a teacher, I returned to this passage numerous times to encourage my students, only slightly tongue in cheek, "Hey, if it's good for Paul, it's good for you. Read your Homer, Plato, and Aristotle."

The point of the story, of course, is deeper than the mere presence of Greek poetry. Paul used his knowledge of Hellenic culture to create an opening for the Gospel of Christ. He did not lambast the Athenians for their polytheism; rather, he pointed out the things they got right. The Areopagites, after all, loved a good conversation, and nothing shuts down discussion faster than off-the-cuff dismissal of someone else's position. It would seem, then, that if we look to this episode in Paul's ministry as an example, cultural literacy does not automatically equate to a personal embrace of each and every tenet of that culture; one would be hard-pressed, for example, to argue that Paul was a polytheist merely because he commended the Athenians for their (famously polytheistic) piety.

Which brings me to feminism.

Given the fallout of recent elections, revelations of the prevalence of sexual harassment and abuse, and, of course, the perennial problem of women in the Church, the feminist movement is having a moment. Tempted though we may be to roll our eyes and move on ("Aren't we past this yet?"), perhaps we should ask why. Why, one hundred and sixty-nine years after Seneca Falls and ninety-seven years after the ratification of the Nineteenth Amendment, did millions of American women take to the streets on January 21, 2017?[1] Rather than dismiss out of hand our friends, neighbors, and sisters (because several of us Christians marched, too), let us take a page from Paul. Let us seek to understand to such a degree that we, too, can quote their poets to them and so seek the Gospel reconciliation of the sexes.

The F-Word

In the ultra-conservative Evangelicalism of my childhood, feminism was a bad word. In fact, we never really used it, unless one can count putting others down with the pejorative "Femi-Nazi." Generally speaking, feminists were part of the monolithic left; they were identifiable by their hatred of men, their nonchalant murder of babies, and their tendency to burn undergarments. We were taught Jesus is, of course, opposed to all of these things, so we were safely on his side so long as we showed up at church every Sunday and voted Republican in November.

I did not question this narrative until relatively recently. The truth is that I made an uneasy peace with the tension that I have always experienced as a Christian who was made female. When I read the Bible for myself as a child and recognized my place in the ecclesiastical pecking order, I was angry at God for making me a girl. I did not want to be in charge, but I did want to be just as human as the boys. As a literal-minded kid in an uber-fundamentalist denomination, I read the Bible through that lens: women were second-class citizens. Growing up almost helped a little, as the arguments about ultimate value versus roles were explained to me. With maturity, however, came the concomitant problems of sexuality and modesty. I was told that, just like the males, I was made in God's image; however, should the shameful two inches of skin above my knee become visible when I took a seat in Sunday school, I would be a heartless temptress, responsible for the stumbling of my brothers. We spent a lot of time in our youth group discussing modesty. I do not recall a single class on the imago Dei.

I was essentially taught a theology of separate but equal, which, though I could not articulate it in my youth, I instinctively knew meant unequal.[2] Yet despite my conviction that, since God loves a gentle and quiet spirit, I was probably eternally lost, I stuck with church. In that milieu I believed embracing feminism would necessarily entail a rejection of faith, so intricately were my politics and theology entwined. I had internalized the toxic patriarchy of my youth so profoundly that I thought it better to have a slim, if highly unlikely, shot at heaven than to experience gender liberation on earth; the two were mutually exclusive.

Renewing My Mind

I was not raised in the Reformed tradition. At my hard-core Arminian alma mater, a professor actually told us that John Calvin overemphasized the grace of God. I was puzzled. What did that mean? Is that possible? It occurred to me at the time that perhaps someone staunchly opposed to Calvinism was not the best source of information about Calvinism. Much later, I skipped the biased middleman and read some Reformed thinkers for myself. Embracing the doctrines of grace in adulthood radically realigned my religious beliefs and brought immense spiritual relief. Here was a theology that truly relied upon God's mercy rather than brushing past it in a race to the to-do list. My soul relaxed. I could stop trying to bootstrap this quiet and gentle thing, and instead rest in the finished work of Christ.

However, religious conditioning dies hard. As Elizabeth Edman said, "Once a religious community steps in to tell you what to believe about yourself, what to hope for, what hope *is*, it is very hard to put those ideas down."[3] Despite my newfound, mostly consistent security in my eternal destination, I still labored under the false proposition that meekness means silence and, preferably, if at all possible, blending into the woodwork. Better to pursue peace at all costs rather than be labeled a contentious woman.

My moment of clarity came in the midst of a marital crisis. I discovered that my husband had been trapped in a damaging pattern of sin. It became abundantly clear to me that God had given me a strong personality and an aptitude for standing my ground precisely for this moment. *Ezer kenegdo*[4] does not mean doormat; in fact, in trying all those years to be just a little quieter, to tone it down, I had been actively undermining my own marriage. Not my God, not my husband, and not even I was served when I was silent. In angry conviction I drew a line in the sand, and it was precisely what my husband needed. Healing grace came through confrontation, and God cast me in the role of instigator and, for a time, spiritual leader.

But wait. If God could specifically use my (allegedly) masculine propensity to wade enthusiastically into a donnybrook and see it through to the end, what did that mean about gender roles in my marriage? In my community? And in what other areas of my life had I been sleepwalking? Accepting that God had purposefully made me strong (and occasionally defiant, since iron sharpens iron, after all) meant that I needed to revisit my views about womanhood theologically and, by extension, politically. Never one to tread lightly, I read Simone de Beauvoir's classic feminist tome, *The Second Sex*, and was profoundly impacted by the accuracy of her anthropological and philosophical analysis of the "othering" of women by men. She said that woman "is determined and differentiated in relation to man, while he is not in relation to her; she is the inessential in front of the essential. He is the Subject; he is the Absolute. She is the Other."[5] I found her arguments sound as well as reflective of my own experience in and out of the Church.

It was the perfect providential storm. As I was contemplating the cultural construct we call gender, my husband was working behind the scenes in state politics. In his professional capacity over the next few years, we were privy to interactions and information that disabused me of the notion that the two political parties were easily divisible into moral versus immoral. I had been taught, with unabashedly religious fervor, that the Left was a godless threat to America. It turned out that from the inside, the political Right was just as bad, if not worse, with the added layer of hypocrisy. The inherited bonds that had tied me to theological and political conservatism were quickly unraveling.

Even as I privately soured on the politics of my youth, our church began to embrace the concept of racial reconciliation. A sister in our congregation loaned me her copy of *America's Original Sin* by Jim Wallis. When I finished that, she let me borrow *Just Mercy* by Bryan Stevenson. As a White former prosecutor I felt like I had been gut-punched. I followed these books with *Heal Us Emmanuel*, edited by Doug Serven, my pastor, as well as *The New Jim Crow* by Michelle Alexander. The extent of the racial problem in our nation and my unwitting but culpable complicity in it was earth-shattering. I felt that almost everything I had been taught was verifiably and morally wrong. I felt nauseated and very, very tired.

And then came the election of 2016.

By the time November rolled around, my philosophical vertigo had passed and my paradigms had well and truly shifted. I talked with friends and family who were stunned, not only by the results of the election, but personally by the vitriolic attacks they endured from loved ones. As these conversations progressed, numerous female friends expressed fear. The thin veneer of civility and economic opportunity that allows upper-middle-class women, particularly if they are White, to live comfortably and in denial of systemic injustice, was removed. As my friends and I processed the knife-in-the-gut sense of betrayal, I could not help thinking: Is this what women of color feel all the time? I was ashamed of the privilege our shocked responses revealed.

It was helpful, however, to recognize the dynamic similarities between the fights for racial and gender equality, particularly as it pertained to privilege. Every time a man sighed heavily because we were not yet past discussions of equal pay or offered a glib response to my expression of dissatisfaction with the status quo, I was convicted by the memories of times my blindness to my own White privilege had resulted in similar behaviors by me. Growing up White and well-off in America had normalized for me what turned out to be a very specific and limited set of experiences; challenges to my self-centered narrative left me feeling personally attacked. In the same way, a male was likely to view his own perception of the world as universally normative, rendering my experience aberrant and threatening to him. This is our self-centered human nature; knowing that I share it reminded me to extend grace. Thus I was increasingly determined to push ahead for reconciliation in the arenas of racial and gender equality, which were entwining and becoming more strongly linked in my mind.

Truthfully, I no longer found othering to be theologically defensible, no matter the context; separate but equal means, as it always has, unequal. Whether it results in racism, sexism, or homophobia (or all three), a theology that defines the other based on immutable characteristics for the purposes of cultural demarcation and exclusion fails to recognize the radical reconciliation available in Christ.

Quote Their Poets

Feminism is neither a dirty word nor a movement the Church need fear. "Simply put, feminism is a movement to end sexism, sexist exploitation, and oppression."[6] This is consistent with a Christian ethic. Moreover, the notion that feminists are inherently anti-male is a straw man fallacy that implies equality is a zero-sum game.

In fact, there is much within today's feminism that the Church can enthusiastically support. First, the current wave is "fundamentally anti-racist."[7] The prominent role of women of color distinguishes current feminism from previous iterations. Much has been written about the second wave of feminism that most equate with the sexual revolution of the 1960s and 1970s and the failure of its White, upper-middle-class proponents to divest of White supremacy.[8] After the general cultural backlash of the 1980s and through the third wave of the movement in the 1990s, feminism has gained an increasingly diversified voice. As Brittney C. Cooper argues, not all feminisms are the same.[9] Women experience sexism and racism differently depending on their economic, racial, educational, and marital status, to name just a few intersections. As the Church, we could certainly start by recognizing that our personal experiences of the world are not shared by all; actively designating time and space to listen to and learn from historically silenced voices will deepen our appreciation of God's multiethnic, multi-gendered, and multicultural body.

Second, particularly after the election and revelations regarding widespread harassment and abuse in and out of Hollywood, fourth wave

feminism has come out swinging against sexual oppression and exploitation. The simple truth is that every woman I know, myself included,
could have participated in the #MeToo campaign on social media,
whereby women all over the world indicated that they had experienced
sexual harassment, abuse, or rape. This seems to be a clear-cut arena in
which the Church should take a vocal and unequivocal stand side-by-
side with feminism.

Finally, feminism recognizes that equality does not mean sameness.
With the exception of intersex people, the biological sexes are distinct.
Gender, on the other hand, is a socially constructed spectrum. Acknowl-
edgment of the diversity of gender expression, as separate from but in
addition to the different sexes, is a reflection of the wonderful diversity
of the body of Christ, not a threat to it. The imago Dei is not limited by
the simplistic and inaccurate conflation of sex with gender. The Church
can agree with feminism that the equal dignity of the sexes is promoted
neither by commitment to transitory social norms nor by rigid adherence
to categorical stereotypes. We must decide whether we are committed to
enforcing the curse or to embracing the barrier-destroying unity of the
kingdom.

Although it will be uncomfortable, dialogue is the way forward.
Rather than the Church dismissing feminists as a bloc of man-hating
zealots and feminists dismissing Christians as universally patriarchal
sexists, it is well past time for us to set aside our preconceived judgments
and listen to one another. Just as a Christian might find a theologically
informed feminist more credible than one who dismisses the faith
without examining Scripture, so too a feminist might be more likely to
consider the arguments of a Christian who is conversant in gender
theory than those of one who labels it nonsense without any attempt to
understand. If we wish to be salt and light to our neighbors, surely
educating ourselves about intersectionality, misogynoir, kyriarchy, and
heteronormativity is not too much to ask.

Moreover, perhaps we should take an honest look at where we get
our information. As in my undergraduate work, I realized that it was
ineffective to take an Arminian's word for what Calvinism is, it should
go without saying that restricting ourselves to anti-feminist sources will
not give us an honest picture of what feminism is. While there is undeniably a place in the debate for conservative anti-feminists, relying on
them exclusively to tell us what, for example, intersectionality means, is
lazy at best and disingenuous at worst. This is particularly true when

one can simply search the internet for Doctor Kimberlé Crenshaw, who coined the term "intersectionality" in the late 1980s, and watch a brief TED talk in which she explains the concept.[10] Allowing our fellow human beings the dignity to explain themselves in their own words before we label them rebels, Marxists, or antinomians (as the case may be) should be the bare minimum required by Christian charity. Paul, after all, quoted Aratus and Epimenides directly and respectfully.

If we truly listen, without prejudging, we may discover there is much that is true, good, and beautiful in feminism. When bell hooks encourages us to "imagine living in a world where there is no domination, where females and males are not alike, or even always equal, but where a vision of mutuality is the ethos shaping our interaction,"[11] surely we the Church, of all people, can relate to the longing for the coming kingdom. When Mary Wollstonecraft insisted in the eighteenth century that the equation of women with angels was a sexist subterfuge to justify unequal treatment,[12] we can certainly concur. In fact we can do more than simply nod in agreement; like Paul in Athens, we can offer a profoundly rich and nuanced explanation of why these women are right.

For far too long the Church has leaned heavily on the law in its dealings with women. Our bodies, our roles, and our choices are policed with a moralism more reflective of secular 1950s America than the radical love of Christ. As the Church, we should remember Jesus came to make all things new, "far as the curse is found,"[13] and this promise is for our sisters, too. It is well past time for the Church to reconsider its commitment to the patriarchal norms of the ancient world and to offer to all women the true freedom and God-imaged equality found only in Jesus Christ and his kingdom.

---

1. Erica Chenoweth and Jeremy Pressman, "This is What We Learned by Counting the Women's Marches," *Washington Post*, Feb. 7, 2017, https://www.washingtonpost.com/news/monkey-cage/wp/2017/02/07/this-is-what-we-learned-by-counting-the-womens-marches/?utm_term=.f9290d53892d.
2. Michelle Higgins, Christina Edmondson, and Ekemini Uwan, "Gender Apartheid," *Truth's Table*, podcast audio, March 25, 2017, https://soundcloud.com/truthstable/gender-apartheid.
3. Elizabeth M. Edman, Queer Virtue, (Boston: Beacon Press, 2016), 55–56.
4. Genesis 2:18
5. Simone de Beauvoir, The Second Sex, trans. Constance Borde and Sheila Malovany-Chevallier (New York: Vintage Books, 2011), 3.
6. bell hooks, Feminism is for Everybody (New York: Routledge, 2015), 1.
7. hooks, Feminism is for Everybody, 58.

8. bell hooks, "The Promises Feminism Made and Broke" in Women of the Revolution, ed. Kira Cochrane (London: Guardian, 2012), 213–14.

9. Brittney C. Cooper, "Five Reasons I'm Here for Beyoncé, the Feminist," in *The Crunk Feminist Collection*, ed. Brittney C. Cooper, Susana M. Morris, Robin M. Boylorn (New York: Feminist Press, 2017), 228.

10. https://www.ted.com/talks/kimberle_crenshaw_the_urgency_of_intersectionality

11. bell hooks, Feminism is for Everybody, xiv.

12. Mary Wollstonecraft, *A Vindication of the Rights of Woman*, ed. Eileen Hunt Botting (New Haven: Yale University Press, 2014), 79.

13. Isaac Watts, "Joy to the World! The Lord Is Come" in Trinity Hymnal (Suwanee: Great Commission Publications, 2007), 195.

A CHURCH CULTURE THAT VALUES WOMEN

WENDY ALSUP

Wendy Alsup is a mom, math teacher, and author of Bible studies. She has her MEd from Clemson University and teaches math at a local community college. She is the author of Practical Theology for Women *and* Is the Bible Good for Women? *She worships at New City Fellowship, a church plant of the Lowcountry Presbytery of South Carolina.*

A decade ago, I entered the doors of the Presbyterian Church in America (PCA) as a wounded woman, limping in after pouring myself out as deacon of women's theology and training at a Reformed, nondenominational megachurch that would eventually crumble. At that megachurch, I was taught for the first time from Genesis 3:16 that a result of the fall of man was that women desired to control the men in their lives. I had been around enough nagging, manipulative women over the years that I bought into that interpretation hook, line, and sinker. I bought into it for others, becoming suspicious of women in our church who disagreed with male leaders. I bought into it for myself too, suspecting any pushback I had against teaching from the pulpit was ultimately tied to my desire to take over the church.

The problem was that I didn't actually have any desire to take over the church. But I must, right? Genesis 3:16 taught I inherently wanted to wrestle control from the men in my life, didn't it?

I grew suspicious of myself and other women, even those I was, in theory, discipling as a deaconess, when they or I had concerns about our senior pastor. I submitted to our elder board, believing they were holding each other accountable even when I couldn't see any restraints on the pastor from the pulpit. Then the church fell apart, crumbling under the strain of its abusive leadership. Had my concerns about leadership perhaps not come from a sinful desire to control? Had some of those concerns been based on a love of the church and a God-given desire to help?

In that season, I began re-examining Genesis 2 and 3. What did it mean to be a helper created in the image of the One True Helper, God himself? What did God mean when he warned the woman that she would desire her husband but he would rule over her in return? I found comfort and encouragement by going back to the historic understanding of these phrases. And my fears of inherently nagging and manipulating in the church, rather than loving and helping it, faded.

Around this time I stumbled into a small PCA church in the heart of Seattle and hid with my family on its back row. I later had to apologize to a kind church brother who greeted my family warmly that first week and received back anything but a warm and welcoming response. We were tired. We had poured ourselves out in service at another church but could only bring ourselves to soak in grace at this new one. We hoped nobody would notice us and shied away from attempts to welcome us into the congregation. It wasn't fair to this church, but they took it in stride and gave us time to sit on the back row, using up their resources rather than contributing to them.

Over time and through careful shepherding, I unfurled my self-protective wings and engaged again in ministry. Pastors sought me out to help with a Sunday school class. I led several morning Bible studies for moms. I can't remember if the pastors and I ever had an explicit conversation on the subject, but over time I noted the stark difference in their stance toward me from the one I experienced at the megachurch that had imploded before.

My pastors weren't suspicious of me.

It was that simple. My pastors were, in a 1 Corinthians 13:7 kind of way, ever ready to believe the best of me. Even more so, they needed me.

In a Genesis 2:18 sense, they saw me as a help provided them by God. I had gifts. They had needs. What more needed to be said?

When I eventually moved across the country back to my hometown in South Carolina, I was surprised to find the same stance in my pastors there. They needed me and weren't suspicious of me or my gifts. This should not be confused with them always agreeing with me (or me always agreeing with them). Both my pastors in Seattle and South Carolina have confronted me and occasionally redirected me. We've had pointed conversations, and I've submitted to their spiritual authority when it was called for. But they value my gifts and calling in the church as I, most assuredly, value theirs.

How do we create such a church culture throughout the PCA? How do we promote a culture that values both the discipleship of women in the deep things of the Word and the use of women's gifts as co-laborers in Christ? How do we create a church culture where women can sharpen their male cohorts, even disagreeing with them at times, without being viewed with suspicion as nags or control freaks?

First, we need our views of women in the mission of God to be shaped by the whole scriptural narrative, rather than cultural pressures or our own baggage against the opposite sex. We need to lean into and learn from the Bible's examples and instructions after the fall of man of the two sexes redeemed by Christ laboring together for the furtherance of the Gospel. This is the foundation of a church culture that sees both biological sexes flourishing together in the Church, not in competition but in cooperation for the Kingdom of God. Let's take a short walk through this narrative.

In the beginning, God created humankind in his image, his *tselem*. Humans were created as the Triune God's representative rulers in the world, commanded to go out and continue to do as he had modeled before them. God created and subdued, and humans were sent out to do a version of the same according to Genesis 1:28. Genesis 2 then zooms in on the creation of these humans, image-bearers of God, in a more detailed way, focusing particularly on the creation of the female human in relation to the male human. Before God made her, creation was not yet fully good (Gen. 2:18). It was incomplete. The sole human in the Garden wasn't yet ready to be sent out into creation to do as God had modeled before him.

God created a *helper* that *fit* the male human. As Ligon Duncan and Susan Hunt point out in their book, *Women's Ministry in the Local*

Church, God gives us great insight into woman's creation in the image of God by calling her a helper (Hebrew *ezer*).[1]

The Hebrew word *ezer* means to help, nourish, sustain, or strengthen.[2] It is used most in the Old Testament to describe God himself, reflecting the fact that the woman was created to bear the image of God. Consider the use of *ezer* in Deuteronomy 33:29: *"Blessed are you, O Israel! Who is like you, a people saved by the Lord? He is your shield and helper and your glorious sword. Your enemies will cower before you, and you will trample down their high places."* (NIV)

In Exodus 18:4, God our help *"delivered... from the sword."* Instead of attacking or ignoring the fight altogether, God defends his own and protects them from their enemies. In Psalm 10:14, God our help sees and cares for the oppressed. Rather than being indifferent or unconcerned, He is the *"helper of the fatherless."* In Psalm 20:2 and Psalm 33:20, God our help supports, shields, and protects. In Psalm 70:5, God our help delivers from distress. In Psalm 72:12–14, God our help rescues the poor, weak, and needy.[3]

This female helper, created to reflect our One True Helper, fit the man. She helped him in ways he particularly needed. Sadly, before we could see examples of that fitting help in the image of God, everything changed in Genesis 3. After Adam and Eve believed Satan's lies and sinned against God, God turned toward Satan and cursed him. Satan would be at war with woman (Gen. 3:15), because despite the fact that her unbelief helped usher sin into the world (or maybe precisely because it did), she would also help usher in the Savior as well.

Jesus eventually was born of a woman. He lived a righteous life, died in our place, and rose again from the dead. In the moments before he ascended to heaven, he left instructions to his disciples that sounded quite similar to God's instructions to Adam and Eve in Genesis 1 and 2 —go and do what he has already been doing, making disciples in his name (Matt. 28:16–20). Instead of staying on earth physically and continuing to make disciples himself as he had done the last three years, God the Son left earth, instructing and empowering his disciples, male and female, to continue in the same model, empowered by the same Spirit that raised him from the dead (Eph. 1:18–20).

The Apostle Paul clarifies this relationship between Genesis 1 and 2 and the New Covenant in the book of Ephesians. After going into detail about all Christ has accomplished for us on the cross in Ephesians 1 and 2 and the reconciliation it brings between God, others, and us in

Ephesians 3 and 4, Paul opens the next chapter with the amazing words, *"Therefore, be imitators of God"* (Eph. 5:1). Our imago Dei identity as male and female humans, marred by the fall of man, is redeemed and restored through Jesus Christ. The cooperative mandate of God to humans at creation is seen in a new light and fueled with a new energy after Jesus' return to heaven.

In our modern churches, we are living out the book of Ephesians as male and female image-bearers, marred by the Fall but redeemed and restored by Jesus Christ. Brothers and sisters in Christ, putting their hand to the plow together in local churches in light of the Great Commission of Matthew 28, can also look also to Genesis 1 and 2 to understand our mandate. We work together in joy as we were created to do in the Garden, as we are redeemed to do through the new birth. We are equipped once again to go, have dominion over the earth, and make disciples in Jesus' name.

This understanding of the Creation Mandate through our new birth in Christ gives us insight on the men and women working together in obedience to God in the Old Testament, looking forward to the Promised One. It also helps us understand the men and women working together in the New, looking back to Christ's life, death, and resurrection. We are reminded at various points of the stories in Scripture of the utter necessity of two biological sexes, working in unity as one set of image-bearers, all submitted to Christ.

At the highest and again the lowest points of the history of God's children in the Old Testament, we see two of the most inspiring and instructional examples of two sexes working together to bear the image of God into humanity—Rahab and the Israelite spies in Joshua 2 (the high point of the conquest of the Promised Land) and Rahab's son, Boaz, and Ruth in the book of Ruth (the low point of the time of Judges). These female image-bearers, just one generation apart from each other, are *ezers* in the image of the One True *Ezer* who helped in ways that fit or were suitable to the gifts of the male image-bearers in their stories.[4]

In the book of Joshua in particular, it is easy to imagine a scenario designed by God in which the spies did not depend on a foreign woman to help them to safety. But that wasn't the scenario God chose. God chose circumstances in which these obedient men needed this obedient woman. Eventually, God even used her to continue the line of Christ, as she later gave birth to Boaz, great grandfather to King David. God could have done a lot of things without two biological sexes, but he didn't. And that in itself is noteworthy as we decide whether we are or aren't ourselves going to value the need for the gifts of two biological sexes in our own local churches.

The pattern of Genesis 3-type relational fallout is seen throughout Scripture. But where sin abounds, grace much more abounds. When we look for it, we see a lot more of Genesis 1 and 2-type relational image-bearing through faith in Christ in Scripture. Rahab helped the Israelite spies. Abigail helped David. Ruth helped most everyone she met, as did the Virtuous Woman of Proverbs 31 whom Ruth fleshed out in real life.[5] Deborah helped Barak, and indeed the entire nation of Israel. Mary of Bethany ministered to Jesus as her sister Martha did to the rest of the disciples. Priscilla helped Aquila disciple Apollos. Phoebe helped Paul, perhaps carrying the book of Romans to the Church at Rome. Euodia and Syntyche, for all of their personal problems, labored with Paul in the ministry of the Gospel. Paul needed them in Gospel work, in the ministry of discipleship, which is why he found their internal conflict so harmful. Both men and women were crucial to the Gospel going forward in the early church.

Here we are two thousand years later, working the same work for the same Christ by the same power of the Holy Spirit. Our churches too are discipling men and women, and we need both biological sexes cooperating together, not suspicious of one another, using their respective gifts to fully image God into our churches as we disciple the next generation of image-bearers to do the same.

Problems arise in the Church when we allow our own personal histories in churches or with the opposite sex to shape our vision of the joint work in Christ, rather than the scriptural narrative of God's design and our redemption through Christ. For pastors, elders, deacons, and other ministry leaders, this may flow from a troubled history with a mother or female boss. Perhaps a female family member, even a wife, betrayed you or a loved one. Do your suspicions of the female sex stemming from their abuse or betrayal distort your understanding of the work of male and female image-bearers together in the Church? Are you automatically on defense when someone from the opposite sex questions you or doesn't agree with you immediately?

Do you long for help from women in your church like Deborah helped Barak? Do you value the courage that Rahab showed in delivering the Israelite spies? Do you recognize a woman like Priscilla in your congregation who can disciple others with accurate theology? Do you value the Phoebes, Euodias, and Synteches in your congregation for the necessary help they bring in Gospel ministry? The great value of the *ezer kenegdo* is the woman isn't exactly like the man. She isn't exactly opposite either. There is overlap for sure, and there is great value in the two sexes agreeing in the work of the ministry. But if your first reaction to the utterance of a different opinion of someone of the other sex is suspicion, concern, or resentment, you may be undermining the particular value God intended when he created woman as a strong helper in the image of God, not exactly like the man.

Women too can have baggage when approaching male leadership in the Church. Sister in Christ, did you have a father who abandoned you, abdicating his responsibilities in the home? Was he or another male authority in your life abusive or passive aggressive? Perhaps you were sexually abused by an older male family member. Have you experienced men lusting for your body while simultaneously disregarding your mind? These histories can affect our trust of men and their gifts in our churches as well. We must all be informed by the scriptural narrative first in order to have the tools to understand our own experiences, for good and for bad.

Though I know many women in the PCA have had very different experiences than mine, my five PCA pastors in my three PCA churches have consistently valued my gifts, solicited my input, and received my feedback, even when on occasion that feedback has been negative. I too have valued the voice of my pastors in my life and solicited their guidance. I have listened to their teaching and submitted to their leadership. I have a good earthly father, one I trust and respect. And that has helped me trust other men in my life. But I have also sat under spiritually abusive leadership, and I have had to soak my mind in the example of Jesus so that Scripture's narrative informs my relationship with my current pastors rather than my bad experiences years ago.

Practically, I meet with a pastor every few months to review opportunities I have in ministry and ask his counsel. My pastors over the years have helped me think through what opportunities I should and should not take and how to best communicate truth through the opportunities I do have. As an author, I have been blessed by pastors willing to read through my manuscripts before I send them to my publisher. Though I often minister in parachurch situations, I still see myself (as do my pastors) as planted in our church, ministering out from it.

My prayer for our churches is that each biological sex would put away suspicions of the other and embrace each other's gifts for the good of all members in the body. That we would "go" and "teach all nations" as Priscilla and Aquila, Paul and Phoebe, Peter, Euodia, and Syntyche did before us and call us to do still today. In his image, God created us to do this work together, and he is glorified when we put away our earthly baggage and, in Christ, do so in his name.

---

1. Ligon Duncan and Susan Hunt, Women's Ministry in the Local Church (Wheaton: Crossway, 2006).

2. Francis Brown, S. R. Driver, and Charles A. Briggs "Hebrew Lexicon entry for Ezer," The NAS Old Testament Hebrew Lexicon, http://www.biblestudytools.com/lexicons/hebrew/nas/ezer-2.html.

3. Wendy Alsup, The Gospel-Centered Woman: Understanding Biblical Womanhood through the Lens of the Gospel (self-published), Kindle location 264–268.

4. Francis Brown, S. R. Driver, and Charles A. Briggs "Hebrew Lexicon entry for Neged," The NAS Old Testament Hebrew Lexicon, http://www.biblestudytools.com/lexicons/hebrew/nas/neged.html.

5. In the Hebrew Bible, the book of Ruth immediately follows Proverbs 31, emphasizing Ruth as a concrete example of the principles of the previous chapter. Furthermore, Boaz refers to her specifically with the same Hebrew phrase translated "virtuous woman" in Proverbs 31.

THE NECESSITY OF WOMEN IN MINISTRY
SARAH VIGGIANO WRIGHT

A Biblical Theology of Women in Leadership

Sarah Viggiano Wright is a teacher, speaker, and writer who loves sharing God's Word and equipping churches in their educational ministries. She is the author of A Living Hope: A Study of 1 Peter. *She contributed to* Christ in the Coronavirus *and* Beneath the Cross of Jesus: Lenten Reflections *and served as an instructor for the Teaching Women to Teach the Bible initiative through Reformed Theological Seminary. Sarah holds an MDiv and an MAC from Covenant Theological Seminary and serves Reformed University Fellowship (RUF) alongside her husband Lee and their three children.*

∾

Brothers and Sisters in the Presbyterian Church in America:

As I sit down to write this chapter, I wrestle with what to say and how to say it. I want my words to be truthful, kind, wise, and, most of all, biblical. I want to be encouraging and winsome while communicating truths that may be hard to hear, all while challenging readers to implement individual and corporate changes. I desire to be tender, sensitive, and charitable to the views of others while being heard and received well. Yet, I know the fact of my gender, together with my attempts to grapple with Scripture and gently expose wounds so they might heal, may cause offense. In this chapter, I will unpack the findings of my biblical studies and endeavor to lovingly spur the Church on to Gospel-centered applications. Those who feel that women should publicly teach *topics* over *texts* could take offense to a female author exegeting Scripture to show the importance of continued studies and discussions of women in ministerial leadership positions. Fears arise in me.

Will I be misconstrued as anti-man or anti-PCA? Will my husband and I be hire-able after publicly articulating my experience and my perspective? Will this seem like an act of shaming, of stirring the pot, or of being unsubmissive? Will it further hinder the very people and causes I seek to elevate? Maybe most of all, I wonder *will I be heard?* Will these areas of pain be acknowledged? Sadly, I know there could be negative responses to these questions, and I wrestle with that reality in articulating my perspective.

On one hand, I deeply grieve both the offense this may cause, and the fears I have in writing this. I long to have conversations with my brothers and sisters in hope that we would all pore over Scripture and find thoughtful applications rooted in truth. On the other hand, some brothers and sisters have reached and acted on conclusions that stifle my ability to work the way I've been called to serve the Church. The ways God has shaped me, equipped me, and called me are all important facets of my being, so it grieves me to have to defend the legitimacy of these parts of my identity. It also makes discussions of women's leadership in the Church vital for me. Without brothers and sisters courageously wading into the waters of such murky, emotional, conflicting issues, women who are called and trained like I am will not have places to exercise their callings in the local church.

So, with fear and trembling, and with fond care and deep respect, I am imploring my brothers and sisters to sit down at the table so we can have a "family conversation." This family discussion begins with the hopeful result of unity in Christ, the edification of his Church, and the continuance of his mission with all people participating in the ways that they have been called and equipped by God, all under the authority of his Scripture.

Before diving into the text, I want to make a few points abundantly clear. First, I affirm the pre-Fall representative headship of Adam as a good part of God's created order. Second, I affirm biblical submission of wives to husbands, of children to fathers, of congregants to elders, and of Christians to one another out of reverence to Christ. Third, I want to highlight a pattern of servant leadership in headship taken from the sacrificial example of Christ himself, as noted in Philippians 2:5–12 and Ephesians 5:25.

The servant leader aspects of headship are pivotal. Christ emptied himself and laid his life down for those under his care. Adam, like Jesus, was to lead in love and in service of another. We tend to elevate the language of leadership and dominion over the language of service and nurture, especially when it comes to headship. But I believe they are inseparable: to lead is to serve; to have dominion is to render care. These activities of service, love, nurture, leadership, and stewardship are viewed with equal importance under the Cultural Mandate. While engaging this chapter, please keep these presuppositions at the forefront of your mind.

Our Context

As Christians, we gather much of our history, our identities, and our worldviews from the first three chapters of Genesis. Many theologies find their origins in Genesis: sabbath, the Trinity, marriage, vocation, covenant, and headship, among others. Genesis begins with the unfolding of a benevolent God's great, grand narrative that encompasses all of redemptive history, known by the markers of Creation, Fall, Redemption, and Consummation. In this grand scope, we can know the thrust of the whole Bible and all of history, starting with how all things were intended to be, but then how goodness was shattered and disconnected from that original beautiful design. God didn't leave us there in our sin and rebellion. He began (as he always had planned before the foundation of the world) a comprehensive plan of rescue for his people and his creation. This incredible redemption will have a glorious culmination with the end of all wrong things. This is a final, holistic restoration, and it ends with the flourishing of all of creation in the new heaven and new earth. So, when asking about women and their roles, we must see how woman was created and what roles she was given. From there we can then assess how we are doing in the here and now, and correct any areas where we have strayed to better reflect redemption now and the glory to come.

Creation: The Necessity and Ontology of Women

Genesis opens with two perspectives of the same creation account. Genesis 1 is a survey of God's whole creative effort. This is viewed in broad strokes and summaries, with emphasis on God's creative power. We also see how the humans God created resemble his image in representing his dominion and in harmoniously relating to him. Genesis 2 zooms in closer on the creation of man and woman to give us a fuller picture of the heart of God. In Genesis 2, we see in more depth the uniqueness of humans from the rest of creation, as well as how they are to relate to God, to each other, and to all creation.

From the broad perspective, we see that on each day of creation, God ended the day with a proclamation summary over his creation: *good*. Out of his great benevolence, God was filling the void with goodness. The vegetation and the creatures[1] in their habitats all harmoniously existed as one grand, good community. And, on the sixth day, God created two caretakers. These guardians of his creation, a man and a woman, bore the very image and likeness of God himself. These stewards were commissioned with the task of representing God's goodness and dominion over all God had made. As the Lord God lovingly created and cares for all of his creation, clothing the lilies and shepherding the lambs, so too humanity is to represent and reflect the goodness of our Servant King through acts of love and stewardship.

Many have wrongly assumed that Adam alone was given these duties, and that Eve acquired her mission through Adam's headship. Singular language like, "Eve was created to help Adam with *his* mission" has led us to think that Adam was solely commissioned, and that Eve subsequently came along as Adam's assistant. Though Adam is the covenantal representative head of humanity, as he was created first and he was alone when God first issued the prohibition (and thus we see he has ultimate accountability in Gen. 3:9–11), the mandate is not solely given to Adam and then disseminated to Eve. The commission is given to *them together*. They are co-recipients and co-heirs of the Creation Mandate. In Genesis 1:26–31, the triune, communal God purposefully uses corporate language, the repetition of the plural pronouns *them* and *you* along with the plural imperatives *be fruitful, multiply, fill, subdue*, and *have dominion*, to affirm Eve's inclusion.

Then God said, "Let us make man in our image, after our likeness. And let them have dominion over the fish of the sea and over the birds of the heavens and over the livestock and over all the earth and over every creeping thing that creeps on the earth."

So God created man in his own image, in the image of God he created him; male and female he created them.

And God blessed them. And God said to them, "Be fruitful and multiply and fill the earth and subdue it, and have dominion over the fish of the sea and over the birds of the heavens and over every living thing that moves on the earth." And God said, "Behold, I have given you every plant yielding seed that is on the face of all the earth, and every tree with seed in its fruit. You shall have them for food. And to every beast of the earth and to every bird of the heavens and to everything that creeps on the earth, everything that has the breath of life, I have given every green plant for food." And it was so. And God saw everything that he had made, and behold, it was very good. And there was evening and there was morning, the sixth day. Gen. 1:26–31 (emphases mine)

Eve's inclusion in the Creation Mandate is a part of her created context, with implications for her personhood and her purpose. In using the corporate language, God self-identifies with Adam and Eve, giving them the unique function in creation as those who resemble his image and as benevolent caretakers to the world. Thus, image-bearer and co-heir are central to the identity of Eve. Now let's examine two other critically important facets of Eve's identity: Eve as woman and as *ezer kenegdo*.

The closer perspective of creation in Genesis 2 shows us more relational components of man and woman, and how they are inextricably connected to each other. Though each day of creation ends with the declaration, good, we get to the sixth day in Genesis 2:18 and things are not good because Adam is alone. Not just lacking in goodness, but not good and incomplete.[2] To complete man and creation, God addresses Adam's need in verse 18, *"Then the LORD God said, it is not good that the man should be alone: I will make him a helper fit for him."*

The benevolent triune God knows the remedy for the lone man is community. God fashions for Adam a woman, who is obviously anatomically different from Adam, however she is of his same substance—she is human. This *ezer kenegdo* is meant to be man's complementary counterpart, and their differences are benefits to the other.

Ezer kenegdo is a phrase that has had a variety of translations: *a help-meet for him* (ASV, ERV, KJV); *a helper suitable for him* (NASB, NIV); *a helper fit for him* (ESV); *a helper as his compliment* (HCSB); and, *a suitable companion for him* (CEV). There have also been scholarly studies that have yielded additional translations or dynamic equivalencies like "a life saver,"[3] "a 'strength' or a 'power' to him,"[4] and "a necessary ally for him."[5] Furthermore, what has accompanied the different translations are a wide range of applications and implications, ranging from the scripturally faithful to the incorrectly suppressive, or the sinfully abusive.

The Meaning of Ezer Kenegdo

So, what does *ezer kenegdo* mean, what does it mean for Eve, and what does it mean for humanity? For an accurate translation of *ezer*, its connection to *kenegdo* provides context for Eve along with her being named "woman," her bearing God's image, and her being included in God's Creation Mandate.

The lexical range of *ezer* includes the senses "help or succour,"[6] "wall-builder," "strengthener," "assistant," "rescuer," "lifesaver," "leader or ruler," and "Ezra" (the name).[7] While all of those are in the lexical range of *ezer*, not all are appropriate or accurate for defining the usage of *ezer* in Genesis 2:18. Let's examine defining *ezer* in Genesis 2:18 as a "strength" or "power," for example.[8] Though "strength" is a true option of the sense of the word *ezer*, and while it is true that women and men can fortify each other, it is not the most accurate translation contextually. Thus, to understand the intended meaning of a word usage, like "helper" of Genesis 2:18, we must obtain our definition from a combination of *sense* and *reference*.[9]

The *ezer* of Genesis 2:18 is grouped with the sense defined as helper or "one who helps," along with Genesis 2:20, Exodus 18:4, Deuteronomy 33:7, 26 and 29, Isaiah 30:5, Ezekiel 12:14, Daniel 11:34, and Hosea 13:9. The contextual commonality of these passages is that help is needed, and that a helper comes to aid. The Lord is referred to as Israel's *ezer*, and God references himself as *ezer* in Hosea 13:9. With respect to the woman introduced in Genesis 2:18, *ezer* is accompanied by *kenegdo*, literally translated as in correspondence with him, or at his side, or a meet for him (to match him).[10] It is an expression for anything correlative and parallel.[11] The Enhanced Browns, Driver, Briggs

Lexicon notes in Genesis 2:18 that Eve's correspondence to Adam is "equal and adequate to himself."[12]

Implications of Ezer Kenegdo

There are several points of significance to note regarding God's fashioning of Eve and his introducing her as *ezer kenegdo*. First, *ezer kenegdo* is not a statement of ontology, rather it is a statement of relatedness to Adam.[13] Thus, helper is not Eve's entire identity or her total functionality, nor is it a full summary of her relationship to Adam. Rather, *ezer kenegdo* is one of many facets of Eve, along with her womanhood, image-bearing, and her responsibility as co-heir of the Creation Mandate. It does not solely mean that she was biologically compatible with Adam, nor that she was solely there to support Adam in his work. She was made for community and she was of communal and personal necessity to man, so to only emphasize (or overemphasize) just one of her facets diminishes all God intends for Eve. Old Testament scholar Claus Westermann counters reducing Eve by this assertion:

> The words *fit for him* refers neither to the sexual nature of woman... nor to the help which she could offer the farmer. Any such limitation destroys the meaning of the passage. What is meant is the personal community of the man and woman in the broadest sense—bodily and spiritual community, mutual help and understanding, joy and contentment in each other.[14]

Second, these broad identity categories of image-bearer, *ezer kenegdo*, woman, and co-heir allow us to extend the Creation Mandate to functions and roles not named in Genesis 1 and 2. The brevity of these accounts alone proves they were not meant to be extensive or exhaustive records of the function of man and woman, of the roles they were to play to each other, or of how they were to function in God's creation. The Bible is authoritatively *ostensive* (pointing us in a direction), and because it is so, we can gather many different theologies, truths, and systems of thinking from the first two chapters of Genesis. Thus, we don't need linguistic stretches of the translation, like "necessary ally,"[15] to recognize that there are ostensive extensions to *ezer kenegdo*. For example, though Adam and Eve are married, the communal necessity men and women have for each other is not limited to just the context of marriage, but rather it pertains to all human relationships.

Third, helper is not inherently a term of inferiority, but rather a term of neutrality.[16] Helper can be used for equals, or, depending on context, can be designated a term of inferiority or superiority if aiding someone of unequal status.

However, when twenty-first century Western people hear helper, we mostly assume a helper is an assistant, someone of lesser status than the superior. Helper has a negative, inferior, or condescending connotation, like "Mommy's little helper" in the kitchen, or a "classroom helper" to pass out the activity. Or, we assume the majority of the task falls on one person with the helper contributing a reduced portion.

Yet, we have an elevated view of helper in reference to God helping his people. When God lovingly helps Israel, he does not subordinate himself to them, nor to their cause. He provides aid and he gives himself for the sake of another, but Israel does not do the greater share of the work, nor does Israel have a position of superiority over God. No, help is not inherently concerned with status of superiority or inferiority; it is primarily about "one who uses his or her efforts for the benefit of another."[17] I am my children's helper as they learn tasks like cutting with scissors or tying their shoes. Nurses help doctors in caring for patients, often spending more time with patients than doctors. The people involved provide context as to the type of relationship they have (inferior, equal, or superior); however, the commonality of help is using effort to benefit another.

With God as our help, there is inherent greatness associated with the term. However, when we think of Eve as Adam's help, we often diminish her as helper. We need redemption of the term helper. Just as we contextually elevate our understanding of the word "servant" (and not subservient) in reference to Jesus as our "Servant King," we must similarly elevate our understanding of helper in reference to Eve. In order to expand our narrowed view of Eve as helper, we must recognize her necessity and her equality.

Adam needed Eve, and not just for rectifying his alone-ness or for procreation, though those are important needs.[18] Adam, who was created ontologically communal, needed her for community. Nineteenth-century Hebraist S. R. Driver states:

It is not enough to place man in the garden: further provision is yet required for the proper development of his nature, and satisfaction of its needs: a *help*, who may in various ways assist him, and who may at the same time prove a companion, able to interchange thought with him, and be in other respects his intellectual equal, is still needed.[19]

Not only did Adam need Eve for community and holistic development, Adam needed her for his fulfillment of the human calling. Adam *needed* Eve to fulfill the Creation Mandate of subduing the earth, filling it, and having dominion over it. The charge was given to *them*, and he could not do it without her! She was an absolute necessity to his completion as a communal being and as co-commissioner of executing God's dominion. While Adam was the representative head and accountable for his servant leadership, Eve was his equal and necessary counterpart. It is biblical to affirm both the representative headship of Adam and the necessity of Eve, as she is Adam's co-commissioned, ontological equal. Adam needed her, not as a supplement or an auxiliary, but as an integral, equal partner. Ingrained in our human identity and mission is the necessity of others. "Human beings cannot fulfill their destiny in any other way than in mutual assistance."[20]

Yes, in order for Adam to fulfill his destiny, Adam needed Eve as his partner, "one who by relative difference and essential equality should be his fitting complement."[21] Eve is articulated by God to be Adam's ontologically equal by his use of *kenegdo*, and she is recognized by Adam as his equal, of the same substance,[22] as Adam proclaims, *"This* [feminine singular pronoun] *at last is bone of my bones and flesh of my flesh"* in Genesis 2:23. "With poetry, [Adam] celebrates the bond and equality of man and woman."[23] The argument for Eve's equality is not for her own individualism; it is for her inclusion to fulfill the mandate. The case for Eve's equality is not due to modern hyper-feminist cultural influence, but has been presented by many reputable early biblical scholars. Throughout centuries of study, Eve's equality has been affirmed. One of the earliest examples comes from Bishop Irenaeus of Lyon, who lived from 140–202 AD. Irenaeus demonstrated such high regard for Eve as "equal and comparable and like to Adam"[24] that he even held Eve to be the stronger of the two humans when facing the serpent's temptation.[25] Modern Old Testament scholar Derek Kidner affirms the stand-alone nature of Eve's equality, saying:

The naming of the animals, a scene which portrays man as monarch of all he surveys, poignantly reveals him as a social being, made for fellowship, not power; he will not live until he loves, giving himself away (Gen. 2:24) to another on his level. So the woman is presented wholly as his partner and counterpart; nothing is yet said of her as childbearer. She is valued for herself alone.[26]

J. H. Hertz, the Chief Rabbi for the United Kingdom from 1913–1946, asserted that woman "is not man's shadow or subordinate, but his other self, his 'helper,' in a sense which no other creature on earth can be."[27] Adam needed Eve, and vice versa, for community, in stewardship of creation, and to complete humanity and the creation account. Eve was necessary for the conclusion of all of creation to be *very good*.

However, we know that the story doesn't conclude there, but rather it takes a tragic turn. In Genesis 3, Adam and Eve sin against God, and their disobedience shatters shalom in every extension: man's relationship to God, man's relationship to man, and man's relationship to creation.

Fall: Diminishing the Necessity of Women

One of the more prominent ways we see the effects of the Fall as it pertains to men and women in the Church is that we see Adam's headship of servant leadership turned to domination, a development further complicated by Eve's desire for her husband and him ruling over her (Gen. 3:16). Eve as necessary helper has turned to Eve as superfluous assistant. And, the satisfaction that both the co-heirs were to take in stewarding God's creation and relating harmoniously with each other turned into a perpetual power struggle. A battle waged with weaponized faulty interpretations of *ezer kenegdo* and misapplications of Eve's personhood and purpose.

Many biblical scholars and theologians started wrongfully devaluing Eve and her role as *ezer*. Church fathers, to whom we owe gratitude for their honorable theological and ecclesiological contributions, started diminishing women's necessity by diminishing Eve's womanhood, her ontological equality, and her roles as *ezer* and co-heir of the Creation Mandate. They were not merely expressing Eve's subordinate role, but were espousing her substandard nature to Adam's.

Reformer Martin Luther viewed Eve as an inferior image-bearer compared to Adam in the same way that the moon is an inferior light source compared to the sun. In his commentary on Genesis, Luther contends:

> So [God] gloried in it and was more delighted in the creation of man, whom he made in his image, than in that of all other creatures. [Animals display God's almighty power], but only man is called God's image, because in him, especially Adam [before the Fall], He was truly revealed.[28]

Luther says that though the woman is not excluded from the "glory of the future life" she is not ontologically equal to man. "The woman certainly differs from the man, for she is weaker in body and intellect [than he]."[29]

Along with being devalued in ontology and image-bearing, women, as a gender, have been villainized, and have often been considered corrupt or morally dangerous. Women have been cast as seductresses who lead men astray, an idea connected to Eve's culpability at the tree of the knowledge of good and evil. Latin church father Tertullian held Eve responsible for the fall of humanity, and he would have *all* women diminished, in more capacities than their dress alone, as a way of demonstrating their perpetual penitence of Eve's and (by proxy of gender) their sin. He expresses this belief with his opening of *On The Apparel of Women*. Paraphrasing the first part, he says, beloved sisters, would it be that you would walk around in an unattractive appearance so as to mourn, like Eve, and atone that you originate from her, as hers is the worthy shame and disgust for being the cause of human perdition. Then he continues:

> And do you not know that you are (each) an Eve? The sentence of God on this sex of yours lives in this age: the guilt must of necessity live too. *You* are the devil's gateway: *you* are the unsealer of that (forbidden) tree: *you* are the first deserter of the divine law: *you* are she who persuaded him whom the devil was not valiant enough to attack. *You* destroyed so easily God's image, man. On account of *your* desert—that is, death—even the Son of God had to die.[30]

Along with the devaluing of women through the attack of their image-bearing and ontological equality, the necessity of women and their role as commissioned co-heirs has also been diminished. African church father Augustine of Hippo asserts that keeping company with men was the only way to be emotionally, mentally, and relationally satisfied. He didn't see the helpfulness of women beyond procreation, and he definitely did not honor the dominion aspect of Eve's call in the Creation Mandate.[31]

The very facets of Eve's nature that God established at creation were the very aspects diminished by some of the most important leaders of the Church. Women have been devalued, demonized, and regarded as dispensable. So, it's no wonder we find ourselves confused and conflicted to this day. The above examples are very overt in their attacks and disdain of Eve, but more covert practices, some rooted in these overt ideologies, are effective today. And, to make matters even more complicated, misapplications can happen at the hands of very well-meaning, well-intended Christians. Misapplications of the Genesis account have affected the Church deeply as they have been applied to women and co-gender relationships in the Church.

First, some still regard relationships with the opposite gender as dangerous. While there are necessary perimeters, and each person ought to honor wisdom, God-given convictions, and always remain above reproach, women have often suffered the consequences of overly rigid, unloving boundaries. Moreover, they have been treated as though they were responsible or deserving of such rigidness, leaving many women feeling shame, confusion, rejection, and dejection.

Second, Christians have gender-ized (assigned a gender to) personality traits, characteristics, and gifts that were never meant to be primary or exclusive to one gender or the other. For example, qualities of nurture and gentleness are assigned primarily to women. While it is undeniable that the nature of the woman's body lends itself to different kinds of nurture, like that of nursing an infant, it does not relegate a woman's function primarily to nurture, nor does it exclude men from nurturing. Giving a "female" assignment to nurture can cause us to neglect the fact that all Christians are called to be nurturing, patient, kind, and gentle. Similarly, matters of contentment, joy, hospitality, and beauty, among other topics, are primarily aimed at women or women's issues. Conversely, notions of leadership, strength, boldness, and the gift of teaching are often primarily associated with men.

In part, carving out explicit gender differences was in an attempt to showcase the distinctiveness between men and women, especially when confronted with cultural movements, like the feminist movement of the

1970s. Historically, there were corporate perspectives that gave women jobs, and positions of civic and domestic leadership without conflict, because it was the most beneficial to our society as a whole, and the need was publicly recognized. Such was the case during the Cold War, when women were needed in both domestic and industrial capacities as it pertained to a larger sense of "home."[32] However, "the gender discussion shifted in line with social developments, involving a move away from this corporate perspective and changes in the understanding of the home. Growing individualism... and also the value of the home in terms of women's identity would exert a profound influence on how Evangelicals viewed gender."[33] These gender views got further complicated in the feminist movement, and the Church wanted to define more absolute statements of masculinity and femininity. God did create men and women to be compliments to the other, but constricted gender-ized distinctions are likely rooted in a reaction to a cultural movement and have gone beyond what is biblically prescribed. And, the truth is that men and women have more commonalities because of our humanity than we have differences because of our genders.

Third, and related to the second, women have been relegated to positions in the Church that are less controversial, instead of positions that require boldly but humbly continuing difficult conversations where there is disagreement. And nothing showcases this debate more than women teaching: what women can teach (*topics* over *texts*) and the audiences women are allowed to teach.

Teaching has been primarily viewed as a man's gift or role, particularly in the PCA, mainly due to how we have interpreted 1 Timothy 2:11–14. The applications of 1 Timothy 2:11–14 range from having only male teachers for any age or audience, to women teaching or co-teaching in any capacity that a nonordained person has access to. Some extend male-only teaching and leadership into the workforce and governing agencies as well, believing that only men should be in any leadership position. Scottish Reformer John Knox held this prohibitive view of women in leadership positions, claiming female leaders were "repugnant to nature" and an insult to God.[34]

While thorough examination of 1 Timothy would be helpful in illuminating its meaning, I will summarize by saying the context of the passage is crucial, and by highlighting that the permission of *let a woman learn* (along with the men of the Church instead of learning being men-only) is critical (cf. Mary at Jesus' feet in Luke 10:39). An extended application of this permission is the ability of both women and unordained men to teach under derived authority or oversight, except from the pulpit of the assembly. Also we should note Paul's praise of other women in ministry or teaching capacities, like Phoebe, Mary, and Junia in Romans 16, or Lois and Eunice of 2 Timothy 1. Teaching children Scripture would have been part of the normal care of Hebrew mothers as well. Jesus used the public spoken testimony of the Samaritan woman of John 4 to bring her village to belief. Many women are due credit for biblical and theological understanding and dissemination of the Bible. Women knowing Scripture has been and continues to be integral to the spread of Christianity.

Woefully, as a woman pursuing a Master of Divinity, I was told several times that the primary function of an MDiv and the primary function of seminary was to equip *men* for pulpit ministry. I was also told that if I wanted to be a *real* benefit to the Church, I ought to pursue a master of arts in educational ministries. This degree might be seen as more applicable to women because of its focus on didactic styles, group discussions, and curriculum, while also seeming less authoritative because it did not require Greek and Hebrew. The MAEM is a phenomenal degree, and were I to have more time to get an additional degree, a MAEM would be at the top of my list! However, the subtext of that comment was that women don't need to engage the languages, nor be taught by a woman who engages the languages. The trajectory of that subtext is that current teaching practices that solely rely on men for exegesis, like reading books together or putting in a pastor's DVD series, should suffice. However, women are hungry for wider variety and deeper impact than that! Women desire an interactive setting to be sharpened in, and some desire that the teacher be a woman. The women who have blessed me in my classes sharpen me with their questions, insights, and takeaways from us diving into Scripture together. My ladies love Hebrew and Greek, historical context discussions, and word-studies along with their love of practical applications! They want it all because it all nourishes them! So, as their teacher, if I'm going to faithfully prepare a lesson on the Bible, I'm going to the original manuscripts in their original languages, the place where seminarians are instructed to start. I am blessed to have the ability to use Greek and Hebrew languages. And while not necessary for knowing and loving God, they are incredibly beneficial tools for my understanding of what God is communicating as I teach his Word to others. And all are called to use the gifts they've been equipped with to serve the Church (Rom. 12:6–8).

Fourth, with regard to topics, we have also falsely gender-ized issues we see as important to women. As much as I love teaching on "Beauty, Bodies, and Femininity," there are more issues for women to discuss. We need to address other women's issues like: Scripture, justification, sanctification, glorification, sin, christology, soteriology, eschatology, ecclesiology, covenant theology, Christian ethics, suffering, and sovereignty. You know, *real* women's issues!

As a parent would never feed her child cereal for breakfast, lunch, and dinner every day for years on end, so too women should not be "fed" a limited amount of topics. For well-rounded growth, we require more nourishment than what conversations on "femininity" offer, and although it is a *good* topic, it is not a complete diet. We need all the categories for health and flourishing. Similarly, the Church should expand the "diet" for men as well. I am so thankful for men's fellowship events in the PCA, but I am unaware of any event where the keynote teaching or theme has been hospitality, even though it is a requirement of elders in 1 Timothy 3:2. Women ought to address issues like contentment, joy, and hospitality, but these are not solely or even primarily "women's issues." They are *Christian* issues! Everyone in the Church is equally called to them.

Fifth, churches have put women in positions irrespective of their God-given calls. Again, I believe this is done because it is seen as the least controversial way of letting women serve; however, it diminishes a woman's gifting and calling by presuming the decision makers are more discerning of the woman's call than she is. Though the process is not the exact same as a Teaching Elder being called to shepherd and preach, God's Holy Spirit does equip and guide *all* believers. There are internal and external components to women's calls to ministries, too.

I felt led to pursue seminary education, a call that was affirmed by many pastors, mentors, and friends who knew the heart, desires, and ministry callings God had given me. But a woman who wants to teach the Bible and theology can feel threatening, and I know of women made to feel as though they were wrong or that they had somehow misjudged their calling because their church context wasn't open to women teaching beyond certain levels. I was once told that if Christ were my true contentment, I would be just as fulfilled teaching a first grade Sunday school class as I would be going to seminary, a comment which initially devastated me and caused me to question my discernment of God's call on my life. I do love teaching children the Bible, because I love teaching the Bible, but that comment wasn't based on how God equipped me or called me. It reduced my calling from vocational to volunteerism.

This issue is not easy, but if we elevate safety and comfort over the proper placement of women leaders according to their callings, we are not only being unfaithful to God, but we are sinning against our sisters and squandering their gifts.

Finally, the Church has not been biblically faithful in exercising its *need* of women. Eve was necessary for Adam pre-Fall, but many churches operate with all-male leadership, excluding talented and equipped women from nonordained positions. Meetings and decisions take place with no female input or consultation. Some of this happens because we assume men are self-sufficient while simultaneously assuming women are not. Some of this happens with men believing themselves to be representing and acting "on behalf of women," which is true *if* they are regularly and systematically consulting women. Some of this also happens from a desire to let the elders lead. However, some of this happens because women are not seen as necessary as they ought to be.

Obviously, no one is sufficient alone. Also, getting female input does not negate male eldership, but rather enhances it and makes it more holistic. The wisdom, opinions, and expertise of women is not something that should be occasionally tapped into as a resource. That's tokenism. Women are not necessary *when* you need them; women are necessary *because* you need them! The voices, thoughts, feelings, experiences, and wisdom of women ought to be craved, sought after, and treasured. Female leadership and input should be routine and regular in all church operations. I am even aware of senior pastors who have weekly committees comprised of wise men and women in their church for the pastor to go over his sermon series, brainstorm, get feedback, ask for sensitive issues or blind spots, and then seek prayer over the preaching of God's Word in their church!

In summary, we have a lot of room for growth. As a result of the Fall, women can be dominated and diminished, even in the Church. They can be relegated to positions of ministry that are "safe" but not necessarily according to their gifting or calling. Certain gifts, like teaching and leadership, have been elevated and designated to men. Simultaneously, we have a lesser view of gifts like nurturing and hospitality, which have been relegated primarily to women. This false gender-izing of gifts has led to a lot of women feeling misunderstood (or wrongfully made), and a lot of gifts being unused or squandered.

Many recognize the benefits of the whole body of Christ serving one another and have sought to give women positions of ministry in the Church. However, when it feels like biblical fidelity is being threatened or infringed upon, conversations have closed down, and women have been given positions that seem more culturally comfortable. This is not the most biblically faithful practice. We need to return to our created intention to rightly relate to each other as necessary co-heirs, especially in the Church.

Redemption: Reaffirming Each Other's Necessity

We need to venture back to Eden, where man and woman needed each other. We need to elevate womanhood and the role of helper back to their original states. We need to fight against the diminishing of women and recognize them as ontological equals and as necessary co-heirs in accordance with the creation account. We need to seek reconciliation for the ways we have hurt and limited women. We need to continue to have conversations on how to work out biblically faithful relationships and leadership positions for women. We need to engage fears when they arise and pray for Spirit-led guidance with our actions and executions. We need to be charitable with those with whom we disagree, realizing that all are trying to work out Gospel-centered, God-honoring applications for women using their gifts and answering their internal and external callings, all under the authority of Scripture.

We need to bear the burdens of our sisters and love them well. For women like myself, who long to have more avenues and opportunities for teaching, we are in a perpetual state of discomfort, and we would like our brothers to enter into the struggle with us. If more were aware that these issues are consistent vexations in our daily church participation and are constant limitations to the holistic functioning as the Church, it would likely be much more urgent to resolve them. We need to create more teaching and leading opportunities for women, and have men demonstrate their need for women by assisting in these endeavors. One potential way of doing this is by utilizing overseers and shepherds to assist and guide women in teaching contexts. This could open up nonordained teaching contexts that women have formerly been excluded from, all while under derived authority from the overseers. Women who are keen teachers, whether they be parishioners, women's ministry leaders, or seminary students, could go through teaching internships with equipping and mentoring in tandem (and offering a stipend, honorarium, or salary wouldn't hurt either). Women who are called to ministry are being dissuaded from going through seminary training, not because their calling is unaffirmed, but because there are too few paying jobs on the other side of seminary. Let's change this!

Finally, we need to stop extra-biblical gender-izing and be more open and inclusive of the variety that God allows us in relating to one another. We need to live more communally and interdependently. We need to live out the creative blueprint for humanity: that we are better together than we are separate. We need to need each other. We need to *need* women.

Questions for Reflection:

- Do the ways we conduct our church life and leadership reflect our innate communal needs of the other?
- Do we have a collection of men and women fulfilling their roles in synergistic ways?
- Are we seeking counsel, prayer, and mentorship from all wise leaders in the faith?
- Do we see raising up female church leaders as pivotal as we do male leaders?
- Does your church or ministry have visible leaders who are women?
- Are women being quoted and referenced from the pulpit?
- Does your pastor regularly visibly and verbally demonstrate his need of women (and not just for behind-the-scenes servant positions)?
- Is your church sending, supporting, and investing in (in prayer, finances, and tangible logistical needs) women to be trained?
- Does your church have paid internships, staff, or other nonordained pastoral positions for women?

Consummation: Perpetual Appreciation

There will be a day when the struggle ends and the order of all of creation is fully and finally restored. In our glorified state, the ontological equality of all brothers and sisters will be plain and indisputable. Jesus, the true head, will come back to dwell with mankind, exercising his dominion, care, love, and service to us still. And after all sorrow and strife is wiped away forevermore, we will abide in a perpetual state of worship and appreciation of our Servant King. May God, who is our Help, come quickly and make it so! And may we love each other well, and co-labor to live out *"Your kingdom come, your will be done, on earth as it is in heaven"* (Matt. 6:10) in the meantime.

---

1. Franz Delitzsch, A New Commentary on Genesis (Edinburgh: T. & T. Clark, 1888), 101. *Adam* refers to man, the species.
2. Bruce K. Waltke, Genesis: A Commentary (Grand Rapids, MI: Zondervan, 2012), 88. Waltke asserts *"lo tov* is highly emphatic." In his footnote of this remark, Waltke states, "the usual way of expressing a less than ideal situation is *en tov,* "it is lacking in goodness." C. J. Collins believes that *lo too* would have been the common way to express it; however, the consensus is that man being alone is NOT good! Not good at all!
3. John D. Garr, Coequal and Counterbalanced: God's Blueprint for Women and Men (Atlanta, GA: Golden Key Press, 2012), 140. Hebraist Dr. John D. Garr references the Eldridges' book *Captivating* in his book *Coequal and Counterbalanced*. Dr Garr's own personal translations is "I will make a help as his partner," but he agrees with the thrust of the Eldridges' translation on *Coequal and Counterbalanced* page 135.
4. David R. Freedman, "Woman, a Power Equal to Man," Biblical Archaeology Review 9, no. 1 (1983): 56–58. Freeman's translation is "a power equal to him."
5. John McKinley, "Necessary Allies–God as ezer, Woman as ezer" (lecture, Evangelical Theological Society, Atlanta, GA, November 17–19, 2015).
6. Sense means multiple meanings of the same word. For example, the word "wicked" has multiple senses. "Wicked" can mean evil or morally wrong (ie. the *wicked* [man] will perish), intending harm (ie. he has a *wicked* tongue), or extremely unpleasant (ie. the heat is *wicked*). However, if you find yourself in Boston, you may encounter a *wicked-*smart (extremely smart) person, a *wicked* (extremely good) cream pie, or a person with a *wicked* (clever) sense of humor. Even though all those senses are in the lexicon under "wicked," only certain senses apply based on the context.
7. Francis Brown, S. R. Driver, and Charles A. Briggs, A Hebrew and English Lexicon of the Old Testament: With an Appendix Containing the Biblical Aramaic (Oxford: Clarendon Press, 1952), 740–741. In the BDB, the lexical range for *ezer* is found on pages 740–741, with the sense for Genesis 2:18 found on page 740.
8. Similarly, *ezer* is not translated as "partner" nor "ally," as both of those are not lexical options for *ezer.* "Partner" is used in Prov. 29:24 *chalaq.* Ally, in many instances, is translated as "friend" (i.e. friend or foe) or "one who loves" if used as a noun, and as a verb has an broad variety of phraseology. Both "partner" and "ally" come from attempt of using dynamic equivalencies of *kenegdo.*
9. Martin Joos, "Semantic Axiom Number One," *Language* 48, no. 2 (1972): 257–265. Both *sense* (meaning) and *reference* (context) are important for gathering which definition(s) applies and which does not. Linguistic principles like *Joos' Law* confirm that in

order to define a word's usage, the word contributes some of our understanding, and the context fills in the rest. The misapplication of sense and reference can lead to translation errors. One common translating error is to assume that all of the lexical entries are equally viable definitions for each usage of a word. However, only certain definitions are best, and the context is key as to which options best apply. C. J. Collins summarizes Joos' Law "for the sense of a word we seek that which contributes the least to its context (which is another way of minding the distinction between sense, contributed by the word, and reference, contributed by the context.)." CJ Collins (Professor of Old Testament at Covenant Theological Seminary), interviewed by the author, St. Louis, MO, May 18, 2018.

10. Joseph Herman Hertz, The Pentateuch and Haftorahs. Hebrew Text, English Translation and Commentary (London: Oxford University Press, 1940), 22.

11. Delitzsch, 140.

12. Francis Brown, S. R. Driver, and Charles A. Briggs, *The Enhanced Hebrew and English Lexicon of the Old Testament: With an Appendix Containing the Biblical Aramaic* (Oak Harbor, WA: Logos, 2000), http://judaisztika.hu/downloads/BDB.pdf.

13. Collins, interview.

14. Claus Westermann, Genesis 1–11, A Continental Commentary (Minneapolis: Fortress Press, 1994), 232.

15. I deeply appreciate John McKinley's scholarship and his intent to have a translation that reflects the thrust of what the Bible is communicating. While "necessary ally" stretches beyond the lexical senses as a translation, the application of his translation "necessary ally" *does* reflect the truest sense of how to regard *helper*, as depicted in Genesis 1 and 2.

16. Westermann, 227. Westermann asserts that the neutral sense of *ezer* is "used deliberately" and that the "majority of interpreters have stressed correctly that the meaning is not just help at work [sites references of proof], nor is it concerned merely with the begetting of descendants; it means support in a broader sense."

17. Collins, interview. In Collins' book, *Genesis 1–4*, which was published in 2006, Collins wrote, "A 'help(er)' is one who takes a subordinate role (which is why it is so startling to read of God being the 'help' of his faithful ones, as in Deut. 33:7 and Ps. 33:20)." However, in a private communication, used with permission, Collins stated he would no longer use the word "subordinate" today due to the amount of negative baggage it has compared to when he wrote *Genesis 1–4*. He says, "Subordinate (as it is used today) is not part of the *sense* of the word 'help/helper.'" While his word choice has changed, the consistency of his message has not, as on the same page Collins affirms Delitzsch's statement that "'helper' will be 'one who by relative difference and essential equality should be his fitting complement." *Genesis 1–4,* 107.

18. John Calvin, A Commentary on Genesis (London: Banner of Truth Trust, 1965). "[The faithful rendering of *kenegdo* is] 'Which may be like him' for Moses intended to note some equality. And hence is refuted the error of some, who think that the woman was formed only for the sake of propagation, and who restrict the word 'good,'... to the production of offspring."

19. S. R. Driver, The Book of Genesis: With Introduction and Notes (London: Methuen, 1913), 41. I would note the word "assist" does not go far enough.

20. Delitzsch, 140.

21. Delitzsch, 140.

22. John Skinner, A Critical and Exegetical Commentary on Genesis (Edinburgh: T. & T. Clark, 1980), 69. Skinner notes that "Bone of my bone" expresses that the members of a kindred group are parts *of the same substance.*

23. Waltke, 89.

24. Joseph P. Smith, St. Irenaeus: Proof of the Apostolic Preaching (New York: Paulist Press, 1992), 55–56.

25. Irenaeus of Lyon, Fragments from the Lost Writings of Irenæus, New Advent, last updated 2017, http://www.newadvent.org/fathers/0134.htm. Of Eve's fortitude,

Irenaeus writes, "Why also did [the serpent] not prefer to make its attack upon the man instead of the woman? And if you say that it attacked her as being the weaker of the two, [I reply that], on the contrary, she was the stronger, since she appears to have been the helper of the man in the transgression of the commandment. For she did by herself alone resist the serpent, and it was after holding out for a while and making opposition that she ate of the tree, being circumvented by craft; whereas Adam, making no fight whatever, nor refusal, partook of the fruit handed to him by the woman, which is an indication of the utmost imbecility and effeminacy of mind. And the woman indeed, having been vanquished in the contest by a demon, is deserving of pardon; but Adam shall deserve none, for he was worsted by a woman—he who, in his own person, had received the command from God."

26. Derek Kidner, Genesis (Downers Grove: InterVarsity Press, 1967), 65.
27. Hertz, 22.
28. Martin Luther, Luther's Commentary on Genesis, vol. 1 (Grand Rapids: Zondervan, 1958), 34.
29. Ibid.
30. Quintus Tertullianus, De Cultu Feminarum (On the Apparel of Women), New Advent, last updated 2017, http://www.newadvent.org/fathers/0402.htm.
31. Saint Augustine, Saint Augustine: The Literal Meaning of Genesis, vol. 1, trans. J. H. Taylor, Ancient Christian Writers Series (New York: Newman/Paulist Press, 1982). From Chapter 5 section 9 of his 9th book on the meaning of Genesis, Augustine says, "Now, if the woman was not made for the man to be his helper in begetting children, in what was she to help him? She was not to till the earth with him, for there was not yet any toil to make help necessary. If there were any such need, a male helper would be better, and the same could be said of comfort of another's presence if Adam were perhaps weary of solitude. How much more agreeably could two male friends, rather than a man and woman, enjoy companionship and conversation in a life shared together... Consequently, I do not see in what sense the woman was made as a helper for the man if not for the sake of bearing children."
32. Michelle Lee-Barnewall, Neither Complementarian nor Egalitarian, A Kingdom Corrective to the Evangelical Gender Debate (Michigan: Baker Publishing Group, 2016), 33–34.
33. Barnewall, 34.
34. John Knox, "The First Blast of the Trumpet Against the Monstrous Regiment of Women, Selected Writings of John Knox: Public Epistles, Treatises, and Expositions to the Year 1559," Presbyterian Heritage Publications, updated 1995, http://www.swrb. com/newslett/actualNLs/firblast.htm. In his writing, The First Blast of the Trumpet Against the Monstrous Regiment of Women, Knox argues the inferiority of women's nature by saying, "For who can deny but it is repugnant to nature, that the blind shall be appointed to lead and conduct such as do see? That the weak, the sick, and impotent persons shall nourish and keep the whole and strong? And finally, that the foolish, mad, and frenetic shall govern the discreet, and give counsel to such as be sober of mind? And such be all women, compared unto man in bearing of authority."

THE AFRICAN AMERICAN
SINGLE MOM

SUZANNE R. BATES

Reconciliation and Justice

Suzanne Bates is a Licensed Clinical Professional (LPC) and she serves as Assistant Professor of Counseling and Associate Dean of Students at Covenant Theological Seminary in St. Louis, Missouri. For more than a decade, she has served as a part-time Staff Counselor for New City Fellowship-St. Louis. In the fall of 2017, Suzanne began her doctoral studies for the Philosophy of Education in Counseling degree at the University of Missouri-St. Louis. She is a native of St. Louis, has four grown children, and two grandchildren.

During his campaign for the 2016 election, candidate Ben Carson said: "We need to face the fact that when young girls have babies out of wedlock, most of the time, their education ends with that first baby. And those babies are four times as likely to grow up in poverty, end up in the penal system, or the welfare system."[1]

Ben Carson's words create a host of emotions. This quote raises the question: Who is he talking about? In fact, what came to your mind as you read this quote? Who came to mind? We do not want to admit it, but quotes like this often result in concluding that the "young girls" indicated are African American. Research suggests this is true for young girls of any race. And yet, societal views about single moms in the Black community place having babies out of wedlock, dropping out of school, living in poverty, and ending up in the penal system, as the image and decline of the Black family. The African American single mom is often held responsible for the plight of and moral temperature of the Black community.

What was in the mind of Ben Carson when he made such a statement? Made at the time when he was campaigning as a presidential candidate, he did not explicitly say, "This is the African American single mom." And yet, Carson's statement raised an uproar within the community, especially the community of African American women, who argued that although research would support his statement about young girls having babies out of wedlock, this does not completely define the African American single mom or the destiny of her children. As you read further, consider what you have believed about African American single moms, their impact on the Black community, their view of themselves, and their need for reconciliation and justice. As a Black single mom, working with single moms for many years, hearing their stories and knowing my own, I find myself having to consider my own heart and attitude about our experience.

Ask yourself the following questions:

- What is your experience of African American single moms, or any single moms?
- What is your experience of the issues they often face?
- What is your understanding of their circumstances and needs in our society today?

Based on your response to these questions and if you will address the issue further, you might ask:

- What have you seen in how your congregation addresses the need for reconciliation and justice for African American single moms? Is there a need?
- What have you seen in the response of your community?

Let me first say, although this chapter is a reflection on the need and blessing of reconciliation and justice for the African American single mom, it is in no way a statement that reconciliation and justice is not needed for *all* single moms. However, beliefs held throughout generations, the history of this nation, and the challenges facing the Black community around issues of racism, slavery, systemic oppression, and marginalization compel us to look more specifically at issues facing the African American woman and the African American single mom and to consider her narrative and the need for justice and reconciliation.

From the mammies, jezebels, and breeder women of slavery to the smiling Aunt Jemimas on pancake mix boxes, ubiquitous Black prostitutes, and ever-present welfare mothers of contemporary popular culture, negative stereotypes applied to African-American women have been fundamental to Black women's oppression.[2]

The African American single mom is first African American. And as such, there are views and responses to her Blackness, her role in society, her dignity, even before she becomes a single mom. We must first look at the views of her as a Black woman to understand more deeply the narrative that is formed by society and by her, as a Black single mom. So, who is the African American woman? What does it mean to be her? bell hooks writes in her book, *Ain't I a Woman: Black Women and Feminism*, "Systemic devaluation of Black womanhood was not simply a direct consequence of race hatred, it was a calculated method of social control."[3] Char Adams resonates with bell hooks, stating:

Having evolved over time, the still-existing stereotypes regarding Black women permeate the psyches of Americans. We see this regularly in popular culture, where news articles and television and movie ads label Black women "sassy" or "strong" and use words like "beautiful" and "elegant" when referring to white women. While this racist propaganda is not as overt as it was in past centuries, it is still very much embedded in American society, and manifests itself in the experiences of Black women every day through microaggressions, oppressive acts and even violence.[4]

The above quote speaks to views often held in our culture; Black women, labeled as sassy and strong, are also labeled as angry and aggressive. I attended a conference recently that focused on some of the challenges and successes of African American women in higher education. The presenter asked participants to write on sticky notes, positive and negative views (personal and otherwise) held about African American women. The notes were placed on the whiteboard for all to view. Although I witnessed others' and my own positive beliefs: beautiful, strong, elegant, educated, smart, persevering, and determined, I was also keenly aware of a deep ache in my soul as I read the many negative stereotypes indicated: lazy, angry, aggressive, loud, over-sexed, takes advantage of the welfare system, and unfaithful. I had the thought that although these negative views are not always true, it is difficult to counter and correct this image in our society.

I have suffered microaggressions and oppressive acts at the hands of those who would make assumptions about my character solely based on my skin color. While teaching a class on Social and Cultural Foundations, a White older student shared his first thought in seeing me, a large Black woman. He thought I would be an angry and loud individual. I also vividly remember a conversation with one of my undergraduate professors. I walked into class early, greeting her as I took my seat. She returned the greeting and then preceded to ask me questions regarding how I speak. She stated that I did not talk like other Blacks and asked if I was from the area. I asked her, "What do you mean?" Of course, I knew exactly what she meant because it was a comment familiar to me. A little more nervously she expounded on her comment and question. Disappointed, I responded that if she had come into contact with any of the Black girls with whom I went to high school, there would be no need for the questions and comment. I did not speak Ebonics, something that at times defined Blacks as *more Black* and ethnic. This must have been her expectation based only on the color of my skin. I attended a predominately White Catholic, all girls, high school. In that context I was not unique and my speech was not unique.

These just give a peek at my experiences as a Black woman; I have many more stories. And I have heard the stories, which resonate with my own, of many other African American women. Although the view of one or two White people does not necessarily reflect the view of all, it is important to give consideration to the historical and current image of Black women in our society to comprehend the nature of these negative stereotypes on the Black single mom. The narrative often given her by society is that:

- She sleeps around.
- Multiple children means multiple men.
- She is dependent on welfare, the system, and others.
- She is to blame for the decline of the Black community by having babies out of wedlock.
- She is likely not educated and/or will most likely stop her education.
- Her kids will end up in gangs and/or jail and prison.

In the accounts given earlier of stereotypes given me as a Black woman, neither of the individuals knew me as a single mom, but I remember fleeting thoughts on what their assessment might have been, particularly around the role I played in my circumstances. In 1989, I moved to the state of Georgia. My marriage was suffering terribly; I decided I needed a separation. I had two children at the time with a third one on the way, which I did not discover until my fifth month of pregnancy. The Lord, through a series of events led me to a fully Anglo, very traditional, Presbyterian church. With each visit I was immediately reminded of being in South Georgia. It was like being in an entirely different culture surrounded by a people who were not like me. I was aware of my Blackness and my circumstances: coming into an all-White church with two kids, one on the way, and no husband. "What are they going to think of me? Would I be a statistic to them: another Black single mom with no baby daddy in sight? These thoughts flooded my mind and heart. I walked into a place where the people loved and served God, but they didn't look like me.

I remember going on my first women's retreat with a colleague from work who invited me. New to the Church and not a regular attendee, I did not know the other ladies, nor did they know me. On their behalf, my colleague asked me questions about my life. There was a strange awkwardness. I was the only Black attendee; they had seen me with my kids and no husband. It appeared no one felt comfortable to ask me questions about my life like: "Where is your husband?" The Spirit told me they were afraid to ask me questions about my children and marriage, questions that women would normally talk about.

I leaned over and whispered in my colleague's ear that they should feel freedom to ask me questions. She shared with me their discomfort and stated they were wrestling with what's safe territory and how to not cause me shame by asking questions around my circumstances as a single mom. They didn't know I was already experiencing shame—not just because of their words or actions. I wrestled with societal perceptions as well as their perceptions about me. Furthermore, I did not want to be a statistic and did not want to be a "project" (sometimes single moms feel this way, especially when ministered to by people from the Church).

Three years after that retreat, my husband and I reunited. I found myself in another shameful position, at least shameful to me. I felt shame for conceiving my fourth child only weeks after he joined us in Georgia. I felt shame because he had been in and out of crack houses where many did not come out alive. I felt shame with adding a fourth child to the financial struggle of caring for three children. What was I thinking? I was afraid, angry with myself, and ashamed. My thoughts were consumed with what my friends at church would think. What would they believe about me, even though they knew me? These questions resounded in my mind and ears daily. I discovered that my view of myself had become more aligned with societal views that Black women just sleep around and get pregnant. Yes, he was my husband, but we had been separated for years. Although he had been clean (without using drugs) for a year, he practiced a risky lifestyle, and I should have given more time to see how he had changed before getting pregnant. It was four months before I could tell anyone and six months before the fog of depression lifted.

My husband was with me, but I still felt like a single mom. A friend of mine would often quote Nehemiah 8:1o to me: *"The joy of the Lord is your strength."* I would get angry and impatient with her lack of understanding. But she was correct in the end. That child, my youngest, brought incredible joy to our household. Sadly, it was not enough to persuade my husband to continue to do the right thing and care for his family. By the time my youngest was fifteen months, he was back on the street engaged in drugs and again abandoned me and our four kids. It was the last time we lived together as husband and wife, and from that point on I raised my kids as a single mom.

Single moms, especially African American single moms, do not want to be a statistic, a project, someone to be pitied, or judged. Often they have what I call "Single Mom Syndrome." Urban Dictionary defines Single Mom Syndrome as, "When a single mother begins to dwell on being alone for the rest of their life and starts paying more attention to men than their children," but this is not what I mean.[5] The

Single Mom Syndrome I am referring to is the attitude adopted by the single mom as a defense mechanism and way of protecting her kids and self. It's an attitude of, "I can do it. I don't need your help. Maybe I do need your help, but I do not want to ask because I do not want you to judge me. I do not want to be, nor am I, a statistic." Time and time again I would witness this in my own attitude and in the attitude of many other Black single moms. The African American single mom wants to be valued—respected as a contributor to society and a vital participant of the community. One benefit of working with single moms was that we offered these gifts to one another: value, respect, acceptance. We were vital to each other and together raised our kids and encouraged one another. Based on societal influences and beliefs, I as a single mom would and should be a statistic. My kids, especially my sons, should be a statistic, whether by gangs, drugs, or incarceration. But by the grace of God, we are not.

Historically, and sadly still today, societal views hold that African American single moms are scapegoats. They are often seen as irresponsible, and responsible for the decline of the Black community at large. The Black single mom is seen as inferior, nonproductive, dysfunctional, and is to blame for the poverty, drugs, and crime in the Black community. Rasheena Fountain, evolutionist and social justice advocate states, "Black single mothers are more than scapegoats." She goes on to state that if she "had a dollar for every time a single mother got blamed for the problems in the African American community," she would be rich.[6] In her dissertation, Timeka Tounsel states:

> An intriguing pattern in U.S. news media regarding professional black women emerged in the years from 2008–14—there were a lot of them. These women held titles like attorney, teacher, writer, and engineer; they were attractive and compelling on screen and in print. The reason they had become the center of multiple headlines, however, was not because of what they had achieved, but because of what they lacked. In 2006, the U.S. Census Bureau released data from its American Community Survey showing that 45 percent of black women in the country had never been married. The trend was said to be most prevalent among black women who were also professionals with college degrees and careers, a combination that some suggested caused them to delay marriage and motherhood. It was Hannah Brueckner, a sociology professor and researcher at Yale University,

who linked the census data to attainment of post-secondary education, and she declared in 2009 that professional black women's achievements had "come... at the cost of marriage and family" (Yale University 2009). Thus black women found themselves, yet again, at the center of a crisis concerning the black family, and like so many times before, it was all their fault.[7]

Tounsel's statement is a reflection of the issues African American women face as a result of media and societal views. The African American single mom, whether uneducated or rising to the middle class through her achievements as an educated, professional single mom, is held responsible for the decline of the Black family and community. Reversing the stigma society has placed on Black women and the Black single mom seems almost impossible. Daniel Patrick Moynihan's report, *The Negro Family: The Case for National Action* (also known as *Moynihan Report, 1965*), addresses issues and trends concerning the Black family. With a focus on the family structure of the Negro home, the report purports that the socialization and economic lack and failure in these families is due to female-led single-parent homes. In Section IV of the report, "The Tangle of Pathology," he argues:

> In essence, the Negro community has been forced into a matriarchal structure which, because it is so out of line with the rest of the American society, seriously retards the progress of the group as a whole, and imposes a crushing burden on the Negro male and, in consequence, on a great many Negro women as well. There is, presumably, no special reason why a society in which males are dominant in family relationships is to be preferred to a matriarchal arrangement. However, it is clearly a disadvantage for a minority group to be operating on one principle, while the great majority of the population, and the one with the most advantages to begin with, is operating on another. This is the present situation of the Negro. Ours is a society which presumes male leadership in private and public affairs. The arrangements of society facilitate such leadership and reward it. A subculture, such as that of the Negro American, in which this is not the pattern, is placed at a distinct disadvantage.[8]

Although it is stated in the report that some families, particularly middle-class families, break out of this pathology, also indicated is the following:

> Nonetheless, at the center of the tangle of pathology is the weakness of the family structure. Once or twice removed, it will be found to be the principal source of most of the aberrant, inadequate, or antisocial behavior that did not establish, but now serves to perpetuate the cycle of poverty and deprivation.[9]

What is being said here is that within the Black community our own beliefs about the family structure and the role of fathers in and out of the home, which is not based on societal norms, adds to the cycle of poverty and deprivation within the Black family structure. And it seems, again, that the African American single mom bears the burden of much of this dynamic. Writers of the *Moynihan Report, 1965,* came to this conclusion:

> Three centuries of injustice have brought about deep-seated structural distortions in the life of the Negro American. At this point, the present tangle of pathology is capable of perpetuating itself without assistance from the white world. The cycle can be broken only if these distortions are set right. In a word, a national effort towards the problems of Negro Americans must be directed towards the question of family structure. The fundamental importance and urgency of restoring the Negro American Family structure has been evident for some time. E. Franklin Frazier put it most succinctly in 1950: "As the result of family disorganization a large proportion of Negro children and youth have not undergone the socialization which only the family can provide. The disorganized families have failed to provide for their emotional needs and have not provided the discipline and habits which are necessary for personality development. Because the disorganized family has failed in its function as a socializing agency, it has handicapped the children in their relations to the institutions in the community. Moreover, family disorganization has been partially responsible for a large amount of juvenile delinquency and adult crime among Negroes. Since the widespread family disorganization among Negroes has resulted from the failure of the father to play the role in family life required by American society, the mitigation of this

problem must await those changes in the Negro and American society which will enable the Negro father to play the role required of him."[10]

So what are the implications? The words used here, "Because the disorganized family has failed in its function as a socializing agency, it has handicapped the children in their relations to the institutions in the community," implies the Black, largely matriarchal, female single-parent household is deficient.

Research states there is a high percentage of children born to unwed mothers within the African American community. A summary of the 2011 Census Bureau data compiled by Kids Count, a project of the Annie E. Casey Foundation, found of single-parent families, 67 percent were non-Hispanic Blacks.[11] New data from the US Census Bureau reports that "only 38.7 percent of African American minors live with both parents."[12] In a 2017 article written by Walter Williams, he states "children from fatherless homes are likelier to drop out of school, die by suicide, have behavioral disorders, join gangs, commit crimes, and end up in prison," and indicates these children are most likely living in "poverty-stricken households." Williams concludes that decimation of the Black family is more the result of the welfare state rather than slavery, racism, and Jim Crow laws.[13]

Cultural perspectives regarding the African American family also play a role. Without going into major detail here, there are three cultural perspectives regarding the African American family that help shape views on the Black family and add to the societal narrative of the African American single mom. Two of these perspectives, the Cultural Deviant and the Cultural Equivalent perspectives, are both deficit models. The Cultural Deviant orientation holds that the African American family is basically dysfunctional and abnormal; it does not uphold and keep traditional, mainstream, societal norms of what is good. Unfortunately, this model is the one often used to study the Black family. The Cultural Equivalent model seeks to place the African American family up against the standards and norms of the dominant culture. This view holds that as long as the African American family can operate, function, and adhere to the normal and mainstream societal traditions of the dominant culture, then they will be OK. Adhering to the mainstream traditions would also mean forsaking cultural values. The Cultural Equivalent perspective ends up encouraging and exalting the dominant cultural traditions while diminishing, and in some ways destroying, cultural differences. "Conformity is best and if not conformity then the AA family is deviant, invisible, irrelevant and unimportant."[14] I once heard a reporter state, "Just because you can go out and have babies, doesn't mean you should." Although his statement was not directly presented to the Black woman, it is implied based on these deficit models. It is assumed that the African American single mom is a single mom because she lacks self-control and is out just having babies, lots of them, because she can. She is considered deviant.

The third cultural perspective regarding the African American family is the Cultural Variant perspective. As a kind of 1970s response to the Moynihan Report, this view holds that we need to view the Black family as culturally distinct; its functions are different. This perspective proposes not looking at the African American family against the norms of the dominant culture, which allows for reevaluation of the conditions of the family, the role and impact of the African American single mom, and any thoughts and ideas associated with the African American family.[15]

Herein lies the reality of the need and blessing of reconciliation for the African American single mom. She carries the burden of blame for economic suffering, crime, welfare, deteriorating families, broken relationships, abandonment, incarceration, drugs, and even death. These are burdens that even I, as a single mom, would not necessarily consider on a day-in and day-out basis. Why? As a single mom, my life and time was filled with surviving, caring for my kids, increasing my education, managing work and home. I rarely took the time to consider the many stressors of my life dictated and shaped by societal views; I was caught up in the cycle. The African American single mom deals with societal views and stereotypes, sexism, racial prejudice and profiling, especially for her sons. She has to be aware of and potentially engage the "School to Prison Pipeline" and "Zero Tolerance" policies,[16] struggling to see and know her own worth and value, practicing self-care, and caring for her children—their provision, health, safety, and education. She often faces emotional challenges and distress, and of course she certainly faces her share of shame. As stated previously, I was not always aware of all of these issues operating and tugging at my heart on a continuum. But I was aware of the need for a reprieve, the need for "something to give," the need to be seen, heard, and valued.

Reconciliation means restoration, bringing back together again; it means "the action of making one view or belief compatible with another."[17] The Scriptures speak to reconciliation as well, reminding readers of the need for reconciliation with God and one another. Ephesians 2:14–17 reads:

> For he himself is our peace, who has made us both one and has broken down in his flesh the dividing wall of hostility by abolishing the law of the commandments expressed in ordinances, that he might create in himself one new man in place of the two, so making peace, and might reconcile us both to God in one body through the cross, thereby killing the hostility. And he came and preached peace to you who were far off and peace to those who were near.

And Colossians 1:20–22 states:

> And you, who were alienated and hostile in mind, doing evil deeds, he has now reconciled in his body of flesh by his death, in order to present you holy and blameless and above reproach before him.

The need for reconciliation suggests something is broken and thus needs to be restored, redeemed, made better, or made whole. For the African American single mom, so much of how she is perceived, addressed, and interacted with by others, and at times herself, is broken. The narrative given her by the dominant culture, by social media, politics, and societal paradigms needs to be changed. She needs a new narrative that allows for her personal beauty, intelligence, and hard work, one that allows her to be free of the blame for the decimation of the Black family and community. She needs a narrative that does not tell her who she should be based on others' view and who she is based on systemic oppression, racism, sexism, and others' prejudices, fears, attitudes, or cultural perspectives. Although it is often not addressed or considered, the African American single mom may have many reasons for why she ended up a single mom—like the reasons people believe a White woman is a single mom. Her husband must have died, or something else went terribly wrong. This too, could be the reason for the state of the African American single mom. But typically, this question is not asked. Most often with Black single moms, the question is, "Do all of the kids have the same father, the same last name?" And they wonder, "How many baby daddies?" So, the narrative must change. Nicole Rodgers and

Rashad Robinson in their article, "How the Media Distorts Black Families," state:

> If our country hopes to close cultural divides and create solutions that make all families strong, the media cannot continue to perpetuate false narratives that cause so much harm, while allowing the truth of the economic and social forces that drive family dynamics to remain invisible. The news media must help the public understand the systemic barriers that impede well-being for so many families and the policies that could improve them. The time for the media industry to reckon with how it covers families is long overdue.[18]

Moving in the direction of reconciliation would mean resisting the myths and stereotypes imparted to African American single moms. It would mean recognizing, naming, and addressing systemic oppression, and issues of education and work within the Black community. Writer and activist Sincere Kirabo discusses four common lies about single moms, which he challenges readers to stop believing: (1) they cannot raise their children properly, (2) fatherlessness leads to inner city youth delinquency, (3) a father-figure is needed for the Black child to be reared correctly (traditional family values), and (4) Black single moms are to blame for the state of Black America.[19] The Church should be at the forefront of this movement, living out the Gospel to minister to African American single moms, offering reconciliation and justice to these moms and their families, and therefore, to the Black community. The wrong in how these single moms have been perceived and treated needs to be restored and made right. Where there has been gross injustice, justice is needed. A commitment to honor, integrity, and the offer of equity must be upheld.

As mentioned earlier, Scripture has a lot to say about reconciliation and justice. The Psalms tell us:

> For you have formed my inward parts; you knitted me together in my mother's womb. I praise you, for I am fearfully and wonderfully made. Wonderful are your works; my soul knows it very well. My frame was not hidden from you, When I was being made in secret, intricately woven in the depths of the earth. Your eyes saw my unformed substance; in your book were written, every one of them, the days that were formed

for me, when as yet there was none of them. How precious to me are your thoughts, O God! Ps. 139:13–17a

God speaks right into these issues; Jesus speaks right into these issues. We have a model through whom we are given wisdom to know how we can begin to be agents of reconciliation and justice in the life of the African American single mom and how we can encourage her in faith, hope, and love. We begin by recognizing who she is and to whom she belongs. For some, this may be challenging as there was a period in our history when Blacks were not considered human, not given dignity, not seen as created by God, not equal to other men and women in the created order of things. But here, in Psalm 139, the psalmist shows us that all are "fearfully and wonderfully made." Here, we see the African American single mom, formed in her mother's womb where all the days of her life are written by God himself, before she is one day old. Here, we see her being fully known and fully seen, with a purpose for each day of her life. We see her dignity, worth, and value. She is a fearfully and wonderfully made creation of God; she is his. Holding this view is imperative if we are going to respond to and enter into the life of the Black single mom. As we recognize our own need to be reconciled and recognize what Christ has done in reconciling us to himself, we are better able to see the need for reconciliation for God's beloved African American single mom and others. We are able to see as well, the need for justice.

Justice, fairness, equity, just behavior or treatment is also a great need of the African American single mom. Already indicated in the pages of this chapter, the unjust views society has held regarding the Black single mom has created disparity in the way she is treated compared to other non-Black single moms. Unlike the White single mom, she is not celebrated for being an unwed mother, having children out of wedlock, for achieving, for pressing through hard places to care for her children. She is not recognized as a valuable contributor to society. This was the presentation given based on the false TV show character Murphy Brown. Although society was not ready to see this White, single woman have a baby out of wedlock and celebrate, and although there was political pushback, when character Murphy Brown began singing "Natural Woman" to the child while in the hospital, there was a shift. She became celebrated for her boldness and independence in response to the political pushback; society began to celebrate her for having and keeping the child. And later, she became the positive icon for White single moms. Alisha Gray quotes several writers stating, "well-known examples of 'Independent Single Mothers,' such as Murphy Brown, are often praised; while Black single mothers seem to be continually correlated with Patriarchal deviance—no matter the popularity."[20] In the meantime, African American single moms are still being held hostage to the negative societal stereotypes. Where is the justice?

Micah 6:8 calls us to do justly, to love mercy, and to walk humbly with God. In many cases, to do justly for the African American single mom would mean praying and asking God to restore the years that the locusts have eaten in the life of these moms.[21]

Several passages in Scripture also give us a vivid picture of God's reconciliatory work and justice with single moms. In 1 Kings 17, we read of the Lord's word coming to Elijah to go to Zarephath where he (the Lord) has already gone before him to have a widow feed him. One might ask, "Is this account about God's provision for Elijah, or for the single mom?" His provision is for both, through both. He has already gone before them both; He sees and hears them and is moved with compassion. God uses his people from all walks of life to bless others and reveal the Glory of Christ. Elijah finds that the widow and and her son have nothing but a handful of flour and a little oil left to make one small cake. Seeing the lack, Elijah still asks the widow to make him a cake and encourages her to not be afraid as the oil will not run dry.

Now, all know that it would take a tremendous amount of faith to believe that there would be enough for her and her son, much less the prophet, to eat. In faith she responds, and as the narrative continues we read that God fulfilled his promise to provide. The author tells us that after she has offered everything, her son becomes ill. The woman is afraid and asks Elijah, "*What have you against me, O man of God? You have come to me to bring my sin to remembrance and to cause the death of my son!*"

Can you imagine what she must have felt? A single mom, with nothing but a son to carry her deceased husband's name and perhaps care for her in her old age, is left to believe that something she did wrong must be why this trouble has come forth. She must be thinking, "How am I going to make it? How am I going to survive?" We see Elijah caring about this woman's heart. He takes the son into the upper chamber and cries out to the Lord on behalf of the widow. He enters her story, her narrative; he validates her heart cry by responding and crying out to God. The Lord hears the cry of the widow, and Elijah and restores her son. He does not allow her to hold the belief that her sin, her brokenness, would cause the death of her son. Elijah brings her son back to her restored. And the widow believes the prophet is from God and believes the words he spoke. Her faith was renewed, and she believed God's care for her and her son.

We see another account of God's mercy for the single mom in 2 Kings 4:1–7. In this account there is another widow crying out to the prophet Elisha. *"Your servant my husband is dead, and you know that your servant feared the Lord, but the creditor has come to take my two children to be his slaves."* Understand here, this single mom is scared. She is grieving the loss of her husband, facing financial burdens, and trying to care for her sons. It's piercing to the heart to hear her cry, *"the creditor has come to take my two children to be his slaves."*

What might this single mom have felt? Fear and grief must have flooded her soul. I can identify with the financial woes and desperation. I, like many single moms, have lived below the poverty line. I know desperation. And there was a time in our history of slavery that the African American woman's sons would have been taken from her, maybe even used as a means of bargaining (really threatening) her for sexual favors. Elisha could have turned a deaf ear. He could have spoken to the woman about using her resources better, or may have resonated with the creditors that the sons should work. But instead, he enters into her narrative. In 2 Kings 4:2 Elisha says, *"What shall I do for you? Tell me, what have you in the house?"*

Again, we see the Lord's compassion and mercy. We see Elisha interceding on her behalf. We see God's provision and restoration. The economic burden lifted, she no longer had to fear enslavement of her sons and was able to focus her energy on caring for her sons.

The accounts given are of women who were married and then widowed. We know Jesus cares about the poor, the widow, and the orphan. He cares about the poor African American single mom, the rich African American single mom, the widowed African American single mom, the never married and poor or rich African American single mom. He cares. He uses his servants to enter into the narratives of these women, to care about their plight, their lack, and to speak to their dignity, worth, and value. In Luke 7:11–17, we see Jesus himself entering into the narrative of the widow of Nain. Her only son was being carried out during the funeral procession. She was left with nothing. Jesus sees this mother, is moved with compassion and acts:

> *And when the Lord saw her, he had compassion on her and said, "Do not weep." Then he came and touched the bier and the bearers stood still. And he said, "Young man, I say to you, arise." And the dead man sat up and began to speak, and Jesus gave him to his mother.* Luke 7:11–17

Herein lies redemption. God is saying, "I care about these things. I care about the widow. I care about the single mom."

The call placed on us, the Church, by God himself, is to be part of changing the African American single mom narrative. We are called to be part of providing for her and the Black family a corrective emotional experience. A corrective emotional experience is a term used in counseling that refers to clients having a real-life experience of change in the here-and-now relationship with the therapist. Working collaboratively with clients, the therapist helps to identify and provides a new, more enjoyable or pleasurable response to clients' faulty expectations or schema and old relationship patterns.[22]

For the African American single mom, a corrective emotional experience is taking what was once polluted through stereotypes, racism, prejudice, and oppression, and speaking into that horrific brokenness and bondage, beauty, worth, dignity, and God's glory. As change agents, we can provide a different response to this single mom—one that builds hope. We must first open our eyes to see and name the real issues, recognizing our own biases and prejudices, and become self-aware. We must see these moms as individuals created in the image of God.

In moving toward reconciliation and justice, there needs to be an eradication of the myths and stereotypes, and this must be done on corporate, institutional, and personal levels. We need to get to know the African American mom for who she is rather than on what society has dictated; we need to enter her story and life. As we enter her life and share her burdens, we help to defend the cause of the fatherless. Remember, apart from what society often speaks and holds as a belief, not all African American single moms became single moms because they just wanted to have lots of babies and different baby daddies. There is a grieving for those who have lost their husbands or those who have deeply desired a lasting relationship with the father of their children and, for whatever reasons, were not granted this experience. We must weep, grieve, and mourn with the African American single mom when she weeps, grieves, and mourns. And we must rejoice with her when she rejoices. Finally, we need to be Boazes.

The blessing of reconciliation and justice is revealed and experienced when we open our eyes to see the African American single mom, to hear her heart, to have compassion, and to act. The blessing comes as we are willing to be as Boaz—kinsman-redeemers. If I am honest, I confess I would have loved to have had such a man as Boaz. When my children were small, and even now at times when they are grown and with children of their own, I long to have in my life a kinsman-redeemer. My personal story is a triumphant one in that the Church, the people of God, did come around me in so many situations. My children are thriving.

And I can say I never felt like a project, a statistic, or an "Oh that poor single mom!" But I can also say I have not specifically known a man to enter my personal life and world and to speak against the many lies I have heard—lies I sometimes listened to, believed, and also fought around my marriage. I've not known a man who might have provided for me a corrective emotional experience for lies that hit hard as a result of a broken marriage and societal paradigms. So, in this, I would have wanted a Boaz. This is not to say I or other African American single moms need a man to be redeemed and whole. But for me personally, I would have liked this type of experience.

However, African American single moms do need men and women in the Church to act as Boaz did when he encountered Ruth and Naomi in the book of Ruth. He stepped in and stepped up to care for these women, not just materially or physically, but also for their reputations. Ruth and Naomi had nothing, only each other. Ruth was a Moabite, a foreigner among Naomi's people. They were open to mockery and scorn. There may have been whispers that they must have sinned greatly to have lost their husbands and Naomi her three sons. When Naomi returned to Bethlehem with her daughter-in-law, she knew she had a kinsman-redeemer, but she did not know how events would unfold. She was grieving, bitter, and felt as if God had forsaken her and Ruth. Boaz entered when Ruth came to his field. From the moment he heard of her and all she did for Naomi, he entered their lives. He concerned himself with their provision, going before Ruth and considering situations she might encounter before she even gave them thought. Boaz, by the Spirit of the Lord, was ahead of Ruth, working and seeing to her good and to Naomi's good.

What does this all mean? Simply stated, the *blessing* of reconciliation and justice for the African American single mom is first in being seen, and thus having dignity restored. It's in helping to carry her burdens, recognizing her gifts, and giving her freedom to use her gifts to serve others. When we commit ourselves to seeing the need and being part of the blessing, we reveal God's glory and express his love. And the world sees Jesus in real and tangible ways. To God be the glory.

---

1. Marina Fang, "Ben Carson Suggests Some 'Lifestyles' are More Valuable Than Others," October 7, 2015, https://www.huffingtonpost.com/entry/ben-carson-traditional-values_us_5615b2c2e4b021e856d38c35.
2. Patricia Hill Collins, Black Feminist Thought: Knowledge, Consciousness and the Politics of Empowerment (*Perspectives on Gender*) (New York, NY: Routledge, 2000), 5.
3. bell hooks, Ain't I a Woman: Black Women and Feminism (New York, NY: Routledge, Taylor & Francis Group, 2015), 53.
4. Char Adams, "Black Women In Our Society Aren't Allowed To Be Angry," *Bustle*, March 27, 2017, https://www.bustle.com/p/black-women-in-our-society-arent-allowed-to-be-angry-44219.
5. "Single Mom Syndrome," Urban Dictionary, https://www.urbandictionary.com/define.php?term=Single%20Mom%20Syndrome%20%28SMS%29.
6. Rasheena Fountain,"Black Single Mothers are More Than Scapegoats," *Huffington Post*, April 7, 2015, https://www.huffpost.com/entry/black-single-mothers-are_b_9619536.
7. Timeka Nicol Tounsel, The Black Woman that Media Built: Content Creation, Interpretation, and the Making of the Black Female Self (Ann Arbor, MI: University of Michigan, 2015), 1.
8. Daniel Patrick Moynihan, "Remembered and Reclaimed," BlackPast.org, written 1965, http://www.blackpast.org/primary/moynihan-report-1965.
9. Ibid.
10. Ibid.
11. Laura Speer and Florencia Gutierrez, "2015 Kids Count Data Book," The Annie E. Casey Foundation, July 21, 2015, http://www.aecf.org/m/databook/aecf-2015kidscountdatabook-2015-em.pdf.
12. Zenitha Prince, "Census Bureau: Higher Percentage of Black Children Live with Single Mothers," Afro: The Black Media Authority, December 31, 2016, https://www.afro.com/census-bureau-higher-percentage-black-children-live-single-mothers.
13. Walter E. Williams, "The Black Family is Struggling and It's not because of Slavery," September 20, 2017, https://www.dailysignal.com/2017/09/20/black-family-struggling-not-slavery.
14. Bette J. Dickerson, African American Single Mothers: Understanding Their Lives and Families, 1st ed. Vol. 10 (Thousand Oaks, CA: Sage Publications, Inc, 1995), 1–20.
15. Ibid.
16. School to Prison Pipeline and Zero Tolerance policies have become prevalent in school districts across America. Due to the concern of crime within schools, districts implemented the zero tolerance policy, which means a child committing a crime, no matter

how minor or unintentional, will be suspended or expelled and in some cases turned juvenile criminal system. This process basically moves kids out of schools and into prisons. For more information, see https://www.thoughtco.com/school-to-prison-pipeline-4136170.

17. Merriam-Webster Dictionary (2018), s.v. "reconciliation."

18. Nicole Rodgers and Rashaad Robinson, "How the News Media Distorts Black Families," December 29, 2017, https://www.washingtonpost.com/outlook/2017/12/29/a374a268-ea6d-11e7-8a6a-80acf0774e64_story.html?utm_term=.6643abdbd3c6.

19. Sincere Kirabo, "4 Common Lies You Should Stop Believing About Black Single Mothers Right Now," *Everyday Feminism*, January 2, 2016, https://everydayfeminism.com/2016/01/black-youth-fatherless-homes/.

20. Alisha Grey, "A Thesis on Black Single Motherhood From Slavery and Beyond," http://www.academia.edu/5595066/A_Thesis_On_Black_Single_Motherhood_From_Slavery_and_Beyond.

21. Joel 2:25. God's promise to restore provision to his people after using a plague to bring his people to repentance.

22. Edward Teyber and Faith McClure, 6th ed. Interpersonal Process in Therapy: An Integrative Model, 6th Edition (Belmont, CA: Brooks & Cole, 2011), 28–31.

WHERE ARE THE WOMEN?

CAROLINE WEST

Caroline West is a student at Johns Hopkins University, where she majors in international studies and sociology. She is a member of Lookout Mountain Presbyterian Church and regularly attends Faith Christian Fellowship in Baltimore, Maryland. At Hopkins, she is the editor-in-chief of The Dialectic, *a journal of Christian thought and serves on the Undergraduate Academic Ethics Board.*

Before I entered university, I was not equipped with all the tools and terms necessary to carefully and thoughtfully examine two important facets of my identity: being female and being a Christian. I understood them solely as subjective concepts, not as objects of study, and it was difficult for me to conceptualize their overlap. I have since muddled through the works of Judith Butler, written a research proposal that introduced me to the measurement of religiousness as a variable, and pondered the connections between capitalism and the doctrine of predestination. In each year of my schooling, my mind has expanded to accommodate new ideas, new perspectives, and new modes of expression. I have developed clarity on some things and wallowed in confusion over others. Throughout everything, I have sought to appreciate complexity, nuance, and deep, critical thought. I have much still to learn, but I hope this chapter reflects some ability on my part to parse the finer points of gender and its manifestations in my denomination, the Presbyterian Church in America (PCA), without fear or favor.

A fairly basic but revealing question borrowed from feminist scholars is useful to pose as we begin our examination: Where are the women? In applying this question to the sphere of Christian faith, we find that the location of women in churches varies widely across the United States. In some churches, women deliver sermons, lead prayers, and exercise authority in decision-making processes. In others, they head committees and teach Sunday school. And there are some churches, of course, where women sit in the pews, work in the nursery, and cook in the kitchen.

I don't provide this series of images to suggest levels of oppression, only to demonstrate that Christians disagree on the positions women should occupy in the Church, often because of different views on scriptural teaching about the role of women. These differences have certainly manifested in the PCA, where my essential question is best rephrased to read not simply "Where are the women?" but "Where (and how) should the women be allowed to serve?" The PCA has wrestled with that question for the past several years; the following is a chronicle of that exploration and how denominational leaders have shaped it.

Understanding the source of the exploration requires knowledge of how, when, and why the denomination itself was first founded. In early 1973, the founding delegates of the PCA were still members of the Presbyterian Church in the United States (PCUS), which merged in 1983 with the United Presbyterian Church in the USA (UPCUSA) to form the Presbyterian Church in the United States of America (PCUSA).[1] By December 1973, the first members of the PCA had broken away from the PCUS in opposition to what they considered "long-developing theological liberalism" in their mother denomination. In their view, the fruit of that liberalism was diminished belief in the "deity of Christ" and in the "inerrancy and authority of Scripture." Furthermore, while the PCUS moved toward sanctioning the ordination of women, the founding delegates of the PCA adhered to the "traditional position on the role of women in the Church offices." They believed ordained church offices should be open exclusively to men.[2]

The ordination of women in the PCUS was certainly not the sole or primary catalyst for the founding of the PCA. Nevertheless, the issue was significant and alarming enough to warrant mention in the first documents released by the newly formed PCA. The ordination of women was listed, along with other practices considered problematic by the PCA, as the direct result of accepting "a different view of Scripture"[3] from that held by "[the PCA] and by the Southern Presbyterian forefathers." This link between disallowing the ordination of women and belief in Scripture's inerrancy is highly significant. It excludes the possibility of variation in interpretation of Scripture, at least in relation to passages on the role of women in the Church. The PCA believes that Scripture teaches, unambiguously, that women are not meant to serve in ordained positions within the Church body: to prevent women from being ordained is to respect biblical principles, thereby maintaining the centrality of Scripture's inerrancy. This principle affirms that the Bible, in its original form, is without error. It also establishes that the "written word of God" is "the only rule of judgment." Accordingly, the Church rests on the foundation of "express revelation" and relies on human reason and philosophy only as it is "reproduced in the [Bible]."[4]

This last point is critical to contextualizing the debate over women's ordination in the PCA: the strength of belief in scriptural inerrancy has led many to equate exploration of this issue with rejection of biblical centrality. Many are frustrated that the PCA, somewhat unique among Protestant denominations for its commitment to the traditional position on women's ordination, appears to be drifting toward what they perceive to be theological liberalism. And they are fearful that revisiting our stance on this one issue might lead us toward an abandonment of other important biblical doctrines.

This was significantly revealed in statements made by church officers at the General Assembly debate on the formation of a study committee on women in ministry in 2017. Consider the following, from Teaching Elder Roland Barnes:[5]

> And lastly, I might say that it could also be dangerous.... When I was considering coming into the PCA, I was told I needed to study the Book of Church Order, carefully, and the Westminster Confession of Faith, the Larger and Shorter Catechisms. I studied them carefully and was thankful that the PCA was holding fast to the Word of God on the role of women in the Church. I came into the PCA because of its position on the role of women in the Church, particularly with regard to the offices of elder and deacon. So, the committee of

commissioners is opposed to this recommendation and urges you brothers, hold fast, do not be conformed to the image of this world. Do not recommit this.[6]

The usage of the word "dangerous" implies that forming the study committee would threaten the peacefulness and unity of the Church; it also suggests the study committee represents the top of the "slippery slope." If the PCA will reject Scripture in regards to the role of women, Rev. Barnes suggests, on what foundation will its doctrine rest? And if the Church is not shaped by adherence to Scripture, then it moves toward conforming to "the image of the world," as Rev. Barnes puts it. At the root of this critique, I believe, is fear—fear of liberalism, fear of distorted theology, fear of change, fear of questioning.

Not all such fears are unwarranted. But Rev. Barnes unjustly dramatizes the dialogue. The motion before the General Assembly was not an endorsement of egalitarianism.[7] It did not suggest the PCA immediately begin ordaining women. The debate centered around whether or not the denomination should embark on careful study and prayerful consideration of God's Word, in an attempt to solidify, and potentially adjust, PCA doctrine on the role of women in ministry. Rev. Barnes built a dichotomous relationship between culture and church with his statement, presenting PCA women with a difficult choice: abide by Scripture and accept the traditional position on our role in the Church, or conform to secular culture and seek to expand that role. The first, according to the rhetoric of Rev. Barnes, preserves peace; the second creates chaos.

A second statement, from Teaching Elder Bill Schweitzer, expands on that contrast, once again revealing undercurrents of fear and frustration:

One thing that we can be absolutely certain of that pursuing this issue is in fact divisive. It is. Make no mistake. Pursuing this issue is a provocative move. And if you are for peace, and I've heard many strong and sincere desires expressed for peace and unity.... If you are for peace, fathers and brothers, I urge you, please, do not approve this study committee.[8]

Once again, melodrama escalates the dialogue. Rev. Schweitzer rebrands the opposing side; to be in favor of the study committee, one must also be in favor of chaos and disunity. Furthermore, he suggests that returning to Scripture to examine its teachings is in fact indicative of doubt in Scripture's inerrancy. This is clarified in earlier remarks wherein he states the following:

> Quite simply, it is whether we intend, whether we intend with all of our heart, mind, soul, and strength to submit to the plain Word of God on this issue.... It could not be any clearer. If it involves teaching, or having authority over a man in the Church, it's wrong. Now the world says this is outmoded and abhorrent. Again, the question is whose word are we going to honor? As Christ's Church, whose word are we going to obey? God's or the world's? Now precisely because this issue is so clear in Scripture, it's a bellwether. It's a litmus test. That's the way it's served on this. Where a church stands on this issue manifests your attitude toward Scripture and indicates your future direction.[9]

Rev. Schweitzer has every right to his opinion, but he does oversimplify the debate, presenting it as a clash between secular culture and the traditional stalwarts of the Church. Furthermore, his swift dismissal of worldly criticism is concerning. History is replete with examples in which it was the Church, not secular culture, that deviated most strongly from God's Word. Cultural concerns are not always anti-biblical or anti-religious. Prayerful contemplation and self-reflection are useful and righteous practices, even if their source is cultural outrage. Moreover, it cannot be denied that cultural outrage has spurred progress that greatly improved the lives of women around the world. To treat culture as the eternal enemy is to deny its capacity to accomplish good— it diminishes the struggles that have been waged on behalf of women and other oppressed populations. Rev. Schweitzer is right to emphasize Scripture's centrality in our denomination, but its price should not be the utter dismissal of any and all cultural concerns.

We now turn to the Ad Interim Committee on the Study of Women in the Military, which was commissioned in 2001 in response to fears that men were increasingly less willing to recognize their military duty to defend country and family in "an effeminate age." The final report reveals, among other things, how women are perceived in the PCA. The first two recommendations are particularly interesting:

> 1. Acknowledging that the child in the womb is "a person covered by Divine protection" and that women of childbearing age often carry

unborn children while remaining unaware of their child's existence; and that principles of just war require the minimization of the loss of life—particularly innocent civilians; the PCA declares that any policy which intentionally places in harm's way as military combatants women who are, or might be, carrying a child in their womb, is a violation of God's Moral Law.

2. This Assembly declares it to be the biblical duty of man to defend woman and therefore condemns the use of women as military combatants, as well as any conscription of women into the Armed Services of the United States.[10]

The first recommendation establishes several key elements that comprise the image of women in the PCA. First, it assumes all or most women of childbearing age want to have children. Second, it assumes all or most women of childbearing age are capable of having children. Third, it assumes all or most women of childbearing age have not and will not take steps to prevent the conception of children. Taken together, these assumptions reveal the extent to which childbearing is treated as the primary privilege of all women, regardless of ability or inclination to undertake it.

The second recommendation establishes men as the defenders of women, drawing on biblical texts as evidence for the rightness of such a relationship. By emphasizing the necessity of men protecting women, the second recommendation serves to reinforce the vulnerability of women established in the first. The position created for women by the final report of the Committee was not intended, I believe, to be cruel, discriminatory, or disempowering. Nevertheless, the restrictions it imposes are important to understand, particularly as they relate to where authority and power are concentrated within the PCA church body. Clearly, most, if not all, roles associated with leadership, defense, and protection are designated as exclusively masculine. This is not to suggest that such a designation is without scriptural justification. The Old Testament makes numerous references to male soldiers called to defend their homelands and families;[11] similar instances exist in the New Testament.[12]

I do think, however, that the authors of the final report should consider that generalizations of women as the inherently weaker sex and uniquely vulnerable as child-bearers, though perhaps useful in applying their interpretation of Scripture, do not capture those women who may deviate from this established norm. What message does this send? It's a subtle one, but it indicates that women are not celebrated as distinctive beings, but are rather a monolith of child-bearers too weak to protect others, regardless of individual preference and ability.

There are some official roles, of course, in which PCA women are currently affirmed. As laid out in the PCA's *Book of Church Order*, women are allowed to "assist the deacons in caring for the sick, the widows, the orphans, the prisoners, and the others who may be in any distress or need" (BCO 9–7). Deacons themselves perform the duties of ministering "to those who are in need, to the sick, to the friendless, and to any who may be in distress." Their office is one of "sympathy and service" (BCO 9–1, 9–2). In contrast to the role of deacon, the role of assistant to the deacons is an unordained position, and those who fill the position are not considered officers of the Church. Women in the PCA may also lead (typically) women's Bible studies, teach single-gender Sunday School classes, read Scripture in church, and serve on leadership committees within the Church. None of these positions are ordained.

The 2016 Ad Interim Committee on Women in Ministry did not intend to challenge this principle of exclusive male ordination, but rather to explore ways in which women may continue to serve the Church, without becoming ordained or violating the precepts of Scripture. Chief among those ways is the possibility of allowing women to serve as deaconesses. The Committee paid particular attention to relevant Scripture on this point, including 1 Timothy 3:8–11.

These verses lay out qualifications for the office of deacon: Deacons are meant to be "dignified, not double-tongued, not addicted to much wine, not greedy for dishonest gain." They should "hold the mystery of faith in clear conscience" and should be tested before being allowed to assume their office. These first three verses are straightforward, but 1 Timothy 3:11 presents greater difficulty in interpretation. It demands that deacons' "wives likewise must be dignified, not slanderers, but sober-minded, faithful in all things." The main issue occurs in interpreting the second word of the verse, which is translated sometimes as "women" and sometimes as "wives." We don't really know whether or not Paul was establishing a designated church office for women, with similar qualifications and responsibilities as the office of deacon. Given the shortness of the description, the Ad Interim Committee deemed it unlikely that Paul was establishing the office of deaconess, but instead was extending the characteristics of deacon to include that of possessing a God-fearing wife.

The committee acknowledged, however, that it is not uncommon for these passages to be used as an indication of biblical sanctioning of the office of deaconess. These passages were also taken by the Committee as a broader description of service that pleases God and fulfills his will for Christians on earth.

This rationale was then utilized to justify the most significant recommendation of the Committee at the conclusion of its study: that churches establish the office of "commissioned church worker," to fulfill the role of assistant to the deacon, with many of the same responsibilities and qualifications, but without the accompaniment of formal ordination. This position would be open to godly men and women. It is uncertain, of course, how many churches will adopt the recommendations of the Committee. Nevertheless, the creation of the aforementioned position is in itself a positive step in the direction of affirming women and their talents. But the PCA can still do more.

For instance, PCA doctrine affirms fundamental differences between men and women, but it sometimes fails to see the uniqueness with which we were all crafted. Variation and difference mean that not every man is suited for roles considered "masculine," and, by the same token, not every woman is suited for roles considered "feminine." The PCA rarely embraces that nuance; church leaders are more likely to insist on rigid categorization. And I understand why: if men and women fulfill distinctive roles, then the two sexes must be distinctive. I don't deny this point at all. However, I do believe we show grace toward one another by accepting that we don't all conform to the established norms for men and women. Ultimately, we grow as a body and love each other in a more Christlike manner when it is acknowledged that not every deviation is the product of sin. Indeed, it may be a sign that the norm itself is not in line with biblical teaching!

We also fail to see the nuance in each other's arguments, which is ultimately detrimental to people on all sides of the issue. Complementarians sometimes unfairly accuse egalitarians of attempting to erase all difference between the sexes. Egalitarians are too quick to claim that complementarians reject the fundamental equality of men and women.[13] In the PCA, egalitarianism is so closely associated with extremist feminism that its potential merits are all but erased. Many people fear that changing the role of women in the church will be followed by the endorsement of same-sex marriage and abortion. I understand why some make this leap; there are churches that have followed this pattern in the course of revisiting their stance on women's ordination. Nevertheless, we are wrong to maintain that all questioning and exploration will inevitably lead the denomination down the path of liberalism. This is not the stance of the whole denomination, but there are some who seem to believe this.

Such fear of change is often accompanied by an unwillingness to recognize the flaws in one's own arguments—flaws that stem most frequently, I think, from the natural biases of the human condition. The PCA's firm belief in the inerrancy of Scripture is an admirable one, and it can become dangerous if one takes not merely the Word to be divinely inspired, but oneself as well. No matter how strongly we believe ourselves to be carrying out God's will on earth, we must understand that we are still imperfect and sinful servants. John Stackhouse puts it well: "We dare not flatter ourselves that we sit on some intellectual height, calmly weighing each item in the balance of our finely calibrated intellects and entirely sanctified souls."[14]

The order and decorum of PCA gatherings, which proceed entirely according to strict parliamentary procedure, are easily taken as evidence of that "intellectual height," though we are just as likely to argue with one another from the gutters of prejudice and sinful pride. Prayerful introspection, though certainly no panacea, could produce more honest discussion, and I think it's a practice from which every single member of the PCA, both male and female, could benefit.

The PCA is also sorely lacking in direct action to back up the verbal and written statements made at General Assemblies and by Ad Interim Committees. The wisdom of Stackhouse is again applicable here:

> We are happy to affirm for the record that men are not inherently superior to women, that male and female together are created in the *imago dei*.[15] But then we *act* as if males really are superior: superior as topics for Bible study, superior to lead in church and home, superior to represent all human beings (as in the so-called generic language of "mankind").[16]

Too many people are blind to the fact that affirming complementarianism does not have to mean women always assume the low-power roles, or that we make allowances for different types of men while refusing to accept that not all women are interested in traditionally feminine pursuits. There is room in the Church to delight in women who nurture best or cook best and also in women who are best suited for leadership and positions of authority. And of course, we know many women are multi-talented and at home in both masculine and feminine arenas!

Finally, we must acknowledge that the biblical image of Christian family—of the body of Christ creating brothers and sisters—is unfulfilled in the PCA, and no doubt in many other denominations. This is not to say that Christians do not show love to each other! I have known and received rich, Christlike, joyous love as a member of the PCA. But I sometimes wonder if we are so eager to exist in community that we fail to confront fundamental problems of inequality and blindness. Of course, many do not acknowledge these problems because they do not believe they exist. But we must demand more of ourselves and of men, specifically.

And here I will make two very personal requests to PCA men.

First, please do not tell me the issue of women's ordination is insignificant because your wife, mother, aunt, daughter, or female friend is content with our current system. Your female relative or friend is not the spokesperson for all women—and she probably doesn't think of herself that way. Don't place that burden on her. This inclination most often stems from a desire to minimize the objections of other women by rationalizing that it can't be all that bad if your female friends and relatives are happy. Resist this fundamentally human urge to generalize!

My second request is: please accept that there are certain experiences that as a male, you will never have and will never understand. You will never know what it is like to be discriminated against on the basis of sex. Full stop. Do not misinterpret me here—I am not saying men should be excluded from dialogue on this issue, or they shouldn't get to have an opinion, or their lack of understanding makes them fundamentally inferior. Nor am I saying this lack of understanding inevitably makes men boorish, indifferent, and insensitive (though, sadly, this is sometimes the case). Nor am I saying women are more noble and saint-like because of the discrimination we sometimes face. I am establishing a core difference in our experiences that represents a significant obstacle to full understanding. Importantly, this doesn't take compassion, kindness, empathy, openness, and repentance off the table.

On the contrary, this recognition of privilege makes those options all the richer, because it allows men to move forward, with humility and graciousness, toward a better and more Christlike relationship with women: one that rests on an acknowledgement of the blind spot and a promise to prayerfully consider how that spot can lead to sin.

Let me emphasize that I have my own fair share of blind spots! The sinfulness of my heart means I don't always recognize and acknowledge them. I am always impatient, sometimes unjustly so, but there are some circumstances that demand swift action be taken to correct them, like General Assembly debates, in which women are the topic of the discussion but never allowed to participate (oh, the irony!). There are men who recognize this and want to change it. But there are still too many who continue to pontificate, sometimes with eloquence, sometimes with arrogance, and never bother to wonder, "Where are the women?" For my part, I will continue to ask until they answer and join in.

"Where Are the Women?" by Caroline West was adapted from "Feminism and Women's Leadership in the Church." *The Dialectic*, vol. 1, no. 3, 2017. Used with permission.

---

1. "Church History," *Presbyterian Church, USA*, accessed 23 July 2017, www.presbyterianmission.org/what-we-believe/church-history/.
2. "History," *Presbyterian Church in America*, accessed 23 July 2017, https://pcanet.org/about-the-pca-2-3/.
3. In other words, they believed that PCUS members did not hold to the doctrine of scriptural inerrancy.
4. W. Jack Williamson and Morton H. Smith, "A Message to All Churches of Jesus Christ Throughout the World from the General Assembly of the National Presbyterian Church," *PCA Historical Center*, 7 December 1973, accessed 23 July 2017, http://www.pcahistory.org/documents/message.html.
5. Roland Barnes, "Thursday Afternoon Business," https://livestream.com/accounts/8521918/PCAGA2016/videos/127477377.
6. In other words, do not reopen the issue by approving the formation of a committee to study it.
7. Egalitarianism, to most members of the PCA, represents a rejection of the complementary, biblical roles established for men and women.
8. Barnes, "Thursday Afternoon Business."
9. Ibid.
10. "General Assembly Actions and Position Papers of the Presbyterian Church in America: Ad Interim Study Committee on Women in the Military," *Presbyterian Church in America*, pcahistory.org/pca.
11. Num. 31:3–4, Josh. 1:14, 6:3, 8:3, Judg. 7:1–8, 20:8–11, 1 Sam. 8:11–12, 11:8, 13:2, 14:52, 24:2, 2 Sam. 24:2, 1 Chron. 21:5, 27:1–15, 23–24, 2 Chron. 17:12–19, 25:5–6, 26:11–14, 2 Kings 24:14–16, and Neh. 4:14.
12. Matt. 8:9, par. Luke 7:8, Acts 10:1, 23:23, cf. also Rom. 13:4.

13. John G. Stackhouse, Jr., *Partners in Christ: A Conservative Case for Egalitarianism* (Westmont, IL: InterVarsity Press, 2015).

14. Ibid.

15. Latin for "image of God."

16. Stackhouse, *Partners in Christ.*

WORDS FROM OUR SISTERS: LOVE

～

ENCOURAGEMENT POINTS
BECKY KIERN

An Invitation to Servant Leadership

Becky is a graduate of Covenant Theological Seminary who has served in staff and lay leadership roles in multiple churches. She lives in Nashville, Tennessee, where she teaches the Bible at retreats and conferences, develops church leadership, and writes Bible study curriculum. She is the author of Our Light and Life: Identity in the Claims of Christ *and has contributed to* Beneath the Cross of Jesus: Lenten Reflections. *Becky has been an adult cardiology RN for nearly fifteen years. Above all her favorite roles are that of friend, sister, and auntie.*

"In all the years I have worked with him, my pastor has never once asked me what our women are being taught in our Bible studies."

"I have never been asked to attend a session meeting. Never asked to give a report to my elders or had them offer to pray for my ministry to the women in our church."

"I would say I have around 1,200 women on my roster. Last year the church hired a part-time assistant to help with Women's Ministry, but she is also the assistant for the youth and children's ministry. Becky, I am so overwhelmed. We have a huge weekly Bible study program, but there are so many leaders I can't even train them all. There are eight pastors on staff who are all good men, but each time I ask for help there is no follow-through. Are the women on my roster not the same women on theirs?"

"I asked my pastor for help with a major relational conflict within our women's leadership team. He looked at me and had the audacity to say, 'See that is why I don't touch Women's Ministry with a ten-foot pole.'"[1]

These statements, as unreal as they may seem, come from real conversations I have had with various women on staff at churches in the Presbyterian Church in America (PCA). The beautiful thing is that each of these women are within church systems who desire for the women in their congregations to be nurtured. They are churches that see the value in having women in leadership roles. Each of these churches have used their valuable resources to create staff positions for women and create budget lines designated for the care and development of the women in their congregations. The sad part is these women, who in my estimation collectively serve nearly 5,000 women, each feel devalued in some way. What is the disconnect?

Over the years I have had the great privilege of working with a number of wonderful pastors who saw my gifts as a benefit to their leadership and the body of Christ. I write this chapter out of my experiences with these men and the sessions under whom I have served in Christ's body for nearly fifteen years. But I also write this chapter because I have sat across countless tables hearing the stories of women who have been misused, neglected, and unloved by the leadership under which they serve. Women who love the Lord and seek the good of his Church. I see broken places in the Church, which by God's grace can be healed. So I write this chapter as an invitation into that healing work. To my brothers who feel like they are already in complementarian churches, I ask you to read this chapter and humbly analyze your church system. To my brothers who are scared to begin the process of including women in your leadership (or feel that they have already tried and failed), I ask you to sit with me and use my diagnostic questions to help you begin brain-storming how you can grow in love for your sisters and as an advocate for the women in your churches.

So first let us acknowledge that relationships are hard. Relationships are broken people living life together. At times the brokenness in our stories causes each of us to act out of our fear, insecurity, or shame. All of us can recount ways we have wounded others through our ignorance. We caused pain by not knowing the background of a situation before we made a hasty conclusion, or by attempting to institute changes within a system without knowing the history or traditions already in place. In order for us to move forward with the inclusion of women (and minori-ties in ethnic majority churches) in substantive roles within our churches, each of us must make the effort to dig into both our individual stories and our churches' historical backgrounds. In doing this, we may just find factors driving our decisions that are extrabiblical in their applications. Relationships are hard, but as Christians we are called to help bring Gospel light into the dark, broken, hard places.

At times, personal brokenness can be the main cause of dysfunction in healthy complementarianism. We are broken, sinful people who, even on our best days, make mistakes that affect others. We all have a level of culpability. In my years of service in the Church I have observed that in addition to our brokenness, most often relational disconnect stems from poor evaluation and communication. Thus there are good men who love the Lord and openly value the women in their churches who are making similar mistakes to the brothers who openly devalue the roles of women. How can this be the case? I would argue many of these leaders have poor evaluation and communication practices. Good leaders desire those within their scope of influence to flourish. One of the best ways this growth can occur is by evaluating the work you are doing and taking time to ask how your leadership affects those around you. Communica-tion and evaluation can occur by taking the time to investigate who is doing the work of the Church. Exercise humility while exploring the experiences of those who sit under your leadership by asking good ques-tions—and actually listening to the answers.

On this side of heaven conflict, disappointment, burnout, pain, and departure will occur. I hope by sharing some of my own experiences and attempting to faithfully convey the experiences of others, I can give you some encouragement points as an entry way to help you process through how your own church system functions. I hope the encouragement to pray, communicate, shepherd, invite, and encourage rest are helpful points as you work through healthy complementarian relationships. You will find that much of the material to come is not necessarily gender specific, but many of these suggestions can help foster a healthy church leadership system no matter your staff demographics.

When it comes to practical application of complementarianism within our church congregations, we must learn ways where we are able to exercise courage. Courage helps us enter into hard but needed growth. In this chapter, the complementarian position I am describing is one where "God created men and women equal in being but assigned different—but equally valuable—functions in his kingdom and that this gender distinctiveness complements, or harmonizes, to fulfill his purpose."[2] The men and women on the Women Serving in the Ministry of the Church Ad Interim Committee, formed for the 45th PCA General Assembly, have written a well-researched report on the "Biblical Foundation for the Roles of Women in the Church."[3] I encourage anyone interested in furthering understanding of the denominational position on this topic to take the time to read through this document. You may also use their source materials as resources for further personal study.

Also of note: in this chapter the term "leadership" can mean a variety of things depending on your individual church context. Some churches have the resources to have women in staff positions (Assimilation, Women's, Children's, Youth, Worship Ministry). Other churches rely on volunteers in either titled or untitled leadership positions (Women's Leadership Team, Outreach Team). But one of my main points is that all churches have women who, as volunteers or paid staff, have incurred relational capital. This makes them leaders in your church system. When I speak about your "leaders," I am encompassing all of these roles.

Pray

> "I have never been asked to give a report to my elders or had them offer to pray for my ministry to the women in our church."

A few weeks ago I heard a Sunday sermon that used 1 Thessalonians 5:16–18 to encourage cultivating a robust prayer life: "*Rejoice always, pray without ceasing, give thanks in all circumstances; for this is the will of God in Christ Jesus for you."* In the sermon, the pastor made the claim that "prayer is trinitarian engagement."[4] I agree, but for our purposes I take his teaching point a step further: "prayer is trinitarian engagement" *in praxis.* As we move forward, let us not forget that while this world is broken, while we are broken, we have a Father who is not. God listens when we pray (Ps. 34:17, 1 Pet. 3:12), the Holy Spirit helps us when we are without words (Rom. 8:26–27), and Christ Jesus sits at the right hand of the Father interceding on behalf of his people (Rom. 8:34). Prayer is relationship with the Lord in practice.

God our Father is delighted when we come to him in both our gore and our glory. He is not ashamed to claim his children as his own despite the mistakes we have made and the ones we will make (1 John 2:2). As God's children we are blessed to be able to bring the cry of our heart before our Father. Paul's words to the Church in Thessalonica strongly encourage us to see value in the relational practices of both joy and dependency.

I begin my encouragement points with prayer because grace and kindness must be given to each other as we work through application in our individual churches and presbyteries. None of the work I am suggesting can be done without dependence on the Lord. So as we move forward, let us remember that even in our points of disagreement, we must not forget to respect each other, to pray with and for each other, and to rejoice in the work that the Lord has done and has promised to complete (1 Thess. 5:12–24). Pray and then pray again.

Diagnostic Questions

- Is prayer a fundamental part of your leadership? If not, what prevents you from incorporating prayer as part of your leadership praxis?
- Are you as a leadership team praying for each other?
- Do you know how to specifically pray for those on your leadership staff?
- Do you know how to specifically pray for the population of women in your church? Who are some trusted female voices in your ministry from whom you could learn?
- How can you help foster an environment where your male

and female leadership feel safe to share personal and
ministry prayer needs with each other?

Communicate

> "In all the years I have worked with him, my pastor has never once
> asked me what our women are being taught in our Bible studies."

Communication is a fundamental part of all relationships. Yet as I
meet with women and discuss their relationships with their elders
(teaching and ruling), I am frequently told how isolated they feel in their
ministry work. Starting from the beginning, Scripture paints a picture of
interdependence between male and female (Gen. 2:18). Paul reminds
the Church in Corinth, *"Nevertheless, in the Lord woman is not independent of man nor man of woman, for as woman was made from man, so
man is now born of woman. And all things are from God"* (1 Cor. 11:11–
12). Writing on the Church, theologian Edmund P. Clowney teaches,
"In their fellowship in Christ, men and women need each other."[5] In
Christ we have the ability to exercise interdependence in our ministry
work, but healthy interdependence can only occur with intentional
communication between elders and their leadership.

The sister quoted above felt a lack of relational connection with
her elders, which left her feeling isolated and questioning the value of
her ministry work within the larger church system. Practicing good
interpersonal communication can help leadership know that they do
not function as independent entities. If you have women teaching
Sunday school classes, leading Bible studies, or serving in this sort of
capacity, take time to ask them about their teaching. This may seem
like a given, but you might be shocked how many women have told me
their leadership has never asked and are unaware of what is being
taught to a large portion of their church. I am aware that many
churches have some form of staff report process, but please, take a
moment to think about how much effort it takes to prepare and teach.
What if no one ever showed interest in your teaching, program development, or discipleship work other than having you fill out a form?
After a period of time, how disheartening would that be to you?
Biblical ministry work depends on relationships.[6] Taking time to cultivate interpersonal communication practices of mutual love and respect

amongst your leadership will go a long way in building those relationships.

Communication centered on creating a biblical culture of trust and respect can help a ministry flourish. A healthy culture of trust can allow for safe spaces to talk about a variety of topics, including elements within your worship service. We all have blind spots; I encourage all leaders to seek out perspectives different than your own to help you see areas where you are placing value systems within your worship service. For example, are you only ever praying for women in the role of mother, thus leaving out women who do not have children? Or do you ever name the fact that men can grieve infertility just as strongly as women? Have you asked single church members their perception of how your church deals with singleness in the worship service? Or what is the experience of the ethnic minorities who worship with you? Try seeking out trusted women within your congregation to hear their perception and experience. You may find that they can offer you valuable insight on liturgy, verses, or hymns that speak into various issues that are commonly mentioned (or omitted) in your worship services.

Diagnostic Questions

- Do you have mature women in your ministry whom you seek out because they offer different perspectives than your own? (This can include your wife, but she is only one female voice. Do not put the weight of the whole female experience onto her shoulders. She should be one of many female voices you are seeking out).
- How can you better communicate with the women in leadership at your church? What are your (individual or as a session) current management practices for the curriculum and discipleship that the women in leadership are teaching in your church?
- How does your session currently check in with the women in leadership at your church? Are there ways that you could offer better support or encouragement? Where do they hope to see growth? What ministry or event might need to end or change because it has lost its effectiveness?
- Ask about their needs, but don't forget to celebrate! What

encouraging things are happening in their ministry?
(Remember God is always on the move!)

Invite

"I have never been asked to attend a session meeting."

Jane had been on staff for years with her church. One Sunday after
church she was looking for a missions meeting and accidentally walked
into the wrong meeting room. Upon disturbing a meeting of her session
one of the elders loudly asked her, "What, do you want to be an elder
now too?" Many of the men in the room then began to laugh at the man's
joke. Jane later told me how she smiled and quickly walked out of the
room, but how the experience of being laughed out of a room by her
elders was so humiliating that she couldn't collect herself enough to
attend the meeting she was originally looking for. She then looked at me
and asked, "That was their monthly session meeting. What if I walked
in because I wanted to attend the meeting simply because I care to hear
what the elders have to say? They didn't even ask me what I was doing
there, they just made a joke at a woman stepping into the room."

Years ago I started having conversations with women at conferences,
retreats, and gatherings, intentionally asking them what it was like
working within their church systems. I quickly found a number of
common themes. One theme I found is many of the women serving in
leadership positions don't feel connected to or valued by their session.
Here is where I show all my cards. I am passionate about the sanctification of both men and women in Christ's church. When I hear of a pastor
or session who devalue their women's ministry directors, women serving
the children, youth, or a whole list of ministry jobs, I question whether
they are truly attempting to know the actual people in their congregations. The women who are showing up each week, to serve by employment or on a volunteer basis, can be one of the greatest resources to a
team of elders. These women know the faith struggles of the individuals
in your churches. If you asked, they could tell you who is sick, whose
marriages are struggling, common sin patterns, and the list goes on.

But these women are not just a resource because they are already
involved with the service ministries of your congregation. They are
valued because they are individual people, known and loved by God.

These women are humans reflecting their Creator with unique gifts, knowledge, training, and experiences. Their individual experiences can not only help elders implement the church's mission and vision, but the women in your church are often the tangible hands and feet of Jesus' love.

Here is what I am asking session members to consider. If you have never had a women attend a session meeting outside of a discipline issue, take time to analyze why this is the case within your church system. Use wisdom to discern whether there is a theological reason to discuss, it stems from traditional practices, or has simply been overlooked. If having a female in your session meetings would be a big system change, please care well for your female leadership member by discussing this among your session before asking her to attend. Then extend invitations to the women on your ministry staff to attend your public session meetings. But don't stop there! Ask your women to share their ministry updates. Ask a session to pray for their ministry work, their families, and their ongoing spiritual maturity. The beautiful thing is that exercising interest, giving spiritual oversight, and identifying areas where thanks can be given will have a trickle-down effect on your entire church body.

Diagnostic Questions

- Staff meetings look different at each church, but look around at who makes up your staff members. Are you gathering each week with the pastors who do adult ministry, but excluding the staff member who works with your adult women? What is the cultural tradition, theological reason, or simple oversight that has led to this decision?
- What effect might it have on your church ministries if the women in leadership are around to hear and contribute to the vision and mission of your church? Where do you see vision disconnects in your ministries? Could this possibly be in relationship to how you have included or excluded the women currently in leadership within your church?
- Creating a unified voice among the leadership can increase trust and help create a calm system within your congregation. How can you cultivate trust within your ministry?

Shepherd

> "I asked my pastor for help with a major relational conflict within our women's leadership team. He looked at me and had the audacity to say, 'You see, that is why I don't touch Women's Ministry with a ten-foot pole.'"

This pastor may have a history of being burned by a previous experience with women in his congregation, but this does not change the fact that denying to help heal a conflict in his congregation left a leader feeling powerless and allowed strife to grow among his people. We must remember that for all our planning, reading, and theological study, our ministry only really incurs value when we are seeking to lead those in our congregations toward Christ. This pastor may have strong oratorical skills, he may have great plans for community outreach, he may even have written some best-selling books, but in that moment, his shepherding skills fell short.

Women are on the front lines of congregational care. They are meeting with wives, single women, mothers, and widows. They are mentoring people who are struggling with faith issues. They are encouraging wives in hard marriages to persevere. They are coaching women through sleepless newborn nights and helping women deal with a variety of life disappointments. Encourage them. Sisters, encourage each other; brothers, encourage your sisters. Let them know you are aware they are doing hard yet vital work. Elders, you have been called, as Peter teaches, to *"shepherd the flock of God that is among you... with humility toward one another, for 'God opposes the proud but gives grace to the humble'"* (1 Peter 5:1–5). Women in leadership spaces can help you understand the shepherding needs of a good portion of your church. I have often found that the emotional health and maturity of our women sets a strong tone for the emotional health of a church. Elders can shepherd their congregations well when they take time to be interested in the work the women are doing in their congregation.

Diagnostic Questions

- Write out the names of the women who are in leadership roles in your church.
- What are some ways that your session has overlooked the work and value of these women? Are there places where repentance is needed?
- How are they (or how can they start) being supported, encouraged, or given oversight by the elders of your congregation?
- Do you know what content is being taught in your Bible studies (children, youth, women, and men)? If the answer is no, why is this the case?

Encourage Rest

"I would say I have around 1,200 women on my roster. Last year the church hired a part-time assistant to help with Women's Ministry, but she also is the assistant for the youth and children's ministry. Becky, I am so overwhelmed. We have a huge weekly Bible study program, but there are so many leaders I can't even train them all. There are eight pastors on staff who are all good men, but each time I ask for help there is no follow-through. Are the women on my roster not the same women on theirs?"

As we close out our encouragement points, I find the above testimony helpful as it includes many of the issues we have already discussed. This dear sister has been given a great responsibility. She has been given a role within her church system, but has not been given the support needed to successfully care for the women in that system. Her problems include communication breakdown and a lack of trust among the leadership, inadequate oversight and shepherding care of the women in the congregation, a leadership member who does not feel her voice is heard or does not feel safe in the system to voice her weariness. All of these combined lead to discouragement and possible burnout.

The answer to healthy complementarian relationships within our ministries is not simply giving women more jobs (although this needs to happen too!). True application of complementarianism is men and women co-laboring for Gospel transformation in our ministries. Men and women working together in their appointed roles with mutual respect for the work the other is doing and building trusting relationships within leadership where they are able to come alongside one another to care for the people they serve. Who doesn't long to work with a leadership team that exercises Gospel-centered humility and service toward one another?

The majority of us who are in ministry, both men and women, have a strong sense of the injustices of this broken world. We labor long hours in hard relational spaces, attempting to bring healing into dark places through the light of the Gospel. We all know the dark places of this world are vast. Many of us struggle with guilt or fatigue, not knowing how to create personal patterns of health. I would like to suggest that this can be especially hard for the women within your churches. I have heard of sessions in healthy church systems who hold their pastors accountable to spend time with their families, in personal study, and in exercise. I cannot say for sure, but my hope would be these sessions understand the health of a pastor's ministry is only as strong as the health of his marriage, personal relationship with God, and his physical body.[7]

These are good practices, and I don't want them changed, but my hope is that the women in leadership in our ministries would work with elders who advocate for them in a similar fashion. Keep in mind this looks different for each of us: what is restful for me may be hard work for you. Do not assume that you know how someone else should rest; but we all need to cultivate healthy patterns if we are to sustain our ministry work.

Diagnostic Questions

- Are the people in your leadership making healthy life patterns a normal part of their lives?
- As you already know, our "job" won't be finished this side of glory, so in what ways can we be seeking to rest appropriately?
- What are some practices that you could incorporate into

your ministry leadership that actively encourage your staff to rest?

$\sim$

As I mentioned above, many of these suggestions are not gender specific, but are good tools in general for building healthy relationships within your leadership. Women, whatever their job, are a part of your leadership and help lead your church in significant ways. Women are teaching your children, encouraging and leading women in your congregations, and walking alongside the men in your church whether it be in marriage, friendship, or in vocation. My hope is that these encouragement points may help you work through how you may bring dignity to the roles they are already filling. Like Paul at the end of Romans, I hope you will be able to affirm them for their value in the Lord's body.[8]

Dorothy Sayers may be best known in the literary world as a prolific mystery novel writer. But Miss Sayers, a brilliant mind and lay theologian, was also one of the first females to attend Oxford University. In a book of essays published in 1947 Miss Sayers encourages us to look at the way Jesus interacted with women during his ministry:

> Perhaps it is no wonder that the women were the first at the Cradle and last at the Cross. They had never known such a man like this Man —there never has been such another. A prophet and teacher who never nagged at them, never flattered or coaxed or patronized; who never made arch jokes about them, never treated them as either "The women, God help us!" or "The ladies, God bless them!"; who rebuked without querulousness and praised without condescension; who never mapped out their sphere for them, never urged them to be feminine or jeered at them for being female; who took their questions and arguments seriously; who had no axe to grind and no uneasy male dignity to defend; who took them as he found them and was completely unselfconscious. There is no act, no sermon, no parable in the whole Gospel that borrows its pungency from female perversity; nobody could possibly guess from the words and deeds of Jesus that there was anything "funny" about women's nature.[9]

Jesus' humility, kindness, and inclusion did not change his God-given role, abate his teaching, or diminish the work of his ministry.

Learning from his work, my prayer is that we can find freedom to exercise humility in relationships, courage to admit our shortcomings, strength in our interdependence, and true joy as we labor together.

---

1. The names and some of the individual situations have been changed to protect the women who have shared their experiences with me.
2. J. Ligon Duncan and Susan Hunt, Women's Ministry in the Local Church (Wheaton: Crossway, 2006), 32.
3. "General Assembly Actions and Position Papers of the Presbyterian Church in America: Ad Interim Study Committee on Women in the Military," Presbyterian Church in America, pcahistory.org/pca/aiscwim.html#3.
4. Pastor David Filson, (sermon, Christ Presbyterian Church, Nashville, TN, December 31, 2017).
5. Edmund P Clowney, The Church (Downers Grove: InterVarsity Press, 1995), 189.
6. Mark 12:28–33, 1 Thess. 4:9, Phil. 2:1–11.
7. Duke Divinity School is currently in the midst of the ten-year study to "assess and improve the health and well-being of United Methodist clergy in North Carolina." For more information: http://divinity.duke.edu/initiatives/clergy-health-initiative.
8. Ro. 16:1–16.
9. Dorothy L Sayers, Are Women Human?: Astute and Witty Essays on the Role of Women in Society (Grand Rapids: Wm. B. Eerdmans, 1971), 68–69.

I CAN TELL THAT WE ARE GONNA BE FRIENDS

BRITTANY SMITH

Brittany Smith grew up in Mesquite, Texas, and studied English at the University of Texas. She worked for two years as an intern with Reformed University Fellowship (RUF) at the University of Oklahoma and married her husband, Dan, on the way to Covenant Theological Seminary, where she received a masters degree from Covenant in 2011. Brittany loves college students, teaching the Bible, and the ministry of RUF. Now settled in Tucson and working for RUF at the University of Arizona, Brittany enjoys the desert wildlife, playing board games on the patio, and reading books to her kids.

Relating to the opposite sex has been a rough road for me. I remember in middle school being terrified and completely intimidated by boys and how to interact with them. Once, a boy brought me flowers after school. He knocked on the front door of my house and I answered. He handed them to me with a sweet smile and mumbled something I can't remember, then bolted down the street. I was so embarrassed and couldn't think of what to do with the flowers. I didn't want to answer questions when my mom came home from work, but it seemed cruel to throw them away immediately. So I stuffed them in my bedroom closet and shut the door. They wilted a few days later, and I threw them away. I don't remember talking again to that brave boy who gave them to me.

I thought things would be easier as I got older, but the dating culture in high school and college still created in my mind only one category for a male relationship: boyfriend, and eventually husband. I did have some help from a pastor (more on him later) after college who helped me think about what it means to be a friend to a man I'm dating. I finally started thinking about being friends with a man in a healthy way, and we ended up getting married. Now that I've been married for almost ten years, I've started to think more about healthy cross-sex friendships both before and after marriage and my need for these relationships with my brothers and fathers in the Church.

Whether or not my experience is representative of others in the Church doesn't change the fact that I don't see a lot of healthy, close relationships between men and women in the Church except husbands and wives—and sometimes even those relationships are not healthy. And this is troubling to me because we are not just friends with our fellow Christians—we are sisters and brothers, fathers and mothers to each other in the household of God. Ephesians 2:19 says, "*So then you are no longer strangers and aliens, but you are fellow citizens with the saints and members of the household of God.*" In the Church, there is another category for relating across the sexes besides the romantic. C. S. Lewis writes:

> Those who cannot conceive Friendship as a substantive love but only as a disguise or elaboration of Eros betray the fact that they have never had a Friend. The rest of us know that though we can have erotic love and friendship for the same person yet in some ways nothing is less like a Friendship than a love-affair. Lovers are always talking to one another about their love; Friends hardly ever about their Friendship. Lovers are normally face to face, absorbed in each other; Friends, side by side, absorbed in some common interest. Above all, Eros (while it lasts) is necessarily between two only. But two, far from being the necessary number for Friendship, is not even the best. And the reason for this is important.[1]

In Mark 10, Peter feels anxious about salvation. He also feels the reality of having given up everything—all his responsibilities and privileges—to follow Jesus. Jesus reassures him with these words:

Truly, I say to you, there is no one who has left house or brothers or sisters or mother or father or children or lands, for my sake and for the gospel, who will not receive a hundredfold now in this time, houses and brothers and sisters and mothers and children and lands, with persecutions, and in the age to come eternal life. Mark 10:29–30

So then we all give up something to follow Christ—some of us give up our dearest familial relationships to be a follower of Jesus. But Jesus reassures us—even those who give up our parents and siblings will receive abundantly within the household of God. God gives us to each other as brothers and sisters, parents and children.

In the Church I have seen a beautiful emphasis on maintaining healthy husband-wife relationships. This is certainly an important and a worthy topic of study and emphasis in our church ministries. However, we all spend a significant time of our life unmarried, and some never marry. How do we relate to our spiritual siblings in the Church? How does it look different when we see each other first as brother or sister in Christ rather than a source of a potential romantic connection?

In college I dated a man for a few months. It wasn't very serious. We never talked about marriage, and it ended pretty quickly for various reasons. The one thing I do remember us talking seriously about was my future plans to attend medical school. He was incredibly unsupportive of this plan and called me naive for thinking I could pursue a career as a doctor and also have a family. This man was my brother in Christ. We attended church together and shared community. While he may be entitled to his opinion, he did not love or support me as a sister through my decision toward what God might be calling me to vocationally. He shamed and belittled me, possibly because he was anxious about a future with me and how my decisions might affect that future.

After we broke up I remember meeting with my Reformed University Fellowship (RUF) campus minister and sharing with him how this man had talked to me and the contrast was remarkable. My campus minister (also my older brother in the faith) told me it was unacceptable to be belittled for a career choice. He said it wasn't naive to want to pursue medicine. He acknowledged all of our choices have consequences and affect the life we will live. If the Lord was calling me to work in medicine, he would provide the way. My campus minister cared for me as I worked through the process of making career and future choices with freedom and gentleness. I'm convinced this was easier for him to do partly because he only viewed me as a sister and was not affected by the potential of marrying me someday.

When we only see those of the opposite sex in the category of romantic relationships, we reduce each other to less than human beings in the household of God. If romance and sexual intercourse are the inevitable conclusion to every connection between the opposite sex, then once we are married it would make sense to shut down any other close relationship with people of the opposite sex. But what if romance wasn't always the inevitable conclusion? Dan Brennan argues it is not. Brennan attributes this underlying current of fear to the influence of Freud's theories that sex lies at the heart of everything: "[Freud] posited frustrated sexual desire to lie at the heart of every relational encounter between men and women—libido lurking in all meaningful oneness."[2]

In his book, *Sacred Unions, Sacred Passions*, Brennan writes:

> Any suggestion of an embodied communion between unmarried men and women is often seen as a threat to the mysterious, ongoing, passionate bond between husband and wife. Forming and nurturing a close, embodied friendship openly between sexes may raise suspicion, awkwardness, and fears, and therefore elicit external social pressure from the community beyond the marriage.[3]

In other words, cross-sex friendships are assumed to be a baby and bathwater situation. In our churches we separate ourselves from each other by gender all the time. We have single-gender ministries, conferences, and Bible studies. There are also informal ways we separate from each other. I have had a pastor who never looked women in the face or spoke to them after the service. Some pastors have policies of never meeting alone with their younger or similar-aged sisters in the faith. Some women claim they would feel incredibly uncomfortable meeting with their spiritual brothers and fathers. Many service ministries of the Church tend toward assimilating only one gender—like nursery care, children's Sunday school, setting up chairs or technical equipment, overseeing wedding logistics or church finances, or food and meal organization. There could be benign or fear-based reasons for any of this separation to occur in the body. Even if the reason for separation seems inconspicuous, are we missing out on something? Brennan thinks we are. He writes:

However, mainstream evangelical author Ruth Barton wonders about how "safe" sex-segregated boundaries among male-female friendships may prevent emotional, physical, and spiritual intimacy in faith communities. "If men and women are not free to share thoughts and ideas over lunch, if we cannot talk with enough privacy and safety to work through issues, if we cannot spend enough time together that we feel like we know each other, if we cannot have fun together, if we cannot open our hearts and love each other as friends do, we will keep a safe distance that permits us to communicate only over a chasm of apathy, misunderstanding and inadequate information."[4]

I have experienced the misunderstanding and apathy that comes when men and women intentionally or lazily allow themselves to be separated from each other. When channels and appropriate situations to know and be known by one another are cut off, I have seen resentment and misinformation grow in my own heart toward my fathers and brothers in the faith. I also have seen my own empathy, respect, appreciation, and affection grow when there is instead time and space to develop cross-sex friendships.

When I worked for RUF as an intern for two years, I worked closely with my campus minster. I remember sitting across from Doug Serven for lunch to discuss the ministry on campus. He continually asked for my input and thoughts on the ministry, student struggles, and decisions to be made for planning and executing events. I remember feeling shocked. I was young and brand new to vocational ministry and felt like I had zero to contribute that would be helpful in making ministry decisions. Yet Doug viewed me as intrinsically valuable because I was a unique person with a different perspective than him. He saw this as an asset to broaden his own understanding.

At the time I depended on his perspective as a man, as a seminary-trained ordained minister of the Church, as an older person, as a married person, and all the unique things that made Doug into a ministry colleague. In the same way, he always affirmed me in the ways I contributed as well: my youth, my fresh eyes, my femininity, my single-ness, and all the things that made up my unique self that the Holy Spirit would bring to bear in how we worked together in ministry. Even my inexperience he saw as opportunities to remember what it was like to be a new person. We needed each other because of our differences, not in spite of them. And our team was better when we valued each other's differences and sought out the help of each other as friends and colleagues.

More recently I was blessed to be working alongside a wonderful group of people who serve as founders and leaders of a small Christian school. Because of the nature of my role, I worked very closely with the president of the board, who was also a good friend from church. As treasurer of the board, I spent a decent amount of time one-on-one with this man going over budgets and details for the planning of the school. During our time working together, he also was elected to be an elder of our church, and our friendship grew because of all these crossovers of shared work for the sake of God's Kingdom. I know without a doubt our friendship has influenced each of us for the better regarding our view of men and women working together in the Church. As my older brother in the faith, he has lovingly looked to care for both me and my husband, our family, and our ministry. I have also challenged him on his perspectives on women in ministry and passed along ideas from knowing his wife (one of my dearest friends) on how to surprise her with the perfect Christmas gift.

In her book *No Little Women*, Aimee Byrd addresses how corporately we separate ministry tasks based on gender, and how the body of Christ might be suffering as a result. Byrd argues, we may need to push back against even the benign ways we separate.[5] For example, if the sisters and mothers in our church have historically been the cooks who rock the potluck dinners, maybe it's worth it to encourage and pursue some men attempting to contribute some dishes. What an opportunity for brothers and sisters to connect and share the experience of providing good food to the congregation. Another example would be nursery care. It may be true that women in general have more natural gifts in nurturing and patience with babies and toddlers. But what better way for their brothers to learn that gentleness by working alongside each other. As other chapters have also described, finding ways to pursue the wisdom and leadership of gifted and trained women to serve alongside the session of elders must also be a priority.

This shared work in the ministry of the Church will help naturally create the space for healthy friendships between men and women. The same space can be created in workplaces and other shared endeavors. I'm not saying there isn't a place for women- or men-only events in the Church from time to time. But if we find this happening over and over again in subtle ways, we may want to ask ourselves: Why is this is happening? Is it actually hurting the unity of the body?

I do want to address the issues that often drive the fear behind fleeing cross-sex friendships in the Church. Sexual immorality is addressed over and over again in Scripture and is taken very seriously, especially by Paul. And the consequences of sexual immorality and unfaithfulness are usually devastating. Countless of us have experienced broken families, parental or spousal abandonment, health issues, and disrupted lives because of sexual immorality. I empathize with the impulse to do whatever it takes to never experience those consequences again in our families and churches.

To be sure, in situations where sexual immorality has occurred, having boundaries in relationships is necessary and merciful. This may create barriers to cross-sex friendships when trust has been broken or where sin has been given a foothold. However, there needs to remain the needed and biblical category of healthy cross-sex friendship in our churches. Necessary boundaries erected to prohibit cross-sex friendship need to remain a consequence and guide to repentance for actual sin and broken trust, and not a fearful standard prohibition throughout the Church family.

In recent years, many in the Church have discussed the use of the so-called Billy Graham rule after it was compared to the relationship between Vice President Mike Pence and his wife Karen.[6] Like all things, the Billy Graham rule requires us to understand it in context and on its own terms. Created as part of his Modesto Manifesto, the rule was a commitment made by Graham and his team to never be alone with a woman to whom they were not married.[7] They also made agreements regarding how money would be handled within their organization. These commitments were made because of the public nature of their work in the Billy Graham Crusades, because of the immense failure of other large-scale evangelist preachers who came before them, and because of the great success they were seeing within their work. These particular men felt it crucial to see how others who had gone before them had been so easily entangled in scandal and felt the best way to prevent it from happening in their midst would be to prevent any possibility of doubt from the public.

It was a high cost to pay, and I do not judge whether those commitments had their intended effect or not. Within its context, it at least is understandable. Though surely, it should not be seen as some kind of standard for all Christian men or Christian pastors to follow.

Recently there also has been a rise in interest in the personal life of Karl Barth. While his personal moral failure of infidelity to his wife has been known for some time, more of Barth's personal letters have been released by his children and translated into English by Christiane Tietz in her *Theological Today* article, "Karl Barth and Charlotte von Kirschbaum."[8] Because of the renewed interest of Barth's affair with von Kirschbaum, many have questioned his theology and how we must now view his contribution to Christian thought. To summarize, though married ten years with children, upon meeting von Kirschbaum, Barth began a thirty-year affair with her which included her living in his home with Barth and the rest of his family, including Barth's wife Nelly. Kirschbaum is recognized as being vital to Barth's theological contribution, as she worked as his live-in assistant as well. As translated by Tietz, Karl Barth wrote:

> The way I am, I never could and still cannot deny either the reality of my marriage or the reality of my love. It is true that I am married, that I am a father and a grandfather. It is also true that I love. And it is true, that these two facts don't match. This is why we after some hesitation at the beginning decided not to solve the problem with a separation on one or the other side.[9]

Barth has been heavily criticized for his moral departure from the commands of Scripture in order to maintain his affair with von Kirschbaum.[10] What I haven't seen suggested is a helpful narrative for how Barth could have navigated his relationships with these two women in a healthy and moral way. Barth needed a category for the love, affection, and connection he found with von Kirschbaum—one that didn't include sexual immorality or an emotional connection that tried to mimic or replace that of his wife.

I propose there can be a third option between that of a sexual or emotional affair that crosses one-flesh boundaries and having no relationship at all. Is there a way of closeness and mutuality between men and women that doesn't always lead to affairs? How can we work together to reorient ourselves as brothers and sisters to one another in the Church instead of reducing an entire gender to a source of danger and potential sin? I need my spiritual brothers and fathers, and they need their sisters and mothers. As we look at our churches, where can we start to see places where men and women can come together as a family? Let us build relationships across the genders in ways that help the entire Church to flourish and show the love and unity we have because of Christ.

---

1. C. S. Lewis, The Four Loves (Broadway, NY: Harper One, 2017).
2. Dan Brennan, "We've Been Duped by Freud on Cross-Gender Friendship: A Response," Christianity Today, April 24, 2012, https://www.christianitytoday.com/women/2012/april/weve-been-duped-by-freud-on-cross-gender-friendship.html.
3. Dan Brennan, Sacred Unions, Sacred Passions: Engaging the Mystery of Friendship between Men and Women (Elgin, IL: Faith Dance Pub., 2010).
4. Ibid.
5. Aimee Byrd, No Little Women: Equipping All Women in the Household of God (Phillipsburg, NJ: P&R Publishing, 2016).
6. Brandon Showalter, "Mike Pence Ridiculed for Practicing 'Billy Graham Rule,'" The Christian Post, March 30, 2017, https://www.christianpost.com/news/mike-pence-ridiculed-for-practicing-billy-graham-rule-179044/.
7. Yonat Shimron, "Billy Graham Made Sure His Integrity Was Never in Question," Religion News Service, February 23, 2018, https://religionnews.com/2018/02/23/billy-graham-made-sure-integrity-never-question/.
8. Christiane Tietz, "Karl Barth and Charlotte Von Kirschbaum," Theology Today 74, no. 2 (2017): 86–111.
9. Ibid.
10. Mark Galli, "What to Make of Karl Barth's Steadfast Adultery," Christianity Today, October 20, 2017, https://www.christianitytoday.com/ct/2017/october-web-only/what-to-make-of-karl-barths-steadfast-adultery.html.

JESUS LOVES ALL THE WOMEN
EMILY HUBBARD

Emily Hubbard (neé Chapman) is a White Mississippian now living in Missouri. She is a lifelong member of the Presbyterian Church in America (PCA). Her husband is a pastor at a multiethnic church in St. Louis, and they have four children. She has degrees from Mississippi State University, including an MS in sociology. Her sociological studies focused on race and religion, and though she is out of academia, her marriage to a Black pastor ensures that she uses her degree daily. She is a public school advocate, loves to discuss childbirth, and in her spare time enjoys crocheting, gardening, and reading.

~

I've been a member of the Presbyterian Church in America (PCA) since I was born. I've baptized my children, including two daughters, into it. I also have a sociology degree I'd like to use to look at how our church, your church, treats women. Though women can have unofficial influence in our churches (hey, fellow pastors' wives!), the church structure—and what we find biblical—contains only men in the highest form of leadership. Only men can be ordained elders and ordained deacons. Only men can vote at General Assembly, the yearly meeting that guides our denomination. And given the general nature of the relationships men have with women, many of these men may only be close to two women in their lives: their wives, if they have one, and their mothers. Not all men, obviously—some may have sisters and daughters. But if the majority of leadership in our church is only near expressions of womanhood connected by familial relationships, they are hobbled in their abilities to care for all the facets of female life. And if the leadership is hobbled, the Church is hobbled. The inability to recognize different experiences of the same gender hurts the Church, it hurts women in the Church, and it alienates women from the Church and from each other.

I know, I know, I said gender. It's not scary, I promise. So maybe you've heard "gender is a social construct," and it sounds troubling. If societies construct gender, then God doesn't, right? Where does that leave the folks who believe our lives should be guided by God's Word and will? Here are two things: 1) we are good Presbyterians who know God is always in control no matter what; 2) across the world, across time, and in your local high school, different cultures have different norms for genders. And though it can be more complicated, generally speaking every culture has ideas about what a woman should be like and what a man should be like. If you've ever tried to navigate a high school life between the cheerleaders, the nerds, and the athletes (which is not to say that cheerleaders are not athletes!), you may know what I mean. If you were homeschooled, I'm sorry.

Let's talk about sex and gender. A person's "sex" refers to his or her chromosomes and body parts. And except for the around one-tenth of a percent of people who are born with an intersex condition (so in our country, that number is roughly the size of the PCA), a person's sex is either male or female [Note that transgender issues are outside the scope of this essay—but they do exist, and those folks who struggle with them are made in the image of God.]. The word "gender" refers to the expressions of one's sex. The attributes we associate with either having a penis or a uterus—those attributes are summed up in the word "gender."

Now, here we go: to say "gender is a social construct" is the same thing as saying "societies construct ideas about gender." That's not as scary, right? Amish people have different ideas about what women and men should wear and do compared to mainstream American society. Different countries, different cultures, different subcultures all have different ideas about what they associate with the ideal man or the ideal women, the expectations all men and women face and deal with as they become adults. Not only do different cultures have different ideas, but even in the same culture, the expectations can change over time. In

1920s America, blue was for girl babies and pink was for boy babies. Today in America, if the icing in the middle of the cake is pink, that baby is a girl. We are in a cultural moment where it seems the ideas of gender have both become solidified (if you've tried to buy baby or toddler clothes recently, you know what I mean) but also more individuals are trying to subvert whatever they think traditional gender norms are. I will take one sentence to point out that more solid gender norms are a great way for corporations to make money, like when that pink car seat that big sister used isn't acceptable for baby brother or even by selling pink or blue or camouflage Bibles. More calcified gender norms also make people who don't fit these firm norms struggle with where they belong and who they are. My hope is that the answer to that is always "at church as a beloved child of God," but the Church often doesn't live up to that promise.

The Church is not a corporation, and the Church doesn't have to conform to the world. And in fact, despite whatever gendered norms one wants to use—and doesn't this fit the biblical idea in Galatians 3:28? —when sociologists look at expressions of gender in populations, the average man and the average woman are more like each other than the most gender-conforming woman and the least gender-conforming woman, or the most masculine and least masculine man. Men and women have fundamentally different bodies, but they are actually more alike than different. Considering that Paul's advice to the whole congregation at Corinth was "Imitate me, just as I imitate Christ," acknowledging this sameness between fellow humans shouldn't feel revolutionary.

I'm *not* saying there are no differences, or that the bodily strength most men have doesn't mean they have responsibilities that come with their strength. I'm also *not* saying there are few enough differences that ladies can also qualify for the "husband of one wife" elder requirement. What I am saying is men and women have more in common than our culture (which profits off exploiting the differences) wants us to acknowledge, and men and women can be different from other men or other women without the Church sliding into a morass of subjectivism.

This gender thing matters to men, especially considering how our greater culture's definitions of masculinity can be harmful not only to men who practice it, but also to the women who have to co-exist with them. But this is a book and essay about women—and women in a denomination where the primary leadership in the Church is male—and unless they've made a serious effort, that leadership may not realize that the other sex can actually express their gender in a great many different ways, voluntarily or not.

Let's look at this from a case study of one—me. At the time of this writing, I'm a thirty-four-year-old married mother of four. My hobbies are reading, crocheting, and gardening. And though in some ways this phrase is passing out of use, I am good at being *maternal*. It has been completely natural to use the body God gave me to grow and feed and snuggle our four children. Holding a sleeping baby that I just nursed to sleep is one of the things that made me feel most at peace in the world. But fitting into American cultural ideas of the feminine ideal is a lot harder for me. I don't care about makeup or jewelry or fashion, and I'd much rather be in the room where the conversation is about sports rather than interior design. I like to cook, but I'm not a good housekeeper, and I'm not good at small talk. Though I love being a mother, I have other aspirations, and I really wouldn't mind having a job, even though my kids are young-ish. I don't need those articles about "stop cleaning and hang out with your kids" because there are always dirty dishes in my sink.

Now, just because I don't like something, doesn't mean it's not a great thing for women to pursue! Nobody has to be like me. But if the image of womanhood at your church is in thrall to American culture and consumerism—a Jesus-ified version of *Good Housekeeping*—I'm probably not going to fit into it. If you have your mothers' Bible study while I'm at work, I won't be able to go. There are some amazing women who have a self-concept that is strong and awesome who navigate around constraining definitions of femininity, but most of us need lots of love and patience and to be explicitly told there is a place for us. Whether we are misfits or deep harborers of internalized misogyny, we need to know there's a specific place for us in the pews and programming of our churches.

That's my personal experience, an n=1. It is "my truth" and, I suspect, the truth of too many women who dutifully put on their lipstick and head to the ladies' tea, wondering whether they'll relate to any of the conversations. But for a broader picture, let's examine Mother's Day 2018, especially as it played out on social media.

Over the course of Mother's Day week on social media, I saw as many "Mother's Day is sad and hard" posts as I saw "Happy Mother's Day" or "my mom is awesome" posts. And then there were the thousand

"Get the best for Mother's Day" ads as you scrolled past the yay or nay posts. In my case, many of the posts were not just connected to the day, but also to how the Church treats that day. In our church, we did a special prayer for mothers (and for every possible iteration of mother-hood-hurt), and female parents who dropped a child off for Sunday school received a small gift (magnets—it was magnets). However, if I can trust my social media feeds, other churches' practices elevate mothers in ways that are hurtful to everyone who doesn't have the perfect story.

Your specific church may not have done this, but our church culture has created a situation that equates wifehood and motherhood with womanhood, and along the way, we've become an unsafe place for the lives that don't fit the narrative arc that ends in a minivan full of kids. And this particular Mother's Day, the folks with divergent narratives let us know about it. The Mother's Day backlash is indicative of the way the Church fails women as it perpetuates and elevates the idea that there's one best way to be a woman. This failure hurts women and alienates them from the Church and from each other.

Does your church recognize women who are gifted in nonmaternal ways throughout the year? Are you clear, throughout the year, from the pulpit, in your small groups, in your Bible studies, that all women matter and have value as beloved children of God, not just as carriers for babies or bringers of casseroles? Do you recognize the artists, the lawyers, the social workers, the teachers, the businesswomen—the real-life Proverbs 31 women—and realtors, alongside the stay-at-home moms? If the only time you talk about women as special is during Mother's Day, or the only programming you have for your women is about parenting, no wonder so many women skip church on that Sunday. Especially if you make all the moms stand up. I don't know how to tell you to do it (besides not having Bible studies when only stay-at-home moms can attend), but I suspect we all know it when we see it.

We're Presbyterian; we baptize our babies. When we baptize babies, the parents take vows to nurture their babies in the fear and admonition of the Lord. Additionally, the congregation is asked the question: "Do you as a congregation undertake the responsibility of assisting the parents in the Christian nurture of this child?" From the beginning of a child's life in our churches, we acknowledge that parents don't do this alone. Our liturgy proclaims that parenthood is not a burden borne alone.

But in practice, we often act like only mothers do—and should do—

the bulk of the parenting, and we fetishize the elevation of motherhood as their only identity. "You do x and y and z—you're such a great mom." I've had men at church greet me by saying "Hello, mama," as I held my newborn, as if the fact of maternity had elided everything about me except that baby. That's a huge burden to put on any one person's shoulders. We need to recognize moms, but we need to acknowledge that they are more than moms. We need to consider how many so-called sacrifices are only available to those with abundant resources. And very often, we can laud mothers without noticing all the other women—faithfully keeping their congregational vows or doing their jobs—who raise our children.

This year and last year, at Mother's Day, though I didn't make cards, I sent text messages to my children's teachers, thanking them for the work they do in my kids' lives, because if I were to try to do all the things they did for each kid, I would explode. Does your church cultivate a culture of sharing the childrearing burden? Do you recognize the faithful nursery workers and Sunday school teachers already? The childless or empty-nester women who are willing to get smudged and spit up on so young moms can sit through a whole sermon? Do you acknowledge and recognize all the mothering-by-others that goes on in your church every week? Or do you accept it as a consequence of their gender and move on? My children have been loved well by so many different women while I've struggled to get through those sleepless nights and crumby floors days. Does your church have a culture that honors and cherishes the women who take their vows seriously, even when those vows may rub against great personal pain? Or do you forget them and only honor the ladies with used uteruses or adoption fees... one day a year? (As a side note, men should be doing this work too, of course, but that's not the point of this essay.)

Speaking of pain, as much as we preach against the prosperity gospel at that brown peoples' church down the street, it's in our own hearts and churches too. We are Job's friends, and we've made the Church an unsafe place to talk about all the hard stuff. We point to the one perfect picture of ponytails, college, marriage, children, maybe a fulfilling MLM scheme, without acknowledging that for most people—especially those with fewer resources—the path to that picture is rocky and twisted. So often the message when it comes to brokenness is that it is caused by a personal failing somewhere, or that if you would just do this one right thing, your deepest desires would be answered. "Stop trying and that baby will come." Are you growing a congregation who can love people and listen to their deep wounds without offering ways to fix it immediately or blaming them? Is your church a place where the background narrative is "If you do all these things in the right order, everything will be OK?"

Is your congregation wrapped in Jesus' love so deeply they are a safe place for women in broken situations? Is your church a place where a couple struggling with infertility feels safe enough to have shared with folks who will give them an extra hug in the foyer? Do you know how many folks in your congregation are estranged from their moms and need hugs from nurturing church moms? Are you able to care for widows? But seriously, is your church a place where people's deep hurts are known (at least by some) and their being poked at is anticipated? Do you care for your people?

There's more to be said about fetishizing motherhood and making the moms who are barely hanging on feel more alone, or making working moms feel like they are bad for not spending every waking moment with their children, and let's not forget about churches with terrible maternity leave policies, but that's outside the scope of this essay. To tie together the case study and the wider example, I will just say this: motherhood is the one part of gendered stereotypes I easily fit into, but as my social media feed became increasingly saturated with "Mother's Day stinks" posts, my joy in this one thing I do OK at was dampened. Because the Church fails to paint a wider picture of what a woman can be or do, I felt alienated. I felt alienated by the women who were hurt, and they felt alienated from the Church and from me because all I wanted to do was just complain about their alienation. We can do so much better. We must do better.

I am a White woman, and I struggle with the stereotypes and fetishes of women in the Church. For women of color in predominantly White churches, the struggle can be much deeper, as Black women must navigate between being viewed as an angry Black woman, the strong Black woman, or a needy welfare queen, just to mention a few. Asian women must deal with the model minority myth and creepy sexual fetishization. Latina women are seen as fiery. In our mostly White denomination, minority women will be asked for their origin stories in ways that imply they don't belong. The Church's unqualified love for the 1950s (White) housewife and every iteration since ignores the necessity of working outside the home (and often working inside the homes of White families) that our country has caused by its racist policies.

We must also acknowledge our sisters who are sexual minorities—who if they're in *our* church we must assume desire to follow faithfully the traditional Christian sexual ethic. But they are ignored, shamed, or erased by our insistence on only one picture of a godly woman. They are unlikely to receive the particular ministry they need to be encouraged in their striving. These women exist. The question remains: Will we love them or will our insistence on conformity push them out of the arms of Jesus' body into the ready embrace of the world?

Not every woman has the ability to fit into a single expression of femininity. If the Church values motherhood as the greatest expression of womanhood, the single woman or the infertile woman is going to be left out and feel second best. Alternatively (though I've never really heard of this happening in a church), if the best ladies are the ones with careers and pencil-length skirts with high heels, then the tired and frumpy mother of four whose kids came too close together to think about pursuing a career will be left out.

Our denomination says it can't find biblical evidence for women's ordination—I can live with that. I can't live in a denomination that says there's only one or two ways to be a woman, and those of us who don't match those expectations are left out, kicked out, or abandoned. Your church is a tiny society. It is constructing its own definitions of the best man and the best woman. It could happen because of who you assume is gifted to teach whom, whether you make your meetings accessible to women who work or have small children, and whether you welcome nursing mothers into your sanctuary or send them to the bench in the bathroom.

We worship a God who wasn't afraid to use women to do his work in cultures that didn't think much of women at all. Though embodied as a man, Jesus wasn't afraid to use feminine gendered language, like Matthew 23:37, where he compared himself to a mother hen. We would do well to examine whether we are succumbing to culturally created gendered norms not found in Scripture, or even if we are elevating one kind of woman found in Scripture over others. Note that the Proverbs 31 woman never has to deal with childcare in the scriptural account. Lydia was a merchant. Jael was an assassin. Rahab was a prostitute. Deborah was a judge. Hannah wanted a baby and then gave him away. Anna was a prophet. Rachel and Abigail were schemers. Shifra and Pua were law-breaking, child-saving midwives. Mary sat at Jesus' feet, but Martha could run a household. Prisca was a teacher. Eunice and Lois were faithful (and cross-cultural) mothers. Esther was a brave queen. The list goes on.

Every human woman in your church is an expression of the image of God, no matter how closely or not she hews to your church's conception of the feminine ideal. The Scriptures have space for all possible arcs in a woman's life if we are willing and faithful to pursue them—and if our preachers are willing to look outside not only their male experiences but also beyond the limited experiences of the women closest to them. Then our church, our denomination, will feel like a place that loves women, all the women in the world.

It is imperative for each church to look closely at its plans, expectations, and provisions for women in its church, and to ask and listen to *all* women about how those ideas and plans impact them. And if the women in your church only have one reaction? Ponder deeply whether you're making space for women—women like me, who could even be stay-at-home-mothers of four—who don't fit into the projection of femininity your church or organization is elevating. Gender matters—it matters to God. For those women who long to be faithful but don't fit into the box or two that makes for easy discipleship and programming, the Church's treatment of women matters.

"Jesus Loves All the Women" by Emily Hubbard is adapted from two previously published essays. Used with permission.

MEN AND WOMEN
JOHN HARALSON & DEBBIE TACKE

Stumbling Toward Partnership

John Haralson has served as a pastor at Grace Church Seattle since 2004. Prior to that, he served churches in San Francisco, New York City, and St. Louis. He is a graduate of the United States Air Force Academy (BS, Civil Engineering) and Covenant Theological Seminary (MDiv). He and his wife, Linn, have four children.

∼

Debbie Tacke serves as the Director of Community Formation at Grace Church Seattle. Before moving to Seattle in 2014, Debbie spent thirteen years in Nashville, Tennessee, providing life coaching and consulting primarily within the medical community. She also served as a part-time staff member of a campus ministry at Vanderbilt Medical and Nursing schools. She has held various financial and business leadership positions. She is a graduate of Milligan College and received her MA in Professional Counseling from Colorado Christian University. Debbie is married to John Tacke, and they enjoy exploring the beauty of the Pacific North-

west, entertaining in their home, and watching their favorite TV shows together.

About five years ago, my (John) teenage daughter told me she wished our church had a woman on our staff she could turn to with her questions. She and I have a good relationship, and at that time we had a (male) associate pastor whom she loved. But she really wanted a woman's perspective on things. Her voice joined the chorus of other women in our congregation. Thankfully, God used her spoken desire to wake me up to some changes our church needed.

At that time, I could have argued that we were doing a decent job of encouraging and celebrating the ministry of women for a church in our denomination. We had gifted women who regularly taught Bible and theology classes to men and women, we had women deacons, and we had women helping lead our congregation each week in worship.

But my daughter—along with other women in our church—was tapping into a critical weakness. Outside of children's ministry, we had no group of women in clear positions of pastoral leadership and trust in the congregation. Don't get me wrong; our church has always had godly women who love using their gifts and have been given space to do so. But our system for connecting people to pastorally gifted women was largely invisible and underground.

At that point, conversations and prayer began among our leaders and congregants about desiring to do a better job of recognizing, equipping, and deputizing gifted women to serve in our congregation. We wanted women at the leadership table and began to try to figure out how to make this happen.

At around the same time this light bulb was going off, our long-time associate pastor and his family followed God's call to Brooklyn to plant a new congregation. Instead of seeking a one-for-one replacement for him, we took the opportunity of his departure to ask questions about some of the needs our church had and what kind of staff position we would need to begin to address them.

We began to dream of someone who was gifted at spiritual formation and leadership development. We wanted someone who could help us foster a stronger culture of individual discipleship and envisioned a person who could help us build our infrastructure by building up people. To find this person, we cast our net fairly wide—looking at people who were ordained (or ordainable) in the Presbyterian Church in America (PCA) and those who were not. This allowed us to consider both men and women for the position.

During the search, nonordained folks bubbled up to the top of our list. It has been my experience that typical, MDiv-holding PCA pastors —of whom I am one—are good at preaching and teaching, in addition to possibly being strong at leadership and/or pastoral counseling. However, people like me do not tend to be strong in the areas where our church had significant needs.

At the end of a very up-and-down process, Debbie Tacke rose to the top of our list. She was exactly the kind of person we needed. So, in November of 2014, Debbie joined our pastoral staff.

For me (Debbie), accepting the pastoral role on staff at Grace was the culmination of a roller coaster discernment process and a lifetime of journeying toward vocational ministry. I grew up as a preacher's kid in a series of nondenominational churches in the Midwest, and early in my life I had a strong desire to be in ministry. I witnessed to my friends on the school bus, went "calling" (visiting church members and visitors in their homes) with my dad, and volunteered at the church office whenever I could.

I grew up saying, "If I were a boy, I would become a minister." In the "nondenominational" denomination I grew up in, women often served as children's ministers, music ministers, or missionaries, but not in more general pastoral roles. I also grew up in a time when most women did not work outside the home (late '60s and '70s), and my assumption became that I would marry a minister and that, together, we would have a ministry to a congregation.

When I graduated from college with a degree in business, I took a job in public accounting, assuming I would work for a couple of years, get married, have children, and live happily ever after. I was utterly unprepared for the years of singleness and full-time work in the business and nonprofit world that became the actual story of my life.

During those years, I was an active member of vibrant church communities where I served in various leadership capacities. I led Bible studies during lunch hours at my work places. I became an aunt and threw myself into investing in the precious little lives of my nieces and nephew. But my desire for a more vocational form of ministry was always just below the surface.

God was actively at work during those years, and I assumed things would just gradually unfold according to the assumptions I had for my life. However, at the age of thirty-five, when I was faced with a decision about partnership in the financial planning firm where I worked, I sensed that God had a different plan in mind, but felt a bit lost about what that might be. I sought out a career counselor who, in addition to helping me come to terms with my pastoral gifts and passion for ministry, highlighted a significant tension in my life that needed to be addressed: "You've been trained female, and it's all wrong for you."

He was referencing my pattern of serving as the right-hand person for key (male) leaders in the organizations where I worked, conforming to their preferences and leadership, instead of fully inhabiting the strength and gifts I had to offer. The truth was, I was afraid of my strength. I had seen (and experienced) women using their strength in domineering and controlling ways, and I was determined not to be one of those women. As a single woman, I had received a lot of unsolicited dating advice along the lines of "Men are intimidated by a strong woman, so don't come across too strong or they'll be turned off."

Having grown up in the church, the vision I had of a godly woman was rooted in the unfortunate translation of the word *"ezer"* in Genesis 2:18: *"Then the Lord God said, 'It is not good that the man should be alone; I will make him a helper* (ezer) *fit for him."* Some translations use the word "helpmeet" instead of helper. As a single woman wrestling with what it meant to *be* female (in contrast with *trained* female), I found author and theologian Carolyn Custis James to be a welcome guide through the fog.

As I read her book, *Lost Women of the Bible,*[1] I was captivated by the vision of what she termed the "blessed alliance" described within the creation account in Genesis. As I said earlier, I had no desire to be a brassy, domineering woman, but I also knew I didn't have the DNA to be a sweet, deferential woman (as much as I had tried to fit into that mold). As I read and re-read Genesis 1–3 with the original language of *"ezer"* being more clearly defined and explained, I sensed God inviting me to a third option, one that would require me to fully engage with all of who God created me to be and fully entrust myself to him. Up to this point in my life, I had attempted to fully entrust myself to him and conform myself to the expectations and norms around me. The journey before me involved actually embracing the desires and gifts he had given me, as well as my feminine soul. This journey is lifelong, and as the title of this chapter states, I am stumbling toward the vision I see described in Genesis 2.

Which brings me to accepting the position on staff at Grace. At the time John contacted me to interview for this position, I was part of an Anglican church in Nashville and was in a discernment process about leaving the nonprofit and campus ministry work I was doing and moving toward ministry within a congregational context. Having discerned that ordination was not something I felt called to pursue, I saw myself serving in some form of pastoral ministry role that focused on discipleship and helping people integrate their life of faith with the reality of life the other six days of the week after they left church.

When John sent me the job description for the role at Grace, I knew it was the work God was leading me to. But the road here was not completely smooth. I was deeply rooted in a wonderful community in Nashville, and leaving it seemed unthinkable, especially to move so far away. I also had never been part of a PCA church, and there were some areas of tension between the vision for men and women that was growing in my heart and mind, and some of the PCA practices related to women in ministry.

Throughout the interview process, John, the session, the interview team, and I had some very honest and frank conversations, and I tried to pull out of the process twice. But in the end, I knew God was calling me to step into this role, filled with tensions and ambiguity and the potential for great beauty or great despair. I sensed the invitation to bring all of who I was and to worry less about boundary lines and titles and more about living out the vision of the blessed alliance.

I joyfully accepted the calling to join the staff after a week-long in-person interview visit in August of 2014. On the day I checked out of my hotel, I picked up the *Seattle Times* from underneath my door, and the headline story about a woman receiving her high school diploma fifty-one years after her class graduated read, "After 51 years, now I belong." Having just turned fifty-one in June of that year, I couldn't help but smile as I accepted my first full-time vocational ministry position.

∾

During the interview process that led to Debbie joining our staff team, we talked a fair amount about men and women in ministry. She kept bringing up Carolyn Custis James and her concept of the "Blessed Alliance," which is all about unleashing the powerful blessing of men and women partnering together, each bringing their distinctive gifts to bear to advance the mission of God in the world. Simply put, James advocates that God has created men and women to need one another in the Church as we seek to serve God together.

This is a far more positive vision than merely trying to tiptoe through the various minefields that can often sabotage the relationships between men and women in the Church. It is also a far more powerful ambition than simply "checking off a box" to put a few women in some positions in the Church and call it good. This is actually an invitation from the Lord to something beautiful and vigorous—a godly alliance between men and women, celebrating each other's gifts and being used by God to profoundly advance his kingdom in the world.

Two months later, Debbie joined our session at our annual retreat. It was a bit unorthodox and unprecedented for us to have a woman join us at the retreat. I mean, are women allowed to take part in a session retreat?

At the retreat, Debbie led the session through a half-day period of silent contemplation of Scripture and prayer. None of us had ever participated in anything like this, but it was something she had done in her prior ministry. So we embraced the awkwardness of questions like "Can a woman be here?" and "What kind of weird, Catholic stuff is she having us do?" and gave it a shot. From my perspective, I can safely say God used this time in a powerful way.

Debbie directed us through a Gospel contemplation exercise with the story of Zacchaeus in Luke 19. We spent two hours imagining ourselves in the story of Jesus and Zacchaeus and asked the Lord to show us what was going on inside our hearts.

As I imagined the ensuing celebration going on at Zacchaeus' house, God began to impress upon my heart that I was "there but not there." I was at the party, but I wasn't really joining in the joy of the Lord and the spread of his kingdom. Although I wasn't mad at Jesus, nor was I trying to catch him in a lie or in any kind of blasphemy like the Pharisees, I was struck—and deeply alarmed—by my lack of presence.

The Lord used this experience in a powerful way to rouse me out of my slumber. I began to realize that "there but not there" described significant chunks of how I was living my life. In a response to my own anxieties, sinfulness, and wounds, I had been fearfully holding my breath instead of faithfully and vulnerably entering into the life the Lord has laid before me. Thankfully, the Lord is continuing to wake me from sleep, and three years later, I am still reaping the benefits of receiving the gifts God has given to Debbie.

~

John's awakening was part of a bigger story of God's movement in the life of our congregation. There was a palpable hunger for God and for true relationship with him among the people I met. In the midst of a city where hospitality is not a natural part of the culture, our congregation has been a haven of hospitality and a place of healing for many. But I almost missed all of that because of fear, one of the great enemies of the blessed alliance. Let me explain.

During my interview process with Grace, one of our elders asked me how I would counsel women who might come to me looking for guidance about the possibility of entering into vocational ministry. It was an honest question on his part, asked from a place of desiring to know how I would hold my own convictions about women in ministry as I interacted with others in a pastoral care role. And my honest answer to his question was that I would encourage the woman to enter into a season of discernment with God and others and be open to hearing God's leading for her life.

It was an honest question and an honest answer, but hidden within that interaction were seeds of suspicion and distrust that soon had me reeling in fear. Would the session really entrust the work of pastoral ministry to me, or would there be a hovering sense of being micromanaged? How would we handle disagreements? Would I actually have a place at the leadership table, or would I be a token female on staff?

I almost pulled out of the interview process at that point because of the anxiety I experienced about all of the potential difficulties I might encounter as a woman on staff in a PCA church. Left to my own decision-making process, I probably would have pulled the plug at that point. But through the counsel of others who were journeying with me in my discernment process, and through the consistent prompting I sensed from God to "keep walking," I continued. However, I knew I needed to address these fears and the corresponding seeds of suspicion I had about life in the PCA.

One of my great temptations over the years has been to spiritualize conflict to the point where the human realities are ignored or minimized. For example, if I had a conflict with someone, instead of addressing it directly with the person, I would attempt to "put on" the qualities of patience, kindness, and love instead of honestly dealing with my own heart before God and discerning the way forward in relationship. Discerning the way forward often involves acknowledging the impact of my own story within the relational conflict—how I've been impacted and shaped and wounded throughout life—as well as honest and often vulnerable conversations with the other person. Having these conversations as a woman with men can often seem awkward, uncomfortable, or in many cases, taboo. Maybe in part because of my season of life, and in part because of my desire to bring all of myself to this new role, I knew I would need to step into this awkward, uncomfortable space if I were going to have any chance of cultivating healthy ministry partner relationships.

So I picked up the phone and called John and talked to him about the fears and uncertainties that the conversation with the session had unleashed, and I expressed my concern about moving forward with the process. One of the things I have appreciated about John from the first time I talked with him is that he is a man without guile. He may not always know what he's feeling about a situation, but he will always listen and thoughtfully consider what is being said. John listened to me, and after I had finished listing out my fears and concerns he basically said, "We're not like that." Of course I had no way of knowing that for sure, but I had developed enough trust through my interactions with John to believe him and to continue on with the process and ultimately accept the position on staff.

Trust has been a huge factor in cultivating our working relationships together. And trust has provided the foundation to step into conflict rather than avoiding it. We certainly don't do it perfectly, and there have been many times when we have created more of a mess before things got cleared up. But by and large, we share a commitment to keep short accounts and deal forthrightly with one another, and that has yielded abundant fruit.

And it turns out, John was right. From the day I arrived, John and the elders treated me as a peer and gave me incredible freedom to engage in the work of pastoral ministry. The elder who asked me that question, who I predicted would be a difficult elder to work with, has become an ally and a trusted friend. I have been incredibly blessed by the kindness and respect I have received from John and our session, and they have been used by God to help me grow in confidence and freedom. God has been inviting all of us into deeper communion with him, and as we have taken that journey together over the past three years, our relationships with one another have also deepened and grown in maturity.

Debbie's ministry has not only transformed me personally, it has also brought a very significant change to our congregation's approach to discipleship. Like many churches shaped and blessed by the work of people like Pete Scazzero and James K. A. Smith, our church is beginning to see the wisdom of combining the life-giving, Christ-centered theology of the Reformed tradition with a much-needed emphasis on the absolute necessity of spiritual disciplines. And, with the Ignatian contours of her own background, Debbie has been a key player of our embrace of a contemplative spiritual approach that pushes us to experience the Good News and not merely know it intellectually. In other words, the Lord is integrating our heads and hearts. For example, five years ago, I could have preached a great sermon about Zacchaeus and how he entered the Kingdom of God and threw a party in response. But now, I am actually *experiencing* more kingdom joy as I am learning how to be present to God and his goodness.

I write these things not to canonize Debbie, and I can imagine her discomfort thinking that she is being put on some kind of pedestal. She is only one person, and she is a flawed and sinful human being like the rest of us. But I do want to point out how much our congregation has been blessed by the simple fact that we have received gifts from the Lord that he granted to us through the pastoral ministry of a woman. Our congregation would be greatly impoverished without the many blessings God has brought to us through her labors.

Coming to Grace has been an incredible blessing to me (Debbie). Having grown up in the Church, I had seen some of the underside of what can happen behind the scenes within a church, but my experience at Grace has been redemptive and has greatly contributed to my own spiritual formation and growth.

As I mentioned earlier, John is a man without guile, and I would say that about our session members as well. There is a shared commitment to honesty and authenticity with one another and with the congregation, and that has created a culture where people are safe to acknowledge the reality of struggle with sin and doubt and grief and confusion. At a recent gathering of our discipleship cohort, John shared a portion of his own journey of spiritual formation and growth from the past couple of years, and it is a gift to work with and for someone who does not try to hide the reality of his own story from the congregation he serves. From my experience, that is a rare gift. One of the things that has always been confusing to me is my own tendency to try to look better than I am in spite of knowing the Gospel is for people who know they are messed up and in need of forgiveness and grace. Being part of Grace has encouraged me to be more and more honest with myself and with God, which has opened me up to more and more of his grace.

One of the other unexpected gifts I have received from being a woman on staff at Grace has been the ability to shed some of my hyper-responsibility and hyperactivity. This is very much a work in progress, but it is in progress. I am a doer by nature, and I like to get things done. For many years prior to coming to Grace, I owned my own business and was involved in campus ministry where I had a great deal of autonomy to make decisions, and I loved what I called "life without committees." That's one side of my gifting.

The other side of that coin is I can take on things that aren't mine to do, and I can be too focused on "moving things forward." Becoming part of the staff at Grace has required me to work within a team context where the input and feedback of others—often John or the session—slows down the process and requires me to submit to a different timetable or agenda than my own. This can be frustrating at times, but the longer I'm here, the more it is becoming a gift to me. It's not ultimately up to me to make things happen or move things forward. God is the one at work through our congregation, and he is using the structure of the PCA and the collaboration among the men and women within our congregation to accomplish his purposes. I have found a surprising gift of rest hidden within submitting to this structure.

I (John) am grateful for the opportunity to tell a little bit of our story, because I think it is something that may be helpful to other congregations. But I also want to make it clear that there has been turbulence and difficulty along the way. We have had a few leaders step down because of some of the decisions we have made with respect to women in leadership at our church. And, with my own tendency toward complacency coupled with an anxiety to "get things done," I can overlook things that are significant.

Here's a painful example. Debbie and I meet each week for a check-in. We plan together, critique one another, and wrestle with some pretty big questions about how to disciple and develop our people. For the last three years, there is no one in our church with whom I have worked more closely.

But I had failed to regularly include Debbie in our session meetings. She was a somewhat regular visitor, but was not at our session meetings as a matter of practice. This past fall, we added another person to our pastoral staff who is an ordained pastor in the PCA. One of the first questions he asked me was, "Why isn't Debbie coming to the session meetings?" I looked at him blankly and realized I didn't have an answer. This was my own blindness at work. I was a fool for not having her at our session meetings each month.

Another ongoing tension has to do with language: What do we call her? Debbie is a pastor; she pastors people. In many ways she is a better pastor than I am. At the same time, I do believe the distinctions between men and women in Scripture are real and given to us for our good. And the Lord desires for us to seek to live those out in faithfulness and love. So, there are real distinctions between what she does and what I do. But still, there is something of an awkward tension in my own heart about titles.

To be sure, there have been challenges. I (Debbie) have come to believe that Satan takes great delight in sowing seeds of resentment, discord, competition, and distrust in all relationships, but especially among men and women, and especially within the Church. If Carolyn Custis James is onto something about this Blessed Alliance ordained by God to rule and subdue the earth together—and I think she is—then we should expect nothing less than a full-scale assault from the father of lies to destroy that intended blessing and gift.

There are a lot of tensions in the life of faith, and living out my pastoral vocation as a woman within the PCA context adds a few more to the list. But I have been a part of other denominational contexts where different, but equally real, tensions and struggles existed. One thing I have observed about denominations is that we are all stumbling toward discipleship, with all of our various gifts as well as sinful tendencies, and we are all engaged in the mystery of participating with God in *his* work of making all things new. That's probably one of the main things I would want someone to take away from our story: while we address and deal with the realities of things like the role of men and women in the Church, our primary focus is on deepening our own lives with God and cultivating a posture of ultimate submission to him. That's easier said than done, but from the perspective of where energy and time are spent, it is incredibly clarifying.

I am deeply grateful for the opportunity to share some of our story at Grace, and I look forward to continuing the journey of learning and growing together as participants in God's great mission of love in the world. And I pray that stories of the Blessed Alliance in action will abound, within our congregation, within the PCA, and beyond. Who knows, maybe that will be the subject of another book!

---

1. Carolyn Custis James, Lost Women of the Bible (Grand Rapids, MI: Zondervan, 2005).

SISTER TO SISTER

~

WORKING FOR GOD

ERIKA FORREST

Erika Forrest is a lifelong Presbyterian but relatively new to the PCA, as a daughter of a PC(USA) minister. A magna cum laude and Phi Beta Kappa graduate of Trinity University with degrees in Chinese and economics, she works as a business analyst for software development. She and her husband, Ryan, and infant son have worshiped at City Presbyterian Church in Oklahoma City since 2014.

It's a bitter experience for a young woman at church to know the church thinks you're just "killing time." With few exceptions, unmarried or childless women feel the pressure of their pastors and congregations to wait patiently for the next phase of their lives. Well-intentioned or not, the message sent is that what occupies a woman's time prior to (or instead of) motherhood is not and cannot be the fulfillment of God's purpose. I have seen gifted women go so unsupported in their academic and vocational paths that they leave the Church body completely, convinced they cannot worship God if he gives them "secular" gifts that weren't to be used.

While in college, I was often encouraged to find the "Christian" application of my career path. How can God use my career for his glory? Gratefully, I was never explicitly discouraged from pursuing my degree or encouraged to change my major from Chinese and economics to something more easily conformed to the bringing of his kingdom come (like medicine or teaching, for example). However, there was always the undercurrent that my career choice should be something that I could turn into pro bono work for the Church or leverage into a charitable side project. But when your career path isn't one they talk about on career day and you find yourself regularly explaining your job and its value (sometimes even to your own company's higher-ups), there rarely exists an obvious, or even a less obvious, humanitarian application of your skills. The expectation to turn your career into a nonprofit can be paralyzing. Can I serve God in this job? Is God really calling me to this field? Am I just killing time until I have (hopefully male) children to whom I will pass on my education?

Even the most well-intentioned egalitarian women have made me feel like my true vocation was a mother and my career and education were secondary. While this can certainly be true for some women, I believe that many of us are expressly called to careers outside the home and the Church. But instead, many Christian circles leave us questioning the legitimacy of work outside the spiritual, philanthropic, or domestic world. We find ourselves asking: "Is the work I do itself directly contributing to the Kingdom of God? Or is my work only a means to financially support the work of these vocational ministers? Is my daily work meaningless to God? Am I being disobedient to God by breaking with cultural norms by employing childcare or house-cleaning services to meet the responsibilities of caring for our home and children? Was my work completely in vain before I married and had a child? Where did we get the idea that work is utilitarian and not itself holy?"

It is within my Presbyterian Church in America (PCA) church that I have been taught that kingdom work doesn't require divisions between sacred and secular, for-profit and nonprofit, or home and public work. It is here I have seen both men and women embraced for their God-given vocations, empowered in their daily work in the world, secular or not. Our church has given single, female, professional graphic designers opportunities to design for the church. We've given married, entrepreneurial and business-owning women space to host business events. The church has encouraged them in God's secular calling for the lives of all women. This daily work and passion is not secondary to the work of the Gospel; it *is* the work of the Gospel. When the church fails to support the daily work of women outside the Church and home in the same way it supports those working primarily in the home, it condemns women to a position of second-class Christians and keeps them from Christ's purpose in their lives.

By honoring the kingdom contribution of individuals with secular vocations, we provide all women with purpose and value within the Church, no matter their season of life. We are no longer telling women their contribution to Christ's plan will come later, when they eventually marry. We are no longer telling infertile women their faith needs to grow. We are no longer telling women who do not want children their desires cannot be from God. We are no longer telling women that all women have the same kind of calling. It is critical that we embrace the completeness of God's presence in our world, not just within the confines of the Christian community and the Christian household, in order to create meaningful space for women in the Kingdom of God. A church that fails to acknowledge and encourage the sacredness of secular vocations fails to embrace the omnipresence of Christ.

In John 17:15–16, Jesus prays that the Father not *"take [your people] out of the world, but that you keep them from the evil one. They are not of the world, just as I am not of the world."* It seems clear Jesus does not desire that we live lives entirely apart from this world. We are not to be caught up to heaven as soon as we embrace Christ as our savior, but instead we continue to lead our lives here. We can extend this to include the idea that we are not called to walk out on our previous professional positions and turn to complete religious seclusion. Paul writes in 1 Corinthians 7:12–13 that new Christians are not to leave their marriage to a non-Christian. Similarly, he writes about Gentiles seeking circumcision after conversion, but instead commands them to remain in the condition in which they were called. We can extrapolate from this that when we become Christians and begin following God's calling for our lives we are not to abandon our secular lives for spiritual isolation, but are to remain as productive and engaged members of the wider world.

If we believe we are intended to continue our lives here on earth, and we also believe God cares for us in even the least of our needs and activities (Matt. 10:29–31), then we must believe that how we spend our earthly time is significant to God. Even Zacchaeus wasn't instructed to leave behind his daily work as a tax collector to pursue a less secular, more godly career or to dedicate himself to his family life. Jesus did not call him to abandon his work and become an apostle like he called Simon Peter and Andrew. "Vocation," which is from the Latin, literally means "calling," and we are called to positions outside of church ministry, just like pastors and missionaries are called to positions within it. Therefore, no vocation is secular because all are God-ordained and in use for the furthering of his kingdom.

Teaching young women the importance of their roles outside of the church building is crucial to developing women with a complete and genuine view of Christ and his kingdom. Too often, the message we receive is that the holiest of vocations are ministry-ordained roles in the Church and God-ordained roles in the family unit. This means, in many churches, either by denominational law or by convention, women are limited to only one holy vocation, that of mother. But this is inauthentic to the spirit of the Gospel, for both men and women. This belief requires that both men and women who are not called to formal ministry are outside the reach of a holy vocation until they bear children, or, at the very least, marry. Then, the sole calling of women is to support their husband in his kingdom work and to raise children, who will fulfill the same roles. The sole calling then of men outside of formal ministry is to earn money to support their wives and children.

This was not the case for Joseph, who was clearly called by God to his prophetic and political role in Egypt (Gen. 41). Clearly this was not the case for Rahab, who was called to serve the Hebrew spies (Josh. 2). Clearly this was not the case for Daniel, who was given station under Nebuchadnezzar in Babylon (Dan. 1). Clearly this was not the case for Nehemiah, who was given the task of rebuilding the city of Jerusalem as the cupbearer to the king of all of the Medo-Persian empire (Neh. 1–2).

In John 6:27, Jesus commands us to *not work for the food that perishes, but for the food that endures to eternal life, which the Son of Man will give to you.* It is clear from elsewhere in Scripture that we are, in fact, intended to work and to provide financially for our families (Eph. 4:28, 1 Thess. 4:11–12, 2 Thess. 3:10–12); however, the true purpose of our work is not for financial benefit. This is "the food that perishes." We are not doomed to a life of unholy purpose, toiling in the fields to put food on the table, either our own table or the table of others. Certainly this is valuable and part of the Christian vocation, but our vocations are greater than that. Adam and Eve were given roles in the physical world and purposes outside of providing for their earthly needs. Prior to the Fall, work was innately valuable. Adam and Eve were to work and tend to the land, but not to toil. Because of our disobedience, *"By the sweat of your face you shall eat bread, till you return to the ground"* (Gen. 3:19a).

Work to fulfill our physical needs became toilsome. Simply satisfying our physical needs is not our vocation; it is our curse.

Joseph is a wonderful example of someone following a God-ordained secular calling. After his stint in Potiphar's house and then prison, after all his brothers so kindly tried to do away with him, Joseph finds himself as the second most powerful man in all of Egypt, because God gave him the gift of interpreting dreams. Interestingly, this gift leads to his appointment as a secular government official. His interpretation of Pharaoh's dream does not lead to Pharaoh falling on his face, declaring the Hebrew god the one and only and requesting circumcision. Instead, it leads to his appointment in a position of secular power, which allows Joseph to rescue not only the nation of Egypt, but also the surrounding nations, including his own brothers who despised and rejected him, from famine (Gen. 37–47).

God gave Joseph incredible discernment and wisdom and called him to a necessary and powerful secular vocation. Joseph was not using his position to earn money for the purchase of Hebrew relics, to win people to God with his righteous behavior (although I'm sure this was also a by-product of his work), but instead to improve the physical situation of the nation in which he was placed. He did not work to fulfill a spiritual vocation as husband and father, and did not act as a priest, although he offered spiritual guidance and wisdom. Instead of viewing secular work as just a means to an end, that of either providing for our families or providing for the spiritual work of those ordained to formal ministry, this secular work proves valuable to perpetuating God's creation and his kingdom on earth.

God's first vocation (at least in our view of time) was creation. He spent the first six days creating the cosmos: light, water and sky, land and vegetation, sun and moon, sea animals, land animals and mankind (Gen. 1). Paul calls us *"imitators of God"* (Eph. 5:1–2), a universal vocation that we need to take seriously. This vocation means all Christians have a purpose to further his creation. Adam and Eve were explicitly commanded to *"be fruitful and multiply and fill the earth and subdue it, and have dominion over the fish in the sea and over the birds of the heavens and over every living creature that moves on the earth"* (Gen. 1:28). This command was given to both Adam and Eve, side by side. We have a God-given responsibility to further his creation. Joseph embodies this responsibility by employing the earth responsibly, harvesting and storing in clever and wise ways to assure famine would not destroy the nation. He stewards God's creation and assures that the nation will continue to prosper. By his example, we are called to work within creation in all capacities; we have a secular vocation.

In any and all vocations, we have the capacity to shape God's creation in such a way as to glorify him. We can display God's love, mercy, and salvation through our work, not despite it or regardless of it. Our work is an act of creation, whether it is composing symphonies, wiring office buildings, or washing dishes. Each of us is called to our specific position within creation to display and further the Kingdom of God. We have the opportunity, by doing our work to the very best of our abilities, to shape the world around us into "heaven on earth," to bring God's kingdom closer to us.

It is at my PCA church that I have seen this calling best encouraged and supported. It is here that I have seen the church patronize professional (female) artists, embracing art's (even modern art's) ability to allude to and expose the spirit of the Gospel. It is here I have seen finance professionals tend to the personal finance needs of others, and not for the purpose of assuring that the offering basket is filled. It is here I have seen professional women gather together to connect and encourage one another in their career goals. It is here I have seen women encouraged and empowered in whatever path God has called them, be it a professional homemaker or as a professional lawyer. It is here that I have seen God call men to equal responsibility in childcare and nursery services, where not even the pastors are exempt from their turn serving. It is here I have seen women established as heads of a formal ministry branch. It is here I have seen support for single women called to international missions. It is here I have seen *all* women celebrated on Mother's Day, not just biological mothers. It is here I have been encouraged to pray impossible prayers, be they about my marriage, my job, my finances, or anything else. It is here I was taught that the world outside of the Church was of sacred importance.

All this is not to say parenthood is not a holy vocation. Certainly the likes of Mary, Elizabeth, and Hannah would disagree. Some of the clearest callings, some straight from the mouth of an angel, have been callings to parenthood, both for men and women (lest we forget Joseph and Zechariah). But the Church has historically been very good at encouraging and affirming domestic callings. Here too my church does an excellent job of recognizing and celebrating mothers, providing resources for both homemakers and working mothers. But, critically, there is encouragement and affirmation for women (and men) whose vocation is not parenthood, like Paul, Miriam, and Lydia.

Embracing the validity of vocations outside the Church and household is the only way to fully recognize the completeness of Christ's presence and power. His presence does not end at the church door. His purpose is not limited by the offices ordained by the Church. It is in my PCA church that I have seen both men and women equally encouraged in their roles, in their distinct vocations, both inside and outside the Church. By understanding the breadth of God's purpose in all aspects of our lives, we create station for women within the work of God on earth without limiting us to a single vocation to which all women cannot be called.

God's holy vocations are broader than we can comprehend; encouraging his people in his callings is essential to building up a strong body of Christ. When churches build up their congregations in their secular work, they bring all Christians into the work of God on earth and the furtherance of Christ's kingdom. In order to empower women within his kingdom, we must acknowledge and encourage the work of all women according to his calling, be it inside or outside the home, knowing that any vocation can be God's vocation. In this church, I have seen women of all kinds of vocations affirmed in their callings and assisted in pursuing them. By doing this, we strengthen the body of Christ, engaging all aspects of the omnipresent God as we seek to further his kingdom.

WOMEN OF OTHER
NATALIE WEBSTER

**A Call to More Humanity, More Vulnerability,
Less Baloney, and More Jesus**

Natalie Webster lives in Houston, Texas. She grew up in the PCA, became a Christian through youth group, matured in her faith through the ministry of Reformed University Fellowship at the University of Florida, and later served as an intern for Reformed University Fellowship at the University of Oklahoma. Natalie hopes to finish her counseling degree at Covenant Theological Seminary and open a family counseling practice in her hometown of Tomball, Texas. She is married to Damon, and they are raising their three kids in the suburbs. Natalie's favorite way to sweat is Pilates, her favorite way to create is cooking, her favorite scent is horse musk, and her favorite social media is Instagram.

~

I fit easily into a subset of people within the church I attend in Houston, Texas. I am a stay-at-home mom in my early thirties. I have an undergraduate degree and currently spend my days with my little children. There are many other women like me at my church, and it is easy to make friends who have days structured similar to mine. I legitimately enjoy planning parties (especially kid ones), driving a minivan, making a meal plan, and decorating my house. While I would not say these soft interests truly describe the fabric of who I am, I do think they are easy to relate to and have made it easy for me to make friends at church.

This was not the case for my mom. She was an accountant by trade who worked in corporate America for twenty-six years in finance and treasury. Both of my parents are Christians, and we regularly attended church growing up. My mom did not fit as easily into a subset of people at our church as I do in mine. Most women at our PCA (Presbyterian Church in America) church did not work, and if they did, it was a job that had very defined hours and was close to home. My mom did lots of international travel, and her hours were never defined. She was an enigma at our church, someone defined as "other."

It was not simply my mom's job that made her stick out at church. My mom is comfortable having conversations about politics, finance, and social issues in groups of both men and women. She and my dad love to throw ideas around and have discussions about different topics, many of which are considered taboo or touchy. This made many people at our church uncomfortable. I once heard someone turn to my mom during a discussion and say, "Well, I know you're liberal." The implication was that not only was being liberal different from the crowd, but that perhaps this affected her own faith in Jesus. Submissive, quiet, Republican, and pro-life are all wrapped up in the subculture to which my mom supposedly did not belong.

To be fair, my mom was not the norm in very many settings. While many of her friends outside of church did work, few worked at the executive level, the same amount of hours, or traveled as much as she did. Yet I would still say it was much easier for her to fit into social settings outside of the church than inside. It is not the actual career part of the description that causes the rub, it is all of the baggage that comes with it. Being a career woman at our church did not match common assumptions about women in our church.

I would define the assumptions that my mom experienced regarding what women should do or be at our church broadly as this: quiet in groups of men and women, run the family calendar, volunteer in the children's ministry, and largely uninterested in positions of leadership. Writing them down, it seems ludicrous. These cannot be the only constructs we have to hand women who walk through the doors of churches. I think they have evolved slowly, are an easy pill to swallow, and are ideas that are easy for a large group of women to be OK with, including myself. I love volunteering in the children's ministry. In fact, I served as the nursery coordinator at our church for four years. But children's ministry is not the only place for women to serve in our churches. It is not that any of these assumptions are bad in and of themselves; it is that they have been used to construct a blueprint of women that many do not fit, and as a result, many are left without much of a place to be in church.

It is certainly not our daily vocation, our political views, or our penchant for lively discussion that should establish our worth and qualification to serve at church. And yet those things specifically are used to push women of "other" to the fringes of our churches, making them unknowable. Women who like discourse and discussion are seen as challenging authority, as not being submissive. What a place to be in. The women on the fringes are unknowable to other women, and are disliked by men.

My mom has always struggled to find her place, her ministry at church because her gifts make it hard for her to serve in what would be considered traditional women's roles. She feels comfortable in a boardroom, making decisions, and talking with both men and women as her equals. The traditional PCA church is not comfortable with women in leadership, in making decisions for the church. For a long time my mom felt like the pastors and elders of her church did not care to know her or her thoughts. That may not have been true, but the silence coming from the leadership of the church towards nontraditional women communicated that women who did not fit the mold simply did not belong.

To add a voice of hope to this narrative, late in her adulthood my mom had two pastors see her gifts and asked her to serve out of them. She helped a church plant with their business decisions. Her pastor has sought her advice on a number of issues as they've worked to become a self-sustaining church. In neither the instance of the church we went to growing up nor the church plant my mom goes to now am I suggesting that the solution was better women's programming such as an additional evening women's Bible study for working women. Instead, I am suggesting that where we see women of other, we talk to them. We bring them into our conversations, our decisions, and our framework. I am not even sure whether the church planter took my mom's advice at all. The point is that he asked her, and they had a discussion. She had opinions about church operations, and her expression of them was valued, not ignored or silenced. The blueprint that has slowly evolved to fit one type of woman, even though I myself fit that blueprint, needs to go.

I am thankful to many pastors who have heard my voice, valued it, listened, and given me a chance to serve in the church. I can honestly say that I have been a part of several ministries that took me seriously, valued my gifts, and made it a point to bring me in on decision-making. It was not until well into her adult life that this was the case for my mom; and unfortunately, many women never have this opportunity. Women who are given the gift of teaching have a hard time finding a place to fit outside of the children's Sunday school room in the PCA. Why is this the case? A lot has been written about this by people much more knowledgeable than myself. Drawing mostly on life experience, I want to suggest one reason for this, and one path to resolution.

We look at others, notice they are different than us, have opinions that challenge us, and perhaps even dredge up some shame in us. The easy out is to say: "They just aren't in the same life stage as I am, so what can I learn from them?" I'm going to call baloney on that one. Had my mom and I gone to church together instead of being mother and daughter, I am not sure we would ever have been friends. It would have been easy for me to say, "Well she works all the time and can't join in playgroup, so it is hard to get to know her." Admittedly, I have said this about working women at our church. And she could have easily said, "She's one of those stay-at-home moms and has all the time in the world and doesn't have to juggle work and home." My mom would admit that she did feel that way about women at the church I grew up at. While I incriminate others, I also incriminate myself because I have used these faulty excuses. This is malarkey, hokum, a lie disguised as truth. It simply cannot stand.

Why is it that we feel we have to look the same as everyone around us to be friends with them? Why is it that when a woman speaks her mind we feel intimidated and that ultimately she's "liberal" and clearly does not understand who Jesus made her to be? The women who work, who have a voice in boardrooms and classrooms, who have strong, beautiful, bold voices sadly have been told that their gifts are actually meant for men and they should be quiet and sit down.

If you hear the accounts of women who were told that either their gifts do not fit in or that they could not be used and you respond, "Well, that is too bad," why do you respond that way? I suggest it is because we feel comfortable with our own positions in the church and comfortable with others remaining uncomfortable. Another word would be complacent. It is not that we feel malice toward women who feel out of place or intentionally ostracize them for their different gifts; it is simply that we do not feel motivated to help them find their place. Due to our own privilege, we do not feel any urgency to get up and find a place for women who do not fit the mold we have created for them.

So what is the answer? I have lobbed a lot of stones and mentioned many things I would like to see changed. Before I offer one though, let me say this: I have been guilty of things I have said above. I know I have used my minivan-driving, stay-at-home-mom, party-host-loving self to make someone else feel like the "other." I am deeply sorry for whenever this was the case. I will not absolve myself from responsibility simply because I did not intend for that to happen. There is power in groups, in labels, and by association. If at any point I have used these words to hurt you, I am sorry.

With that said, here is my suggestion for change: vulnerability. No matter how fringe, how complacent, how obscure, how vanilla you feel that you are, we all need vulnerability. I think we can all show Jesus to each other a little more by sharing the unique things he has created in each of us. We do not need to be in the same phase of life, the same occupation, or have the same interests to be friends. When I was ten years old I wanted to spend all of my free time with horses, and often did. The coat I wore to the barn was the same coat I wore to school and it normally smelled like horse, which I loved. It also tended to have leftover bits of carrots and horse treats in the pockets. I showed this to a friend once. She walked away from me on the playground because she thought it was too weird. While I suspected it at the time, she did admit it to me when we were teenagers. I have spent hours thinking about that moment. Ten-year-old Natalie really wanted someone to love the fact that she had horse treat crumbs and moldy carrots in her pockets, and sometimes even as a thirty-two-year-old I still look for this affirmation. So my plea is this: Will you get to know my ten-year-old, moldy-pocket friend? And will you let me get to know whatever version of yourself you are too afraid to show people because you don't want them to walk away? I think Jesus will meet us there and would like for us to know each other.

There is so much dignity in having a place to serve, a place to worship, and a place to be known. The constructs and the blueprint that we have in our churches have not been helpful in allowing all women this dignity. Women who are on the fringes of our community, including my mom, have been left to wonder whether they have a place at church. I confidently say that they do, and we all have a responsibility in making sure that is the case. Vulnerability is the path forward. Vulnerability brings us to a place where we can apologize, repent, be known and move toward dignity. If you see my minivan with the NPR sticker pull up at church, I would love to talk to you about the time I called in to the Diane Rehm show. I would also like to tell you about my horse Chance, what my kids are up to, and what I'm doing in Pilates these days. What would you like to tell me about? I can't wait to hear about it. Then let's go worship Jesus together.

THRIVING WITHIN LIMITS
RONDI LAUTERBACH

Rondi Lauterbach is a pastor's wife who has been a friend and encourager of women in their life's callings. She earned her BA in Slavic Languages from Princeton University and her MA in English: TESOL from Portland State University. Her first book, Hungry: Learning to Feed Your Soul with Christ, *was published in 2016. Rondi loves playing with her grandchildren, teaching Pilates, and traveling to Serbia with her husband to encourage the Church there.*

~

Thirty years ago I was sitting on the church nursery floor, watching my youngest child figure out how to get a toy from a little boy. She did not use tact or discretion. The ensuing fight required intervention.

A visiting pastor's wife sat in the single rocker and started asking me questions. "How's it going with your husband's first senior pastor role?" I told her in sound bites about settling into a new city, new house, and new church, all the while keeping tabs on my busy toddler.

"What do you think your ministry will be? Working with children?"

"Oh no," I gave a little chuckle. "I've never wanted to work with children. It's not my gift. I still can't believe God has entrusted us with three kids of our own!"

"Then do you plan to settle into women's ministry?"

"Oh, I hope not... " I groaned. "I can't stand women's events. Too many high-pitched voices and, well, fluff."

She looked at me, puzzled. "Then what do you want to do? Teach the men?!"

I laughed and shook my head, but I felt both ashamed and trapped. Was I really as proud as I sounded? Was this really the only way to talk about church ministry for women—two open doors and one firmly closed?

Her questions—and my knee-jerk answers—had painted me into a corner that was forbidden to me. Up to that moment I hadn't been confronted with such a stark and discouraging landscape of ministry in the local church.

~

Why does that day stick in my memory? Simply because it was the first time gender roles in the Church had felt restrictive to me. This was the first, but unfortunately not the last time that God's commands, intended for our blessing, were applied in such a way that they felt more like a curse.

Let me back up for a moment. My husband has served as a pastor for more than thirty-seven years in a variety of denominational contexts. We have only recently come into the Presbyterian Church in America (PCA).

Throughout those years, we encountered various types of women's ministry and engaged in numerous discussions about what women could and couldn't do around the Church. The most intense debate was actually not over whether a woman could teach adult Sunday school, but whether she could be an usher! You heard me right. My husband, quietly amused, pushed back with this irrefutable argument, "Well in my view the ushers certainly aren't an authority position, because no one ever pays any attention to them.... "

As I reflect on those years, I can't help but ask, why did some places feel restrictive while others gave me a sense of freedom? The theology was identical. What factors, then, changed my experience?

With that question in mind, I'll first cover my early experiences of freedom, then my later experiences of restrictive limits, and finally I'll conclude by asking what's the point? What is God's purpose in all this?

~

My childhood made me accustomed to open doors.

I was born into a Southern family that valued education, community service, and active church participation. The church that I attended was a mainline Protestant one—neither fundamentalist nor evangelical.

This was both a loss and a gain. The Gospel was fuzzy, but the linguistic baggage was absent. The term "helpmeet" wasn't in my vocabulary. I didn't know what it was nor that I was supposed to become one. All I knew was that my parents took my gifts and aspirations seriously.

Doors were opening for women in those years. My father's Ivy League alma mater began accepting women in 1969. I matriculated five years later. Shortly before I left for college, the Jesus of my Sunday school years became the Jesus of my adult life. He used a broken heart to show me his saving love. Immediately Scripture became alive and wonderful to me. Shortly after that I met the man who was to become my husband.

God breathed life into us both through his Word. It was the foundation of our lives and marriage. When we declared our vows and were pronounced one flesh, we became a team, Mark-and-Rondi, and planned to take our one-flesh calling seriously.

We understood the biblical teaching on women's roles to be a picture of complementary servanthood, with the man taking the lead. The roles were a means to a very good end—one flesh in the marriage, fruitful partnership in the church. We planned to talk theology together, wash dishes together, raise a family together, serve a church together—male and female in Christ—submitting to our Lord by serving in distinct roles at home and at church.

Gender roles, too, felt like an open door to me. I wasn't afraid of being pinched or crushed by the calling to submit to my husband, who happened to also be my pastor. He didn't think God called him to keep me in my place, but to help me thrive. He respected me.

He needed me, too. Not just to wash his socks and make his meals, but to stand shoulder to shoulder with him on the battlefields where we served. He needed me to fight. To watch. To pray. To care for the wounded. To love the stranger. I was his "necessary ally," John McKinley's strong translation of *ezer kenegdo*.[1] Our partnership was necessary for the mission.

Within the limits God had set, there seemed to be plenty of room for both of us to use the gifts he had given. I experienced freedom both at home and at church. But later, church situations arose where, though they claimed to adhere to the same theology of gender roles we believed, the leaders applied it in a way that felt very restrictive.

~

"Are you really saying that women may not teach the Bible, even to other women?" That question was finally spoken out loud at a meeting with church leaders. We waited with bated breath. "Yes. All teaching must be done by the pastors. The women should restrict their teaching to the application of the doctrines."

I was overwhelmed with dismay that day. How can you avoid the default legalism of the human heart if all you can talk about is the dos and don'ts of Scripture? How can you keep Christ at the center without speaking from the Bible itself?

I felt not just silenced but suffocated. It was as if they had stripped me of the sword of the Spirit and placed a plastic child's sword in my hand instead, so I wouldn't hurt myself or anyone else. That church was most interested in keeping me in my place. Its policy conveyed distrust.

By way of contrast, churches can be places that cause women to thrive. Central to such thriving is a deepening and maturing grasp of God's word through active engagement with it. Receiving the preached word must be accompanied by personal reading, study, meditation, and, yes, teaching that word to others. Unnecessary restrictions on women's roles will not just reduce the lives of the women, but impoverish the life of the local congregation.

In the example I cited, no one had tampered with the relevant texts on women's roles. No one had changed the theology. Then what happened?

I came to recognize three ways that biblical limits could become restrictive.

Overapplied Text

Scripture gives rules about men's and women's roles for the ordering of the home and the Church. But in the 1990s those roles began to be applied to society. "Should women be police officers?" One woman asked John Piper. To his credit, he didn't give her a direct yes or no. But the reasoning he presented for her to consider was based on his view of two terms, "biblical manhood and biblical womanhood."[2]

These terms defined the essence of men and women as "leaders" and "followers," a concept that exceeded Scripture and opened up a host of wrong applications for biblical roles, hence the question about women police officers. Such an application violated the intention of Paul's instructions, which were given for the Church. As one scholar puts it: "All Christian teaching on men-women roles presupposes a new creation and a new nature (or to use scriptural terms, new man or person). The teaching is intended for the *redeemed community*."[3]

My sense that this was a wrong approach was validated in a seminary class years later. That class was titled "The Role of Women in the Church, Home, and Society." When the professor lectured on the last topic, it was short and sweet: "Scripture doesn't prescribe or restrict the role of women in society."

Biblical limits become restrictive when they are overapplied, even with good intentions, such as "resisting the culture." Fencing the law is just as dangerous as the slippery slope.

A first call to action, then, is to be vigilant about freedom within the limits God has set. Fear about the "slippery slope" must not be allowed to produce restrictions where God has given freedom.

Patriarchy Replacing Complementary Roles

I remember one Sunday when I looked for one of the pastors of our church so I could apologize to him. I had spoken in anger to him on a recent occasion and my conscience was pricked by Matthew 18 to make amends.

He said he forgave me, but had a strange look on his face. Later he approached my husband and called him to task for not stepping in and apologizing in my place, as was his responsibility as the husband. That, he assured Mark, is what headship is all about. Both my husband and I were shocked by his words. Did that pastor really think male headship meant the wife shouldn't make her own apology? "That's ridiculous!" my husband snorted.

We came to realize, through the same seminary class mentioned earlier, that "complementarity" isn't the most conservative expression of men's and women's roles. There was one farther to the right—hierarchy or patriarchy. That day's lecture clarified our understanding and equipped us to push back against a view that stripped women of their shared status with men before God as fellow image-bearers (Gen. 1:26–27), joint heirs (1 Pet. 3:7), and equally united to Christ (Gal. 3:28).

Biblical limits become restrictive when patriarchy has become the unstated, functional paradigm in a church or denomination.

A second call to action is to watch out for paternalistic attitudes that can show up in paternalistic words or actions.

Male Leaders Treating Women with Contempt

"What are we going to do with the women?! (God bless 'em.)" That's a phrase my husband has heard from an exasperated fellow leader on more than one occasion. It is usually accompanied by a roll of the eyes or a condescending chuckle. It shows that the problem with "women's roles in the Church" isn't always a matter of polity or even of application of polity. It can also be a matter of sanctification.

The sin of contempt is behind those careless words, even if the speaker protests that he is simply frustrated by "the women problem" in the Church. Contempt is real and sinful and must not be tolerated in the body of Christ.

Fueling such words is ungodly stereotyping, proud superiority, and dismissive neglect, all of which will lead to deficiencies in appropriate pastoral care for the women under the charge of the very speaker who has been called to shepherd them. Neglect harms women as much as paternalism.

Our shepherds are called to lead, feed, know, and protect the whole flock. An attitude of contempt will pollute their calling, harm the Church, and bring dishonor on their Chief Shepherd, who will hold them accountable.

What can be done to counter this sin and reverse its evil effect? Polity isn't the answer for such a demon. In Jesus' words, *"This kind cannot be driven out by anything but prayer"* (Mark 9:29). The answer lies in watching. Praying. Confession. And repentance. Biblical limits become restrictive when women are viewed with contempt.

A third call to action is a call to our church officers at the session, presbytery, and General Assembly levels to watch and pray—to examine themselves and seek the Lord for conviction, repentance, and change. This third call must include a call to action for our women as well—to forgive. Even if it happens seventy times seven times.

~

At this point you may be saying, "So what?"

Why have I shared my experience with you, when yours might be quite different? Am I simply being the voice of cynicism saying, "Take heart, it could be worse!" No. I shared because I want to be a voice of change for our churches and a voice of hope for individual women.

First, why is action called for? Why is change needed? Because the goal of male and female roles is a glorious one—it's unity. That's the concept behind the marriage words "one flesh" as well as behind the Church words "one body." The roles are meant to serve the goal of making us one. Stephen Clark puts it this way: "Genesis teaches that unity is God's desire for human beings and for every human grouping. The work of Christ is intended to restore that unity by creating a new humanity, the Church, in which that unity is actualized" (Eph. 5:32).[4]

This has profound implications for our current discussion in the PCA. Unity means if one of us hurts, we all do. If the husband hurts, the wife is sad. If the woman in the pew is treated with contempt, the man in the pew as well as the man in the pulpit takes action. Thus the love of Christ is lived out among us.

Unity also means fruitfulness. In fact it is God's primary means to bring fruitfulness. Apart from a miraculous intervention that has only occurred once in human history, it takes the unity of male and female to have children. And in the Church, Christ's body, it takes the unity of men and women serving and worshiping together to bear fruit for his kingdom.

Second, why do individual women need a voice of hope? Because change comes slowly, and we must trust God in the meantime.

Dear sister, even if the officers in your church seem like they don't get it or appear unresponsive to the plea for change, you have a Great Shepherd. God's sovereignty brings his kingly, kindly rule over all human frailty, mistakes, sin, and fear of slippery slopes.

I can testify that God has used even the difficult situations in churches for my good. I have never lacked opportunity to serve him, even when one or all three of the highlighted problems were present in the church we attended. I found instead that when one door slammed in my face, God opened another one like the Gentleman he is, and I found unexpected joy in unexpected places. Ultimately, he is the one who will cause us to thrive within the limits where he has placed us.

Christ is the husband to us all. As he nourishes and cherishes his Church, may we thrive together under his rule and bear much fruit.

---

1. John McKinley, "Towards a Fuller Expression of Complementarianism in Church Life," a recorded session from the 67th Annual Meeting of the Evangelical Theological Society with the theme, Marriage and the Family, November 17–19, 2015, in Atlanta, GA.
2. John Piper, "Should Women Be Police Officers?," August 13, 2005, in *Ask Pastor John*, produced by Desiring God, podcast, https://www.desiringgod.org/interviews/should-women-be-police-officers.
3. Stephen B. Clark, *Man and Woman in Christ: An Examination of the Roles of Men and Women in Light of Scripture and the Social Sciences* (Servant Books: MI, 1980), 38. My emphasis.
4. Ibid., 39.

1992

RENEE HIGGINS

Renee Higgins has been a PCA pastor's wife for more than twenty years. She currently teaches Bible study and prayer at the South City Church in St. Louis and is an Entrust Coach for Precept Ministries International. She is married to Mike Higgins, the mother of Mary and Michelle, and the grandmother of Moses and Matilda.

∼

"*Because the Lord is my Shepherd, I have everything I need.*" These words from Psalm 23 are my prayer and my song as I come before God for his guidance.

In 1992, my husband Mike and I made a decision to leave the military, along with its financial security, healthcare, and officer housing and return home to St. Louis, Missouri, so that Mike could attend seminary. 1992 was a "clarion call" for us—a call that awakens you and rouses you to prepare for a great change.

We had learned about Black church tradition in both Pentecostal and Progressive National Baptist churches, and God was blessing us to grow in faith by hearing the stories of our elders and leaders who had persevered because of God. Even though they had to endure hardships, their faith had made them strong. So I still praise God for giving me these heroes of faith. Their stories still encourage me, and their strength continues to speak to me. They taught me how to pray.

During the ten years as active duty military, the Lord had sent us many places, and it was about time for another move, or what the Army calls a "permanent change of station." I personally had looked forward to leaving Fort Leonard Wood, Missouri, and going to another part of the country or even having another overseas tour, maybe returning to Germany.

But this was not to be, because the Lord had stirred our hearts for full-time ministry. The Lord had used our time in the Army to expand our views of the world. Even though we learned a lot about geography while attending St. Louis public schools, it was not the same as traveling to some of the places that we had read about.

In 1992, instead of looking forward to a new duty station, we were going back home. Every place that the Lord sent us in the Army he showed us that we were there to be blessed and be a blessing for others. I remember our first duty station, Fort Riley, Kansas. I was expecting to go farther than the next state over from Missouri, but the Army post seemed like a completely different country.

We had barely settled in when Mike had to leave for training, so I was left alone with the girls and the news channel telling us to bring in our small pets because of coyotes. My next-door neighbor invited me to PWOC (Protestant Women of the Chapel) and the sign on the wall of the chapel spoke to me. It was Philippians 4:11, "Not that I speak in respect of want: for I have learned, in whatsoever state I am, therewith to be content." I was blessed by my neighbor to be invited and found out later that she was blessed by me because she did not know how to approach a Black woman. We laughed about it later. Neither of us had ever had next-door neighbors of another color.

God was blessing me to see people of other colors and denominations drawn together because their families belonged to the Army. I joined PWOC and found out about Precept Bible studies. I went with a group of ladies to Chattanooga to attend Precept training, another experience of culture shock for me and those around me. I attended chapel services whenever Mike was in the field for training.

Our second duty station was in Bad Nauheim, Germany. Mike and I spent three years living in Germany, and I had the opportunity to travel to some wonderful places in Europe to attend conferences and take in the beauty of that part of the world. Mike and I, along with our two daughters, Mary and Michelle, have many cool and funny stories from our first ten years in the Army. I now know that it was God's hand guiding us and gently leading us so that we would be able to minister to a diverse group of people and understand the need to be able to work way outside of our personal comfort zones. The military is socioeconomically, culturally, and racially diverse but there is one mission statement: to defend the citizens of the United States from its enemies, to fight and win the nation's wars. The Church is as diverse as the military, but again with one mission: "To make disciples." I often reflect on Paul's words in 1 Corinthians 9:22 where he says, *"I became all things to all men that I might save some."* We don't do the "saving," but we should be passionate about "becoming."

We met others, enlarging our circle of Christian family but still holding tight to our Black Pentecostal roots. We attended the Gospel services at the chapel, which offered services for Catholic, Jewish, and Protestant faiths. One of the Protestant services was called the Gospel service because it was attended by Blacks. That's another story—or maybe now that I look back it is the same story, because we often had a young White chaplain giving the Gospel chapel service who did not know what to do with a diverse congregation. I see now God was using Mike in these services as a way to prepare him to one day become a chaplain. We stayed with the chapel service until a Church of God in Christ opened on the economy, which is what we would call housing, businesses, or land outside of the Army post. We wanted more than the chapel provided so we became members of a church in the German city of Friedberg outside of the post.

Our next duty station after leaving Germany was Fort Leonard Wood, Missouri. It was not what we wanted, but it was God's plan because he had already orchestrated our 1992 move. We did not walk fearfully into 1992; we had faith that God was about to expand our vision of him even more, and we were excited about how he would use us.

We knew St. Louis. We knew that we both had families there. St. Louis was home, and we would receive help from friends and family. We could probably attend our old church and move to our old neighborhood. The switch back to civilian life would not be that hard.

This is where I stop saying "we" because Mike and I were not seeing the same thing.

It was like a tale of two cities. I was calling family and friends reuniting with church members and choirs, and Mike was looking at what school he would attend and where would he work. I joke about it now, saying that I was singing "We've come this far by faith," while Mike was singing "We still have a long way to go."

I was not blind to the fact that moving home without employment or housing weighed heavier on Mike. I knew too that some friends and family were having a hard time understanding why we would leave the Army to minister. Mike was already a minister. But we had prayed, and the Lord spoke peace to our hearts. We had no earthly assurance that a chaplain slot would be open after Mike finished seminary with his Masters of Divinity degree. Mike tells the story of finding Covenant Seminary in the St. Louis phone book after calling Concordia and being told he needed to be Lutheran. We had a good laugh wondering what Covenant would want him to do to prove himself able to attend their seminary.

So in 1992 when we moved back to St. Louis, we did not move in with family. We did not move to our old neighborhood. We did not ask for help from friends to find employment. I was homeschooling the girls so we did not need to be near public schooling. We were depending on God, and God answered, as he always does, in ways beyond our imagination. Because we know God is faithful and trustworthy. He promises to protect us even under conditions of difficulty. He tells us to commit ourselves to his love, to obey, and he will fill our hearts with his love. This is our blessed assurance: we were moving back to our hometown, but God was doing something new in our lives.

When we reported to Covenant Seminary, Mike had been ordained twice by two prestigious Black denominations. He was first ordained in 1981 by the Progressive Baptist Convention, of which the Rev. Dr. Martin Luther King Jr. was a member, and by the Church of God in Christ (COGIC) in 1985.

Neither of us remembered sermons about the Great Reformation or Calvin's Institutes or Luther's Ninety-five Theses. There were names in European and American church history that we did not know. So Mike showed up with the other new students, who were mostly young, White men straight out of college, to attend a Presbyterian seminary. He was a Black Baptist Pentecostal preacher with ten years of military service as a commissioned officer. He would need to learn the new languages of Hebrew, Greek, Reformed, and White Evangelicalism.

I don't remember specific times of going out to Covenant during

Mike's first year of seminary. The girls and I were busy with home-schooling and moving into a new place. I know that I did not have a neighbor to take me to PWOC, or a chapel service that included wives of husbands who were united in training for the Army. I eventually knew that my husband was in a struggle with his experience in seminary.

This was not a speed bump; this was a pothole. Mike would come home, and we would talk and pray. Once he said something I won't forget. He told me I could not understand what he was going through, because I had never been somebody who people said "Yes, sir!" to in the Army and now people get you mixed up with the other Black person on campus. I did not tell him I am somebody, or that what he said to me sounded like he thought I wasn't somebody. But I saw what he had been dealing with trying to be father, husband, student, and provider. I don't know how many other things he thought he needed to be to be some-body. He felt devalued. He was trying to relate, but to do so he had to censor himself, not giving his own perspective or opinions because others might not relate. He had even been asked by one of his professors if he could take his exam outside the classroom because his vocal tics because of having Tourette's syndrome interrupted some of the other students in the class.

I tried to continue in encouraging my husband with songs and Scrip-tures. But he was right. I did not understand what he was going through. I shared with him from Romans 12:9–16:

> Let love be genuine. Abhor what is evil; hold fast to what is good. Love one another with brotherly affection. Outdo one another in showing honor. Do not be slothful in zeal, be fervent in spirit, serve the Lord. Rejoice in hope, be patient in tribulation, be constant in prayer. Contribute to the needs of the saints and seek to show hospitality. Bless those who persecute you; bless and do not curse them. Rejoice with those who rejoice, weep with those who weep. Live in harmony with one another. Do not be haughty, but associate with the lowly. Never be wise in your own sight.

Yes, that was a pothole on my journey. I had heard a sermon illustra-tion about our Christian journey having twists and turns, speed bumps, and potholes. These hindrances are not to stop us, but to help us take note of other people and places. Then we are to stop and fill that pothole. Then we maybe mark it and let others know that someone else has traveled this road and left a few warning signs, so that it will not cause them to stumble or fall.

Some names on my filled-in potholes are implicit bias, social status, injustice, and racial reconciliation. I did not even know that I would stumble on some of those; but if you are not looking, you can stumble on issues that mean more to others, and when you make mention of them their responses can cause pain both ways.

I also had some great things happen in 1992. I praise God for working out things in our lives that put me in greater awe of how he works. When Mike was searching for employment, the Lord blessed him to work at Life-Skills, and he was hired because of what should have been a problem: because he has Tourette's syndrome, he was chosen over others to work with youth with autism.

God used Mike and his dealing with the motor and vocal tics that are a part of Tourette's syndrome to be a source of encouragement for children and their parents who also live with the disorder, because it had not kept him from being an Army officer and a minister of the Gospel.

The Lord opened doors for friendship for the girls and me by placing us in the right place as we were looking for homeschool co-op groups. We joined a group of ladies and their children who we still have relationships with from Memorial and Grace and Peace churches in St. Louis.

So my pothole from 1992 is filled, and our entrance into the Presbyterian world has brought unexpected changes in our lives. In 1994, Mike entered into the chaplain's candidate program. In 1995, Jerram Barrs asked Mike if he would be interested in becoming a part of the Presbyterian Church in America (PCA) because the PCA needed people like Mike. In 1996, Mike graduated from Covenant and received his Masters of Divinity. Mike would eventually transfer his COGIC credentials into the PCA after an hour-long examination on the floor of Tennessee Valley Presbytery in 1997.

As I said before, 1992 was a clarion call for us—a call that awakens you and rouses you to prepare for a great change. You may be a young woman of color coming to the PCA from another denomination. If you have a psalm, a song, a scripture, or a story in your life's journal of what made you aware of God being your friend and guide, keep that in your heart and guard it—it will bring you encouragement.

You will need to encourage yourself if you are a wife or mother, and if you are a wife you will need to know who you are in God because you may be called on to encourage your spouse. You may even find out like I did that people who lack color or rhythm may not lack heart and understanding, and you may find a friend along the way.

To every woman that has ever been told you've never been anything, or you'll never be anything, know this: that is a pothole you need to fill. Because God made you in his image, and you are here because he has called you to contribute to the kingdom. Don't seek to be something great to or for any man. Read Matthew 5:11–16 and let your light shine. The text from Matthew 5 specifically states:

> *Blessed are you when others revile you and persecute you and utter all kinds of evil against you falsely on my account. Rejoice and be glad, for your reward is great in heaven, for so they persecuted the prophets who were before you. "You are the salt of the earth, but if salt has lost its taste, how shall its saltiness be restored? It is no longer good for anything except to be thrown out and trampled under people's feet. "You are the light of the world. A city set on a hill cannot be hidden. Nor do people light a lamp and put it under a basket, but on a stand, and it gives light to all in the house. In the same way, let your light shine before others, so that they may see your good works and give glory to your Father who is in heaven.*

When Mike and I left the Army post to attend a church with people that we had more in common with culturally, it did not bother us to do so. But after 1992 we would be bothered by separating culturally. The directing of the Lord was showing us that our calling was to help others see the greater need of reconciliation in the Church. We now use our experiences to tell others that there is a greater oneness in the church body than color or culture, and that people with different backgrounds can come together to serve the one true God. Jesus prayed for us in John 17 to be one.

All these things we went through in 1992 were God preparing us for the ministry he had planned for us. We needed to have certain experiences to tell others that struggles can make us strong. And we don't deny the real struggles racial minorities face in a dominant culture setting— even in church. We now tell our story of having to cut our ribbons that we had nicely tied around the box where we had placed what we knew about God so we could be ready to present it when asked what our ministry would be. The Lord caused us to go back and see that there was no prepared box that we could give that made our journey an easy road with no potholes. We share how we found out that God works outside of the box, and how important it is that our relationship with him is one of following his lead, even if he takes us back to a former place. He is the Good Shepherd, and he cares for his sheep.

In my journey I will still sing, pray, and encourage myself in the Lord no matter where I am. I still look for potholes, and I try to fill them so that someone else might not stumble. I don't let events, years, or any number of things still my song. I keep in step sometimes by singing an old hymn, "Marching to Zion," connecting it to the Scripture in Hebrews 12 because it speaks about the saints singing together at the New Mount Zion and the New Jerusalem. I am on my way to the City of the Living God, the Heavenly Jerusalem, getting ready to join innumerable angels at Mount Zion.

WORDS FROM OUR BROTHERS

MOTHERS AND SISTERS
SEAN MICHAEL LUCAS

A Personal Testimony and Challenge

Sean Michael Lucas pastors at Independent Presbyterian Church (PCA) in Memphis, Tennessee. He also serves as Chancellor's Professor of Church History at Reformed Theological Seminary. Prior to coming to Memphis, he served on church staffs in Kentucky, Missouri, and Mississippi, as well as a faculty member and administrator at Covenant Theological Seminary. He is the author of several books, most recently For a Continuing Church: The Roots of the Presbyterian Church in America. *He loves to run, and he follows the St. Louis Cardinals.*

In our conservative Presbyterian tradition, we have spent a great deal of time exegeting, discussing, arguing over, defending, and implementing 1 Timothy 2:11–15. Those verses, key for the complementarian position, focus especially on the public worship service and the authoritative teaching of the elder in that context. We believe—rightly, in my view—that Paul is telling us that in that context, male elders are the ones who are to teach and preside, not female leaders. That does not mean that women are never to teach mixed groups, that women are to "be quiet" always in every context, that "full submission" is required in every ecclesial situation. Paul's instruction there is particularly focused on the context of public worship (1 Tim. 2:1–2, 8) and the authoritative proclamation of the Word as an overseer.

As I say, we've spent a great deal of time on that text. But sadly and detrimentally, we have neglected verses a few chapters later that are just as important for understanding how women and men should relate to each other in the life of the Church. In 1 Timothy 5:1–2, Paul instructs Timothy, *"Do not rebuke an older man harshly, but exhort him as if he were your father. Treat younger men as brothers, older women as mothers, and younger women as sisters, with absolute purity"* (NIV). If we are the family of God (and we are), then surely how we treat women in our family is just as important as making sure that our church order is proper and that we ensure that only men are teaching and ruling elders. In fact, if we love to call each other "fathers and brothers," then we should also delight to call the women in our churches "mothers and sisters."

But not just call them—treat them as such. The language of mother takes us to the Fifth Commandment: *"Honor your father and your mother"* (Exod. 20:12). And so, those older women in our congregations are worthy of great honor. In fact, Luther suggests that "it is a far higher thing to honor than to love one, inasmuch as it comprehends not only love, but also modesty, humility, and deference as to a majesty there hidden, and requires not only that they be addressed kindly and with reverence, but, most of all, that both in heart and with the body we so act as to show that we esteem them very highly, and that, next to God, we regard them as the very highest."[1] As elders in Christ's church, we have to ask ourselves, "What does it look like to honor and love the women in our congregations; to show modesty, humility, and deference to them; to esteem them very highly?"

The language of sister, especially with the qualification of "absolute purity," reminds us that we are fellow siblings in God's family. We have an equal share in the Father's love, equal right to the Father's inheritance, equal benefit and blessing from the Father himself. It also reminds that we men treat our sisters with purity of thought, word, and deed, that we do not view them as objects of lust or desire or tools of manipulation or power. Rather, as elders in Christ's Church, we care for them for their own sakes, as those both made in God's image and remade by Christ's blood.

I wonder how adding the language of "mothers and sisters" beside the Presbyterian invocation of "fathers and brothers" would shift the debates that we are presently having about how women might serve Christ's Church within a commitment to biblical complementarianism. For my own part throughout my ministry, I have been taught how valuable mothers and sisters are within Christ's Church by a number of remarkable women with whom God has allowed me to partner to advance his cause in our world. I would like to give testimony and tribute to these mothers and sisters who have encouraged me in the Gospel and who have been a delight to serve with in God's family.

When I served in St. Louis at Covenant Presbyterian Church and Covenant Theological Seminary, God in his mercy blessed me to serve beside Kathy Chapell and Mary Beth McGreevy. Kathy and Bryan Chapell were our backyard neighbors while we worked at Covenant Seminary. And after George Robertson left Covenant Church, and I was thrust into the role of interim senior pastor (while I continued to work at the seminary as a faculty member and administrator), I had the opportunity to serve beside Kathy, who was our church's music and choir director. I'll never forget our staff meetings at Starbucks where she repeatedly reminded me of the Gospel, especially Zephaniah 3:17. Countless times I felt unsure and unable; countless times this Gospel mother encouraged me by reminding me that I was (and am) unable, but Christ is able. And if I listen, I can hear him singing with joy over me.

Likewise, while at Covenant, I got to know Mary Beth McGreevy, one of the more remarkable Bible teachers and leaders in our denomination. It was my privilege when I was academic dean to advocate for Mary Beth to teach in our MA degree programs. She was (and remains) an excellent teacher. She had a great gift of taking material Bryan Chapell taught in his preaching courses and making it accessible for those who would be teaching Sunday schools or Bible studies. She also networked well with our women who held the MDiv degree, encouraging them with her experiences at Tenth Presbyterian Church, Covenant Presbyterian Church, and Covenant Seminary, reminding them that the Presbyterian Church in America (PCA) is a good place for women to do ministry. I learned how to serve with talented women by serving beside Mary Beth.

Such experiences in St. Louis shaped the way I thought about hiring for church staffs. When I got to Hattiesburg, Mississippi, one of the absolute best hires that we made was to bring Kathy Young on board. Kathy is a regional leader in early childhood education, but she is also a creative teacher and passionate advocate for children in the life of the church. While her title was "director of children's ministry," Kathy offered sound, biblical, thoughtful pastoral care to children and their families. She attended our pastoral meetings, providing wise input not only into church programming, but also insight into what was happening in the lives of church families from her unique seat on the bus. We did try to hire other women for our staff, especially one in the position of "director of missions," but having Kathy allowed us to learn much from our sister about ministry.

In 2017, God brought my family to Memphis and allowed me to partner with two remarkable mothers and sisters: Lisa Turner and Casey Cockrum. Lisa has served Independent Presbyterian Church for more than thirty years in a variety of capacities, but also has maintained a singular focus on pastorally caring well for others, whether women or men. Everyone in our congregation knows that if you need help, you'll find it most quickly from Lisa. Since the early 1980s, she has led student ministry, college ministry, congregational care, fellowship events, camping ministry (she leads our partnership with Palmer Home for Children called Camp Palmer), and now women's ministry. Her energy, wisdom, and care are vital to the well-being of IPC; it is inconceivable what our church would be if Lisa were not here. I have learned the art of caring well from watching and serving beside her.

In addition, being able to work with Casey Cockrum is to work with a visionary leader who manifests tremendous care for those under her direction. Casey serves Reformed University Fellowship as Director of Campus Staff, overseeing nearly thirty-five female campus staff members. Her energy and direction, her wisdom about people and situations, her evident love for Jesus—all encourage me in my own practice of leadership and my own discipleship. With her husband Colton, they've modeled to me what Christian marriage looks like and what Christian hopefulness feels like. I know that I'm a better person, a better believer, after I've been with her.

While there are several others I could mention, these five women have been my mothers and sisters in the faith. I've benefited from their wisdom and care. I've gained from their love for Jesus. I've learned how to be a better pastor because I've served beside them in God's family. I very much believe that I would be poorer—a poorer Christian, a poorer pastor, a poorer leader, a poorer man—if I had not served with them.

Which begs the question: Why would anyone want to serve only with fathers and brothers?

Again, the point here is not one of ordination. We firmly believe that the Scriptures are clear that the office of elder is for men, that the preached Word in the context of corporate worship is to be brought by men, that the oversight of the affairs of the congregation are to be conducted by men. None of that is up for debate.

But in a well-regulated family, even though the father is ultimately responsible for exercising oversight, for instructing, for governing and guiding, do not mothers have a place, a role, a contribution? Aren't our children taught more and shaped better when fathers and mothers work together? Would any of us who are fathers—like I am, the father of four children—want to parent, direct, guide, and instruct our children alone without our wives, their mothers?

And in many families, though the oldest sons feel the responsibility of providing and caring for the whole family when their fathers are absent or lost or dead, isn't there a place for sisters? Don't we need our sisters to assist, to counsel, to guide, to offer insight when we can't always see what mom and dad need in a given moment?

So what I am testifying about is the value of having mothers and sisters involved on ministry teams, offering their gifts and graces to advance the work of the Church. How might we come to honor our older women as mothers and our peer-aged or younger women as sisters with all purity in our ministries? Three ways, I think.

First, *intentionality.* We are never going to honor women as mothers and sisters in our ministries unless we are intentional about it. When there is an opportunity to hire a director-level position that does not require ordination, are we intentional about considering both women and men for that position? When we are thinking about speakers for an event—not just an event that would lend itself to women, but an event that requires a general expertise in a particular area—do we consider women as part of the speaking team? When we are forming a committee to deal with an issue, do we default simply to involving only men or do we intentionally involve women? When we need people to pray at staff meeting, small group, large group, or some other venue, do we ever intentionally ask a woman to lead in prayer?

Notice that none of these things requires ordination. All of these things would be open to nonordained men: hiring director-level positions, speaking on a matter of general expertise, involving on a committee, asking to pray. If we are going to show honor, love, humility, and deference to women as our mothers and sisters, then intentionally involving them in these things would be a major step forward.

Next, *humility*. This takes us back to Luther—honoring mothers and sisters requires humility. However, we often think that humility involves something untoward, something that looks like retiring behavior or groveling before another. Not at all. I love how the author John Dickson defines humility in the light of Philippians 2: "Humility is the noble choice to forgo your status, deploy your resources, or use your influence for the good of others before yourself. More simply, you could say the humble person is marked by a willingness to hold power in the service of others."[2] Humility gives power away to others; it does not grasp power or glory, but willingly lets it go to bless another.

Think about how that understanding of humility applies toward our mothers and sisters in Christ. As a man, a teaching elder, a senior pastor, a faculty member, a denominational leader, I have power and privilege; I have resources and influence. As a result, I have choices to make. I can either grasp, cling to, hold on to my power and privilege, my resources and influences. I can grasp glory. Or I can make the decision to let it all go and use it to serve someone else: a woman who has gifts and graces, wisdom and insight. Humility means that I ask the question: "How might I use my power and influence to advance this mother or sister so that she might use her gifts and graces best for God's glory and the church's good?"

Unfortunately, many of us men are not humble enough to ask that question. We cling to our power and status, privilege and influence. We are convinced that if she increases, I decrease. And so, in our pride, we hide behind a misuse of the Bible's teaching on complementarianism to avoid working with, supporting, or honoring a mother or sister by involving her in the Church's work. And that's to our detriment and shame.

Finally, *charity*. The book I use for both premarital and marital counseling is Paul Tripp's *What Did You Expect?* I find that book to be extremely helpful in realistically dealing with the challenges that we face in marriage, challenges that come from faulty expectations. Tripp organized the book around six key commitments. For my wife and me, one of the most helpful was the fifth one: "We will deal with our differences with appreciation and grace."[3] So often in our marriage, we had dealt with our personality or perspective differences as though they were right or wrong. I'm a planner, but my wife is spontaneous—instead of dealing with that difference charitably, I saw it as a massive character failure. My wife is extroverted and loves to have people over, but I'm introverted and easily tired—my wife saw my reticence about entertaining as a disturbing and un-Christian lack of love. Of course, neither case was actually a right or wrong issue; rather, these were simple personality differences that were more like whether someone was right-handed or left-handed.

If we are going to work well as women and men together, we have to deal with our natural personality or perspective differences with charity and grace. That means we cannot personalize what is not personal; we have to see that our differing perspectives are actually helpful angles of vision on the same problem with a shared Gospel commitment. That means that we can't get frustrated with each other's quirks; we have to see that our different personalities and even gender differences add and not subtract value from the conversations we have and the work we do.

It does little good for the kingdom if we can recite the Westminster Shorter Catechism or parse Hebrew verbs or explain knotty passages from the theologian Herman Bavinck, but in the end fail to love well. Part of loving well is honoring our mothers and sisters in Christ. That's not simply by recognizing mothers on Mother's Day, by funding the annual women's retreat, or by quickly passing the women's ministry budget without amendment in session meeting.

Rather, we love our mothers and sisters in Christ well when we intentionally include them in appropriate ministry responsibilities for which they are qualified. We love them well when we demonstrate the humility to give away our power and privilege, our influence and resources, so that they might use their giftedness for God's glory. We love them well when we deal with our natural personality, perspective, and even gender differences with charity and grace. It has been my privilege in ministry to be blessed through the partnership and care of Kathy Chapell, Mary Beth McGreevy, Kathy Young, Lisa Turner, Casey Cockrum, and many other women. Perhaps in this family of God called the PCA we will find a richer blessing if we learn to love not only the language of fathers and brothers, but of mothers and sisters too.

1. Martin Luther, "The Large Catechism of Dr. Martin Luther," in The Annotated Luther, vol. 2: Word and Faith, ed. Kirsi I. Stjerna (Minneapolis: Fortress, 2015), 315.
2. John Dickson, Humilitas: A Lost Key to Life, Love, and Leadership (Grand Rapids: Zondervan, 2011), 24.
3. Paul David Tripp, What Did You Expect?: Redeeming the Realities of Marriage (Wheaton: Crossway, 2010), 67.

ANGEL OF MERCY

OTIS WESTBROOK PICKETT

Dr. Rose Fairbank Beals, American Female Medical Missionary in India

Otis W. Pickett serves as Assistant Professor of History and Director of Social Studies Education Programs at Mississippi College, where he teaches US History, Civil War History, and the History of American Religion. He is also co-founder of the Prison to College Pipeline Program, which provides for-credit college courses to incarcerated learners in Mississippi state penitentiaries. Otis has degrees from Clemson University (BA), Covenant Theological Seminary (MATS), College of Charleston (MA), and University of Mississippi (PhD). He and his wife, Julie, have six children (three living and three who have gone home to be with Jesus) and are members at Redeemer Church (PCA) in Jackson, Mississippi, where Otis serves as an elder.

~

Women in America have been the backbone of the Christian church for almost four centuries now. This should surprise no one, certainly not historians, pastors, church members, or anyone who has ever lived and worshipped in an organized body of Christians for any length of time. The church in America is merely a blip on the radar of the history of the church globally, but the centrality of the role of women to the American church experience displays a historical continuity over time that began at the crucifixion and continues today. Women made up the super majority (75 percent) of the disciples of Christ who were willing to claim him while he was nailed to a cross in Golgotha. For the one man who was there, three women were there. In my limited personal experience, anecdotally speaking (having worshipped in multiple contexts over the last twenty years), I have found these numbers pretty much hold steady when the church doors open on Wednesday nights, for activities on Sunday morning, for VBS, for Sunday school, for the nursery, for prayer meetings, and for pretty much every other event in the life of the church.

Indeed, standing up to and in the midst of Roman soldiers, women were there to be with and claim their savior. As John recorded:

> But standing by the cross of Jesus were his mother and his mother's sister, Mary the wife of Clopas, and Mary Magdalene. When Jesus saw his mother and the disciple whom he loved standing nearby, he said to his mother, "Woman, behold, your son!" Then he said to the disciple, "Behold, your mother!" And from that hour the disciple took her to his own home. (John 19:25–26)

This is just one of the many sections of Scripture that point out the centrality that women play in the life of the Church and in the ministry of Jesus.

As an American church, despite women playing a central role in religious expression during the colonial era, the First and Second Great Awakenings, the reform movements, and every other epoch of American church history, the church in North America has a comparatively poor record of historically appreciating women and valuing women as Jesus would have. For instance, with regard to American religious history, it has only been in the last forty years that historians have significantly addressed the role of women in the life of the Church. Prior histories dealt mostly with male pastors and influential male congregants. Today, we see continuity of this treatment as the summer of 2018, in particular, has displayed continued cases in the American church of abuse, mistreatment, and marginalization of women in a variety of denominations across the United States. Still, despite this record, women have not vacated the church in America, but have continued to serve faithfully.

Given the aforementioned marginalization of the important role of women with regard to their historical significance to the life of the Church, in this essay I would like to highlight the life of the missionary, Dr. Rose Fairbank Beals. Hopefully, as we learn about her experience and the experiences of other Christian women, it will help us consider whether we are doing all we can do, within a biblical and confessional framework, to celebrate our women, appreciate them, highlight their contributions, and to shift the focus of the conversation away from what women cannot do, within the ecclesiastical context, to what they can do, and how we (as brothers) can better support our sisters in Christ to fulfill their passions for ministry and service within the bride of Christ. As Christ will present his bride as holy, spotless and blameless, so must we, brothers, do all we can to reflect our savior in support of our women so that they feel cherished, valued, supported, and empowered members of our churches and denominations.

I first want to say that I am absolutely honored that I was asked to participate in this volume. I do not consider myself an expert on these issues, but only one who is convicted that we are not doing enough to value our women within the Church. Second, I am a firm believer that we do not fully appreciate the contribution of people without understanding something of their history and experiences. When we study and know the history of a people group, we are much more likely to appreciate all they have been through and therefore more likely to listen to them, value them, and not only appreciate their contribution and presence, but be creative in imagining ways in which we can all partner together for the kingdom and benefit from each other's gifts. When we are ignorant of a particular people group's experiences, then we are much more likely to devalue and lack empathy for that group. However, I would also like to share something of my own experiences that compelled me to contribute to this volume.

A Word about My Own Experiences

As a child growing up in the US South, I saw a very strong female presence as soon as I set foot in the church. Watching my great-grandmother attend church faithfully, watching both my grandmothers practice Christianity, and going weekly with my mother to the local Episcopalian church and later to an all African American Baptist Church on the Charleston peninsula gave me a great appreciation for the role of women in the life of the Church. As a child, my impression was that there were few men around outside the pastoral staff, but there were always lots of women working, praying, and serving. I think it is fair to say that I was interested in the kindness and gentleness of Christ because I saw godly women model this to me through their lives. As I have been serving in the Church over the last twenty years, in a variety of ministry contexts, I ask many folks about their experiences in coming to faith and who God used to bring them to faith. I am usually not surprised to find far more women in those experiences than men.

However, something I noticed about the African American ecclesiastical context that was different from my prior experiences in largely Caucasian contexts was that the pastor took time out of the service to highlight the contribution of women's ministry, to celebrate women who worked on behalf of the Church and in the community. The pastor often asked women to give testimonies and offer prayers for the sake of the body of Christ. In short, it was my experience that African American churches valued the contributions of their female members more than in Caucasian contexts and this "valuing" happened regularly in the context of public worship.

I also remember, as a child, falling in love with history listening to Dr. Barbara Fields in Ken Burns' classic documentary: *The Civil War*. For the first time in my short life, I heard about the Civil War from the perspective of an African American woman. Fields was brilliant and the true shining star of the documentary. I would commend her book *Slavery and Freedom on the Middle Ground: Maryland during the Nineteenth Century* to anyone wanting to learn more about the institution of slavery and the experience of African Americans in the nineteenth century. I remember her saying at the end of the documentary that:

> History is not was... it is. The Civil War... is. It is in the present as well as in the past. The generation that fought the war, the generation that argued over the definition of the war, the generation that had to pay the price in blood, that had to pay the price in blasted hopes and a lost future also established a standard that will not mean anything until we

have finished the work.... The Civil War is still going on. It's still to be fought and, regrettably, it can still be lost.[1]

Those words have stayed with me throughout my life and career. She taught me I have a role to play in this great struggle in American life that we are still fighting all these years later.

Of course, my best friend, spouse, partner, and the love of my life, Julie Thome Pickett, far exceeds me in intelligence, skill, ability, and just about everything else. She has been a constant source of inspiration and has been my greatest teacher. Daily I learn from Julie and benefit from her kind and patient example. Julie has continued to encourage me in thinking about ways we can better value women in the Church and in all areas of life. I likely would not have been able to write this chapter if it were not for her, and I have grown as a Christian man because of her.

We think about these issues often for our daughter's sake and for the sake of our sons. I hope my daughter can walk into a church as an adult one day and be seen as a valued member in the work of that body and envision herself as serving that body in a meaningful way consistent with her gifts, which are plentiful. She will have much to offer because she is her mother's daughter, and she is cherished by Christ.

I hope my sons can be effective in the life of the Church and be advocates for women in their lives and in their churches. Julie's example of faith, love for Christ, compassion, and strong work ethic, as an expert in marketing, office management, and as a mother, will no doubt impact my children and their children's children for decades to come. Julie has been a sounding board for struggling women in the Church and has been a constant advocate for the marginalized in whatever context we have gone. Quite honestly, she should be the one writing this chapter.

When we went to graduate school, we first went to Covenant Seminary, as I was considering pursuing a career in full-time vocational ministry.[2] At Covenant, I started in the MDiv classes, which were mostly filled with male students. However, as I continued and thought more about history graduate education, I switched to the MA in Theological Studies degree, where many of my classes were mostly women, including my wife Julie who took several classes with me. In classes and study groups, I began to listen and hear some of the deep struggles that women in Reformed communities were dealing with, especially while in seminary.

I remember several of my professors at Covenant, most notably

Jerram Barrs and Greg Perry, encouraging us in both word and example, through the pages of Scripture and in the example of Christ, to cherish, value, nourish, and encourage women in the Church and on campus. I am very thankful for these professors and their examples, but I am most thankful for the women at Covenant Seminary from 2003–2006 who sharpened my understanding of God's Word, who quickened my theological acumen, who broadened my historical understanding and who were always patient, kind and charitable with the male students, even when these characteristics were not always extended to them.[3]

I have since known several women in a variety of seminaries who have struggled finding a place. These female students' motives are often questioned, and their presence is too often undervalued. To my brothers in seminary reading this, please see your sisters. Please hear them and value them. Please make room at the table for them and welcome them into study circles, conversations, and the community of seminary. Please advocate for them, as your Savior would, if you hear or see they are being undervalued. Many women on seminary campuses feel isolated, lonely, forgotten, and on the margins of that community. A kind word or an encouraging gesture would be Christlike, brotherly, and most appreciated. Remember how kindly, gently, and respectfully Jesus engaged with women in his own context.

Please do your best to make sure women in your classes and on your campuses feel valued and welcomed as a part of that learning community. I think you will find that your understanding will be strengthened, your exposition of the biblical texts will be more fully applicable to your congregation and, guess what, those percentages I mentioned earlier are likely to be reflected in the churches you will pastor. You can learn how to start shepherding and caring for women in your congregations by how you care for women in your seminary training. Instead of looking at a woman in your class and questioning why she is there, you should be praising God that, in his good providence, he has blessed your learning community with the diversity of his creation.

As I moved on into graduate study in history, I took my first course in Women's History at The College of Charleston which has a jointly offered class with The Citadel. Dr. Blain Roberts was the professor of this course, and she not only taught me a great deal about women's experiences in America, but she was the first scholar in graduate school I remember who actually treated me as an equal. She spoke to me as an equal and offered to help expand my interest on female missionaries in the nineteenth and twentieth centuries as a part of the research for the course. Her class ended up being one of my favorites in graduate school, and her advocacy was very important in allowing me to move on to a PhD program. She helped edit my work and has continued to be a great friend and colleague in the field of professional history.

Another of my favorite courses was in the PhD program in history at the University of Mississippi entitled African American Women's History, taught by Dr. Angela Hornsby-Gutting. When I was in graduate school at the University of Mississippi (2008–2013), the history department worked very hard to recruit African American graduate students and particularly African American women. I had the great privilege of having many women and several African American women as colleagues in graduate school (which is very rare for many history PhD programs across the country), and these colleagues taught me a great deal about the field of history, community, and valuing all historical perspectives.

I remain indebted to these women for all they taught me. Dr. Deirdre Cooper Owens, who came to the University of Mississippi later in my graduate studies, was not only a tremendous scholar, but was one who treated graduate students with dignity and respect. I am so thankful for her example, friendship, and scholarship, but most importantly for seeing, valuing, and treating us lowly graduate students with kindness and generosity. Throughout my graduate education, I benefited much from sitting at the feet of and learning from amazing female scholars and colleagues. I also am indebted to Dr. Elizabeth Payne and Dr. Sheila Skemp who taught me so much about American religious history and religion in the early colonial era. Dr. Nancy Bercaw and Dr. Robbie Ethridge, both amazing female scholars in history and anthropology, served on my dissertation committee and offered feedback, support, edits, and recommendations. Were it not for their kind efforts, my dissertation would have failed in many more places than it did. They have continued to be a support in a variety of ways throughout my career.

In 2014, I had the pleasure of co-founding the Prison to College Pipeline Program with Dr. Patrick Alexander. This program offers for-credit college courses at Mississippi state penitentiaries in Parchman and at Central Mississippi Correctional Facility in Pearl, Mississippi. In 2016, I had the great honor to co-teach (with Dr. Stephanie Rolph at Millsaps College), the first, to our knowledge, for-credit college course (from a four-year in-state institution) to incarcerated women in the history of the state of Mississippi. Dr. Rolph and I taught a class on Southern Women's History to incarcerated, mostly Southern, women.

Often, as the only male in the classroom, my education was tremendous as I heard the depth of struggle throughout American history that women in the South have experienced, as well as how modern incarcerated women saw historical continuity with their own situations and experiences. I am absolutely positive that I learned far more from Dr. Rolph and those students than I ever taught them. However, I think those students also appreciated a male professor sometimes just being quiet, listening, and learning from them. This experience left a tremendous impact on my life.

Finally, it has been a great pleasure to know and befriend Dr. Alicia Jackson at Covenant College. Dr. Jackson is also a graduate of the History PhD program at the University of Mississippi, and we have presented on panels together at the Conference on Faith and History and both have contributed chapters to a volume entitled *Southern Religion, Southern Culture: Essays Honoring Charles Reagan Wilson*. One of the great honors of my life was when she invited me to speak at both chapel and at Constitution Day at Covenant College. Her kind and gracious introduction was one I will always remember.

I mention all of these examples because I think it is very important that men continue to learn about women's history, but also that they learn it from female authors and writers. I also think it is important to have professional relationships where men are consistently being taught by and learning from women. This can be hard in a denomination that does not ordain women, so pastors and elders in Reformed contexts have to think creatively about ways they can learn from female peers. This could be befriending and hearing from the experiences of an ordained woman in another denomination, reaching out to female thought leaders in your own denomination, reading female Christian writers, or listening to podcasts from Christian women.

As I have moved in Reformed circles now for the last twenty years, I have come across many learned men. However, few of those men had the opportunity, after college, to learn from women, in an educational context, while pursuing their MDiv or continuing education. I believe this is a major issue facing how those in Reformed circles value women and women's contributions in ecclesiastical contexts.

Throughout my career I have benefited from learning from amazing female historians and scholars. The field of history would be incredibly lacking if it did not have women's voices as women have typically made up the majority of any human civilization. What kind of history would we be writing if we excluded more than half of the population we are seeking to understand from the writing of history? Likewise, if most churches are made up of a majority of women, who are doing much of the work of the Church, then the question must be asked: Are we fully valuing the contributions of women like we should? It is my belief we are not doing all we can and need to do. Christians, of all peoples, should be known for how we value and care for women. At least in the American church, historically speaking, I am not sure this has been our reputation.

I believe it would benefit our pastors and elders, our seminary students, our college students, and our young men in our churches, to find more ways to seek learning opportunities from women. This can happen in conversations, by reading books authored by women, by learning about the history of women, by attending lectures, seminars, and public speaking engagements by women, and by having more women educators in the appropriate contexts in our seminaries and churches. However, one of the best ways we can begin to value women in the Church more is by studying the history of women and how they have faithfully served, often without much acknowledgement.

Having said that, let me now turn to a brief history of the life and career of Dr. Rose Fairbank Beals.

Rose Fairbank Beals

Missionaries have played a significant role in US and world history. Throughout the late nineteenth and early twentieth centuries, medical missionaries brought new medicines, surgical procedures, and advanced medical technology to massive populations around the globe. Dr. Rose Fairbank Beals, one of the first medically trained American female missionaries in India, described her work, writing, "It was because they had heard about the Wai Hospital that they had come," and, "The blind girl is given a cot in the Children's Ward. The nurses are kind to her; she sometimes hears singing. And then there is an operation for infantile cataract; a few days of quiet rest; and the bandages are taken off her eyes." Beals went on to describe the girl's recovery and reaction:

Gradually, gradually—it takes two or three days indeed before the little girl realizes that she can see. And then she begins to make out color and people moving about. And, at last on the day that they go home, the little girl, blind no longer, catches and holds the hand of the doctor standing near her, and with great eagerness shows how she can see.[4]

Her patients and the villagers of Wai called Beals the "angel of mercy," and for many a blind Indian child, indeed she was.

Christian missionary presence has a rather short record in India compared to the country's vast history. Bengal was the first region in India to experience Christian missionaries of the Jesuit Order, coming with the Portuguese in the late sixteenth century.[5] The first Protestant missionary in Bengal was John Zachariah Kiernander, a member of the Royal Danish Mission in 1740. By 1850, more than one quarter of Protestant missionaries in the world were in India.[6] However, the majority of these early missionaries were men, and "main missionary societies largely took the view that only ordained men were fitted to engage in 'spiritual warfare' with the forces of paganism and heathenism in India."[7] However, as the nineteenth century ended, the women's suffrage movement in England began to question the assumptions of women's roles in society, particularly with a concern for medical vocations.[8]

Historian Antoinette Burton wrote, "The conviction that Indian women were trapped in the 'sunless, airless,' and allegedly unhygienic Oriental Zenana motivated the institutionalization of women's medicine and was crucial in helping the professionalization of women Doctors in Victorian Britain."[9] The Indian Zenana women were "imagined as imprisoned and awaiting liberation at the hands of Englishwomen's benevolence," which "exercised a generally powerful ideological force in this period."[10] Indeed, female British doctors relied heavily upon the bodies of Indian women in order to gain clinical experience, but also for training in specializations.[11]

Indian women also provided an audience and opportunity for female Christian missionaries to spread their message. Medical missions provided excellent access, because when a Christian was healing someone physically, they were generally regarded as less hostile. Fanny Butler, one of the first female medical missionaries in India put it this way: "It was a means of approach to many who were inclined to be hostile to [missionaries'] teaching, but could not resist it when it was expressed in acts of mercy."[12] Proceedings of the South India Missionary Conference of 1858 pointed out by G. A. Oddie in his monograph, *Social Protest In India*, corroborated this mentality. Missionaries thought of medical missions as one of the best methods of disarming resistance and intolerance, particularly among Muslims and in isolated areas, and of attracting the people and of disposing them in support of tolerating Christian education.[13]

Known in India as "Dr. Madam-Saheb," Dr. Rose Fairbank Beals' work, faith, family, vocation, and her life as a missionary has left a tremendous impact on the field of medical missions, but also on the Christian witness in India. She was a missionary and practiced medicine in a context of "entrenched patriarchalism of institutionalized religion and institutionalized medicine."[14] It is in this context that Beals labored, and it was here, in her role as a female American medical missionary, that she was able to transcend traditional societal restrictions. Thankfully, largely because of Beals's example, and that of other female missionaries in the early twentieth century, most denominations now support sending female missionaries. Further, Beals's medical ability displayed to hospitals and medical agencies that women were more than competent doctors and were able practitioners of the medical profession, even under the direst conditions.

Rose Fairbank Beals was born on August 1, 1874, in Ahmednagar, India, the daughter of Mr. and Mrs. Samuel Fairbank, who were missionaries in India for more than fifty years.[15] In 1879, Samuel Fairbank sent his daughter Rose back to America to begin her education. She later matriculated at Smith College in Northampton, Massachusetts, and in 1895, she attended Johns Hopkins University Medical School, becoming one of the first women to earn an MD from that institution in 1900.

After medical school, Rose Fairbank returned to India under the sponsorship of the American Board of Foreign Missions to serve as a medical missionary, and she took charge of a Missionary Hospital in Western India called Union. During this time, Rose Fairbank met Dr. Lester H. Beals, they fell in love, and were married in 1905. They settled in the town of Wai in the Satara District of the Bombay Province, and in 1908 the couple opened the American Marathi Mission. It was here that they spent the bulk of their lives working as physicians for the people of Wai, as well as the surrounding villages. Together, the Beals built the mission into the Willis F. Pierce Memorial Hospital, which they managed jointly until their retirement in 1941. Beals wrote, "For here [India] is our home, and the privilege of work, in a corner of the earth where we seem to be greatly needed."[16]

In 1923 the Beals opened the children's ward, and in 1926 the women's ward followed.[17] Rose Beals was in charge of the women's and children's wards, and she performed all manner of surgeries and medical treatments, including cataract surgery, treatment of bubonic plague, dysentery, pneumonia, Caesarean, appendicitis, asthma, abscess of the neck, urine suppression, cholera, abdominal tumors, fractures, heart and kidney ascites, burns, and lockjaw, among others. Nevertheless, cataracts, pneumonia, and the plague seemed to be the most prevalent ailments of Indian people in this district.[18] In a section of *The Silver Jubilee,* a history of Willis F. Pierce Memorial Hospital, some residents reflected on how the hospital helped the people of Wai, especially those in rural parts of India that did not have medical opportunities in the city. One patient recalled:

> As the years have gone by and Government has developed its medical centers in larger towns and cities, mission hospitals in large places had not had such opportunities as the hospitals lying out among the villages where the need is not so well met. And now, with the stress there is on Rural Reconstruction, one sees that the Wai Hospital, gradually as the years went by, has naturally grown and fitted into this need.[19]

The hospital also did well to adapt to village life in India. The staff developed the hospital into a place where it was "pleasant and easy for the orthodox, for the poor, for the very shy and fearful, for veiled women who have seldom if ever been in public places, as well as for the well-to-do and more sophisticated to come here." The testimony went on to report that "it has resulted, in this district, that people like to come into the Wai Mission Hospital. They do not fear operations, but beg for them. They come from far and near, and they find it very hard indeed when sometimes we have to turn some hopeless one away, saying that we cannot help him."[20] Indeed, it was the overall thrust throughout Beals's writings that there was always too much work to do rather than not enough. People came in large numbers to be healed at Wai by Beals, and she remarked, "Endless other ills and ails have a claim on our time."[21]

As a female physician in the early twentieth century, traditional Western gender roles for medicine severely limited Beals's prospects. India was the place that provided Beals the opportunity, as well as the freedom, to practice her vocation. The simple fact was that there were many people in India who needed medical attention, and there were few doctors. This provided Beals an opportunity to practice her discipline (both medicine and missions) in a place of prominence in Indian society. She was known as "Doctor Madam-Saheb" and was treated with much respect even by Hindus, who considered her an "untouchable" due to her low caste. Beals was motivated to help the poor of India receive medical attention, and this moved her to go to rural western India as a medical missionary. Throughout this work, Beals effectively challenged both the traditional roles of women in India as well as in the United States.

Beals was able to help challenge traditional gender roles among Indian people simply by her presence as a female medical missionary. She described in one letter an invitation to have tea and visit the Begam Saheba, who was the wife of the Nawab Saheb, and thus kept in strict "purda" or within the walls of her home. The Nawab Saheb represented the Muslims from Wai in the National Legislative Assembly at Delhi. Beals stated that Begam Saheba "confided to me that her husband was himself teaching her English. And I believe one of these days she will come out of that seclusion and confinement, and shine as the true lady that she is."[22] No doubt, Beals's presence as a female physician with a very public role must have left a tremendous impression on Begam Saheba. Throughout her career, Beals supported the education of women in India and was personally responsible for educating many women herself. By doing so, she showed to the women around her that they had value as image-bearers of God, and her children were watching her example, just as she had watched her father and mother.

In one of Beals's memoirs, entitled "Special Medical Story from India," she chronicled her work in a Zenana Hospital, or a hospital for women only, where she was the head physician of this ward as well as the children's ward. One afternoon Beals was surprised to find "a Mohammedan gentlemen standing inside the gate."[23] She quickly learned that the Maharaja's daughter, a princess who had recently been married, had fallen ill and a "lady doctor" was needed as soon as possible. This princess could only have contact with women, and therefore it was imperative that Beals come to her aid or the woman would die. The sorrowful doctor looked at the dispensary room crowded with patients and refused the request knowing that the princess was more than seventy or eighty miles away in Tikamgarh, the capital of Orchha.

However, after her noonday meal, and after most of the patients had been treated, Beals decided to make the long journey by train, ox cart, elephant, and carriage to Orchha. When she arrived, she found that the patient was under "strict 'purda' (behind curtains) and that no medical man could see her."[24] Beals found that the princess was suffering from dysentery, and she was able to do much for her afflicted condition. After five days, the patient responded well and many in her company offered thanks and respect to Beals.

Beals and the princess became close friends, and the princess told her that she could not read or write. Beals "told her about American girls" and about "why I had come way out 12,000 miles to do what I could for her and for others." Beals became the court favorite on the last day, and the king spoke with her about America. She was compensated a tidy sum of "over 100 rupees a day and 50 rupees bakshish." Beals closed her story with the statement, "Such was India, but now it has developed greatly. And such was and is the life of a woman missionary doctor."[25] We can only speculate as to what kind of impact Beals might have had on the princess or her husband, but we can affirm that only a woman and only a female doctor could have done what Beals did to save this woman's life. Had the practitioners of missions or medicine kept women from participating in either field, then the Gospel might have never gone behind these walls and, likely, this woman would have died.

As an American female physician, Beals was in a special position to help raise women out of isolated positions. While spending time healing the young princess, Beals embodied her willingness to go out of her way to heal people and to be an example of an educated Christian woman. First, her presence proved to Indian women that they were capable of such high scholastic vocations as being a physician. Second, she provided an example to the princess of a Christian woman who was highly educated and had value both inside and outside of a marital context. Third, Beals showed the Maharaja, Prime Minister, men, women, and children of Tikamgarh that she succeeded in her occupation and that other women, if given the chance, could succeed in any number of professions.

As a wife and mother, Beals also transformed traditional roles of women in India and the United States. Through much of the family papers, it was clear from her husband Lester Beals's writings that she was seen as completely equal in skill, intellectual prowess, and spiritual consciousness. For Beals, her "mission" was to help and heal her people by treating their physical ailments while also providing a context where her patients could hear about Jesus and Christianity. Presentations of the Gospel of Jesus took place on Thursday evenings in the Wai hospital. On these nights, "We have some Hindus-Brahmins in to read the Bible. It is called 'reading the Bible,' and that is what we do, but we realize quite well that those who come may not be quite so keen on reading the Bible as they are on getting practice in English. But it gives the opportunity for intimacy, for talk on deep religious subjects, and breaks down barriers, and draws us together. So we do it."[26]

Another characteristic, which seemed to be prevalent throughout Beals's missionary style, was the way in which she shared the Christian faith. Many missionaries throughout history have often been unwilling to accept another's culture as having a place in Christianity. However, on August 20, 1920, in a letter home to friends in America, Beals wrote that "all castes are gathered there from the Brahmin to the outcaste, whatever castes or conditions happen to be in the hospital at the time. And somehow or other we sit together, facing each other, singing together, listening together, and praying together, we are drawn together." She went on to write, "We come away friends. Hindus, Mohammedans, and Christians have joined together in worshipping God. And sometimes I give thanks for the limitations of our hospital."[27]

It was clear that Beals welcomed everyone into the hospital and allowed people from different faiths to participate in Christian worship without forcing them to change who they were, culturally speaking. One scholar has defined missionary work as "an attempt to introduce the Christian religion into a non-Western society, irrespective of whether or not the members of this society are actually in need of being confronted with another religion."[28] However, the healing of many people, both medically and spiritually, in Western India due to the efforts of the Beals and other medical missionaries cannot be underestimated or underappreciated, as this definition seems to do. Rose Beals was willing to give up many of the comforts of home to go into a largely unknown place in order to help people who did not possess advanced medical technology. Further, her presentation of the Gospel of Christ happened in the context of love and care for her neighbor, not as a part of an imperialist agenda.

Noted internationally for their work in fighting the bubonic plague with the use of inoculations, the British government recognized Beals and published her joint notes with her husband on the subject. Further, Beals was honored in many ways upon her return home to the United States. She was invited to speak at a variety of places, including Pilgrim Hall in Boston; Women's Club meetings; various churches, including in East Orange, Newark, and Vermont; classes on Mission Studies; the Smith College Alumnae Council; and on what she called her "speaking tours."

She wrote, "I am starting out this week to try to help the Board by speaking in many places in Massachusetts under a Speakers' Bureau connected with our Congregational Churches."[29] Later she related to her family, "You probably have all heard rumors of the 'speaking tour' which I undertook. Indeed almost everyone wondered whether such a thing were possible; and not a few wrote to Mrs. Carver, the manager of the Speakers' Bureau in Boston, to expostulate with her and tell her that she was expecting too much of Dr. Rose Beals."[30]

Later in her life, Smith College honored Dr. Rose Fairbank Beals with an Honorary Doctorate of Science, a result of her distinguished medical service in India. The Bealses finally retired and settled in California in 1945 in a home known, fittingly, as Pilgrim Place. Dr. Rose Fairbank Beals died on March 24, 1955, leaving behind three children and several grandchildren.

The life of Dr. Rose Fairbank Beals was truly significant and provides an interesting case study of an individual who not only helped to shape the history of women in India, but women's history in America and the fields of medicine and missions as well. Just as Beals went to India and, as the opening story of this chapter suggested, helped the blind to see, would the example of Dr. Rose Fairbank Beals help those of us in the American church with our blind spots? Would we see women in our churches, value them, cherish their work, nurture their gifts, and celebrate their efforts?

Would this brief study of Beals encourage more men to study and examine the history of women in the Church and teach their young men about the contribution of women in Christianity, from the cross at Golgotha, to the mission field, to the ladies in their own churches, whom Christ will welcome in one day with the words, "Well done, good and faithful servant"? Would we be preparing our men to value and treasure women in their churches, because Christ will be treasuring all of us in eternity and we will spend all of time with one another in mutual love and admiration that will be perfect? Let us live into that reality now with the kingdom to come as our focus and with our Savior, Jesus Christ, as our great example.

---

1. *The Civil War*, episode 9, "*The Better Angels of Our Nature*," directed by Ken Burns, aired September 27, 1990, on PBS.

2. I say "we" went to graduate school because I see the degrees I have earned as Julie's as much as they are my own. She labored constantly for many years to help me attain a terminal degree and is deserving of the title and all the honors, rights, privileges, and responsibilities belonging to those degrees. Julie T. Pickett is my love and my hero.

3. I was also encouraged by the recent Covenant Seminary Alumni Gathering at the Presbyterian Church in America General Assembly in Atlanta, GA (2018), where President Dalby announced that the seminary is looking to hire more female faculty. I think this will benefit their students and the seminary community tremendously.

4. *The Silver Jubilee 1913–1938: History of the Willis F. Pierce Memorial Hospital, Memories, and Meditation*, box 11, folder 7, Fairbanks Family Collection, Duke University Special Collections. The Fairbanks Family Collection at Duke University Special Collections will be referred to throughout the rest of the examination as FFC, DUSC.

5. S. K. Bhattacharya, Christian Missions, Missionaries and Indian Society: A Socio-Economic Study (New Delhi: Mohit Publications, 1999), 66.

6. J. C. Ingleby, Missionaries, Education and India: Issues in Protestant Missionary Education in the Long Nineteenth Century (New Delhi: ISPCK, 1998), 33.

7. Ibid., 33.

8. 9. Benoy Bhusan Roy and Pranati Ray, Zenana Mission: The Role of Christian Missionaries for the Education of Women in 19th Century Bengal (New Delhi: ISPCK, 1998), 8.

9. Antoinette Burton, "Contesting the Zenana: The Mission to Make 'Lady Doctors for India,' 1874–1885," The Journal of British Studies 35, no. 3 (July 1996): 369.

10. Ibid., 369.

11. Ibid., 393.

12. Ibid., 378.

13. G. A. Oddie, Social Protest in India: British Protestant Missionaries and Social Reforms 1850–1900 (New Delhi: Manohar Publishing, 1979), 23.

14. Antoinette Burton, "Contesting the Zenana: The Mission to Make 'Lady Doctors for India,' 1874–1885," 381.

15. "Rites Conducted for Woman Who Served in India," 24 March 1955, Claremont, Copy of Newspaper Clipping, box 12, folder 8, FFC, DUSC.

16. Rose and Lester Beals, "Letter to Friends in America," 1 October 1927, box 12, folder 1, FFC, DUSC.

17. *The Silver Jubilee 1913–1938: History of the Willis F. Pierce Memorial Hospital*, box 11, folder 7, FFC, DUSC.

18. Rose Beals, "Letter to Friends in America," 20 August 1920.

19. *The Silver Jubilee 1913–1938: History of the Willis F. Pierce Memorial Hospital, Memories and Meditation*, 1.

20. Ibid.

21. Rose Beals, "Letter to Friends in America," 1 March 1921.

22. Rose and Lester Beals, "Letter to Friends in America," 20 September 1921.

23. Rose Beals, "Special Medical Story from India," 1905.
24. Ibid., 3.
25. Ibid., 15.
26. Rose Beals, "Letter to Friends in America," 1.
27. Ibid.
28. J. Boel, Christian Missions in India: A Sociological Analysis (Amsterdam: Graduate Press, 1975), 69.
29. Rose Beals, "Letter to My Dear Family," February 25 1934.
30. Rose Beals, "Letter to My Dear Family," 16 April 1934.

A THIRD WAY

SCOTT SAULS

Scott Sauls has served as a pastor at Christ Presbyterian Church in Nash-ville, Tennessee, since 2012. Previously, Scott was a lead pastor at Redeemer Presbyterian Church in New York City and planted churches in Kansas City and St. Louis. He has degrees from Furman University (BA) and Covenant Theological Seminary (MDiv) and has written four books: Jesus Outside the Lines, Befriend, From Weakness to Strength, *and* Irresistible Faith. *Scott and his wife, Patti, have two daughters and enjoy live music, reading and discussing books, and hiking Nashville's lovely Warner trails.*

"Dad, why do only men get to be pastors and elders in our church?"

Our oldest daughter was ten when she raised this question at our dinner table. As you might imagine, she caught me off guard. During her lifetime (and also, to this day, during mine), I have served as pastor in churches where only men can be preachers, pastors, and elders. So, you can imagine the challenging—not to mention delicate—discussion that followed as we informed our inquisitive daughter that in fact, many Christian traditions and denominations *do* have men *and* women who serve as their pastors and elders... but ours was not one of them. Further-more, many of our own Christian friends are women who sometimes preach sermons for Sunday worship and sometimes serve as elders in local churches... but ours was not one of them. Her initial response to these realities was one of dismay.

"So," she responded, "you're saying that if someday I decide that *I* want to be a pastor or a preacher, in *our* church the answer would be no? You're saying that I would have to go somewhere else—to a different kind of church than the one I grew up in—to be accepted in this role?"

"Well, I suppose the answer would be yes," I sheepishly replied. Then, I attempted to explain to her the differences between churches and traditions on this particular subject. As I did, I also explained that good-hearted, biblically serious Christians can have differing viewpoints on certain things... and that women's roles in the Church have historically been among them.

Several years later in a similar conversation, I also explained to her how our own church encourages women to exercise their gifts for leading and serving fully, and in multiple ways. Approximately half of the senior directors on our staff are women who lead our women's ministry but also faith and work integration, missional living, mercy and justice partnerships, music and worship, counseling and congregational care, children's ministries, hospitality, and more. Several of our women serve the Church as commissioned deaconesses, alongside and in partnership with our ordained deacons. Many of the advisers to the senior pastor are women. Women lead in our worship services by reading Scripture, leading in the prayers of the people, giving testimonies of God's grace in their lives, collecting the offering, and speaking words of encouragement to fellow believers around the communion tables. Our elder meetings include women who, though not elders themselves, offer their perspective and wise counsel to the elders. The committees of our church, including several chairpersons, are populated with women as well as men. "These are just a few things," I offered to our daughter, "that we do in our effort to follow what we believe is one of God's priorities for his Church—that *every* member, not just the men, exercise her or his spiritual gifts and abilities to the utmost."

"Hmmm... OK," she replied in a partially convinced, yet still uncertain tone. "I'll have to think about that."

On a personal note, I would add that I *love* and wish to honor the inquisitive spirit our daughter brought to the table on this, as well as many other important subjects during her childhood. I want also to add that when I get to heaven, I could discover that I and those who believe as I do on these matters got some things wrong. As I hope the rest of this essay will support, I have come to believe that there are good points to be made from Scripture on all sides of the issue. This is one of those places where Christians ought to be quick to listen, slow to speak, and ever so careful not to pass judgment on others who have drawn different conclusions based on *their* careful study of Scripture.

A Real-Time Debate Among Believers

This same conversation is not limited to family dinner tables, but is also alive in churches, the blogosphere, and on social media feeds everywhere. The debate over gender roles in church, and also home, has become very personal for many believers. Though differences between churches and denominations have existed for quite some time, the debate around gender roles has been highlighted anew—especially in recent years through the publishing of egalitarian books such as *Junia Is Not Alone* by Scot McKnight and *A Woman's Place* by Katelyn Beaty, along with their complementarian counterparts such as *Jesus, Justice, and Gender Roles* by Kathy Keller and *Redeeming the Feminine Soul* by Julie Roys. These and many other books are ones from which I, in seeking to learn from perspectives similar to *and* different than my own, have benefited greatly because of their serious-minded engagement with the biblical text.

On one side of the debate is the *egalitarian* view, which says that both men and women can (and should) exercise their gifts equally and without distinction in both church and home. This includes preaching and formal leadership roles such as pastor, elder, deacon, and co-head of household. On the other side of the debate is the *complementarian* view —which says that while men and women are equals in dignity and gifting, God has assigned the two genders different, and in some cases gender-specific, roles.

Whether we land on the side of the egalitarian or the complementarian view, the types of questions being asked by our daughter and millions of others are important ones that require thoughtful, satisfying —and above all, biblically based—answers. On this subject as well as every other, Scripture's relevance is derived neither from traditional nor progressive assumptions and norms, but rather from its ultimate and infallible source, which is the breath of God's Spirit himself: *"'All Scripture is breathed out by God and profitable for teaching, for reproof, for correction, and for training in righteousness,' says the Lord"* (2 Tim. 3:16).

Indeed, Scripture's relevance rests in its ability, as the inspired Word of God, to stand above our different cultures and experiences and personal feelings about this subject or that subject, in such a way as to *affirm* in us that which is right, good, and lovely, and to *correct* in us that which is not.

In many people's eyes, neither churches nor pastors nor parents have done a great job providing the needed thoughtful, satisfying answers to important and potentially life-altering questions around gender roles and differences. Instead, complementarians are sometimes accused of offering answers that feel, especially to women and girls, insensitive and dismissive to legitimate female concerns, as well as to solid scholarship that has yielded more egalitarian conclusions. Likewise, egalitarians are sometimes accused of offering answers that diminish the authority (and therefore the functional relevance) of Scripture in favor of the whims of popular culture and personal experience and feelings.

While in most cases these sorts of accusations are neither accurate nor fair, the questions keep coming nonetheless. Perhaps more than ever, we need clarity about where *he* and *she* fit in God's picture of church and home—for it still stands that *"in the beginning, God made them male and female"* (Matt. 19:4, Mark 10:6). And as with all contested subject matter, the way that we handle these specific issues will, for good or for ill, have bearing upon the witness of Jesus both inside *and* outside the Church. Therefore, the egalitarian versus complementarian discussion merits serious reflection, a humble demeanor, and a charitable spirit from all sides. For reasons that should be obvious, the conversation must be stewarded from both sides with a shared commitment to biblical tenacity, sincere efforts to understand each other's perspectives, a deep reluctance to judge or to become self-righteous about the issue, and above all, to put on love, which binds God's people—even across the lines of difference—in unity and peace.

We must also revere how personal a thing this discussion is for many. For some, especially women who believe they have been gifted and called to teach and lead in the Church, the questions are not merely theological, but also deeply personal. For them, this is not just an interesting armchair discussion, but a question of life trajectory and calling and—just like their complementarian sisters and brothers—of an eagerness to follow what they believe to be the teaching of Scripture.

The questions that must be contended with by complementarians and egalitarians alike, are as follows:

Regarding leadership in the Church: If men and women are created as equals in the image of God as Scripture attests (Gen. 1:27), and if all believers have been endowed with the Spirit's gifts to be exercised for the good of all as Scripture also attests (Rom. 12:6, 1 Cor. 12:7), then should women be held back from preaching and formal leading roles in the Church?

Regarding leadership in marriage and family: If men and women are equals in the sight of God, and if in Christ there *"is no male and female... in Christ Jesus"* (Gal. 3:28), should wives be expected to submit to their husbands in everything? Or should husbands and wives be seen as co-heads of household (Eph. 5:22–33)?

As Egalitarians See It

According to increasing numbers of women *and* men—especially those who lean toward an egalitarian viewpoint—complementarian role restrictions appear to diminish the place of women in both church and home. Many egalitarians believe that complementarian views represent reductionist misinterpretations of Scriptures that say things like, *"I do not permit a woman to teach or to exercise authority over a man; rather, she is to remain quiet"* and *"Wives, submit to your own husbands, as to the Lord. For the husband is the head of the wife even as Christ is the head of the church"* (1 Tim. 2:12, Eph. 5:22–23). Egalitarians contend that while such statements seem clear when presented apart from their fuller contexts, when presented *from within* their contexts they seem to tell a different story.

The context assumed by egalitarians is essentially twofold. First, these Scriptures and others like them were written from a unique, culturally bound, and therefore temporary context in the same way that the Old Testament ceremonial laws about washing hands and eating shellfish were. "In Paul's day," thoughtful egalitarians might say, "women in subservient roles was standard practice just as slavery was standard practice in first-century, Middle Eastern culture. So, if women are to remain subservient in every time and culture, then we would also have to say the same about slavery."

Second, egalitarians contend that Scripture represents progress *toward* an even greater, more just, and more emancipated ideal that would unfold over time, after the canon of Scripture was completed. "By the time we reach the end of the New Testament," egalitarians might say, "slavery is still a standard, and yet waning, practice. But since that time—and not in spite of Scripture but because of Scripture—greater freedoms have been accomplished in societies, churches, and households by virtue of the fact that in those societies, churches, and households, there are no longer slaves." In other words, scriptural teaching around slavery was intended to *begin* or *trigger* a process that would be completed through the work of Christ in later generations, namely, emancipation and civil rights. *Slaves set free.*

On a similar note, egalitarians assume the same trajectory for women in the Church and home. Written from within a male-dominated, patriarchal, and sometimes misogynistic culture (for example, in those days a woman's testimony in court was not considered valid), egalitarians believe that Scripture also envisioned an unfolding process over time, in which women would be elevated to equal status and also equal roles as men. While the Scriptures don't "finish the job" of empowering women to serve and lead in every way that a man can, the Scriptures nonetheless "start the job" that we, in the name of Christ and by the love of Christ working in and through us, are meant to "finish the job."

Confronting Misogyny?

Hopefully, these and other egalitarian tenets can provide us with some background as to why certain forms of complementarianism create angst for egalitarians. Especially when taught in an unfeeling or unempathetic or paternalistic or chauvinistic way, restrictions on women serving in certain roles can have the additional damaging effect of being stifling, dismissive, and even demeaning toward women. Likewise, if presented in a domineering or overreaching way, complementarian teachings can risk diminishing the very important truth that the most *complete* expression of God's image is one that embodies attributes of male *and* female together. Just as God presents himself to us as "Our Father" *and* "like a mother"—and just as Jesus comes to us as an "elder brother" who longs to gather us beneath his wings "like a mother hen" (Rom. 8:15, Isa. 66:13, Heb. 2:11, Luke 13:34)—men need their female counterparts to rub off on them, and vice versa.

Also, and in more extreme cases, some egalitarians would suggest that the very existence of the conversation is both strange and offensive in our late-modern times. Concerning complementarian beliefs about male and female in the Church, egalitarian author Rachel Held Evans has written:

> I've watched congregations devote years and years to heated arguments about whether a female missionary should be allowed to share about her ministry on a Sunday morning, whether students older than ten should have female Sunday school teachers, whether girls should be encouraged to attend seminary, whether women should be permitted to collect the offering or write the church newsletter or make an announcement... all while thirty thousand children die every day from preventable disease. If that's not an adventure in missing the point, I don't know what is.[1]

Concerning complementarian views in relation to the home and marriage, Evans has also written

> [The] premise—that wives must be subordinate to their husbands—is faulty, and... that premise can actually damage marital relationships by, among other things, impeding honest communication... trying to force first century societal norms onto modern-day marriages have proven... complicated.[2]

It is not only egalitarians like Evans who have concerns about how complementarian beliefs are applied in certain, and especially more culturally conservative, contexts (I use the word "culturally" here, and not the word "biblically," for a very specific reason). There are also women who, while holding complementarian beliefs themselves, have experienced marginalization and judgment as they sought to exercise their God-given gifts within a complementarian framework. One such woman is popular and gifted Bible teacher Beth Moore, who wrote the following in an essay on her blog entitled, "A Letter to My Brothers":

> As a woman leader in the conservative Evangelical world, I learned early to show constant pronounced deference—not just proper respect which I was glad to show—to male leaders and, when placed in situations to serve alongside them, to do so apologetically. I issued disclaimers ad nauseam. I wore flats instead of heels when I knew I'd be serving alongside a man of shorter stature so I wouldn't be taller

than he. I've ridden elevators in hotels packed with fellow leaders who were serving at the same event and not been spoken to and, even more awkwardly, in the same vehicles where I was never acknowledged. I've been in team meetings where I was either ignored or made fun of, the latter of which I was expected to understand was all in good fun. I am a laugher. I can take jokes and make jokes. I know good fun when I'm having it and I also know when I'm being dismissed and ridiculed. I was the elephant in the room with a skirt on. I've been talked down to by male seminary students and held my tongue when I wanted to say, "Brother, I was getting up before dawn to pray and to pore over the Scriptures when you were still in your pull ups."[3]

Such concerns notwithstanding, and in spite of gross misapplication of complementarian beliefs experienced by Moore and the many gifted women she represents, there are millions of believers—both men and women—who still hold firm to a complementarian framework. For example, a well-known and very popular Christian network called The Gospel Coalition (TGC) has made male headship in church and home one of its central tenets. In an article on TGC's website called "To My Egalitarian Friends," Kathleen Nielson writes:

> Complementarians find Scripture to speak clearly and cohesively from beginning to end on the subject of human beings as male and female created equally in the image of God and with distinct roles relating to marriage and the church. The prominence and pervasiveness of this strand of Scripture's teaching... makes this a biblical issue that merits and even requires regular attention and discussion—especially in light of contemporary challenges to centuries-old understandings. The fundamentally crucial issue for all of us in these matters must be to hear and obey the Word of God.[4]

So then, whereas complementarians are saying the issue for them is solely about "hearing and obeying the Word of God," egalitarians are contending that perhaps we may be missing some teachings and trajectories as derived *from* the Word of God that could, if we paid more careful attention to them, lead us to some different and, presumably, less complementarian conclusions.

The Bible and Women

In response to complementarian assertions about women's roles in the Church, egalitarians appeal to the Bible in several places. Some common examples cited include the following:

Women Speaking to the Gathered Church

In several instances, the Bible encourages women to exercise their teaching and speaking gifts when the Church is gathered. Specifically, women are empowered to exercise the gift of prophecy—or speaking God's word to the community—in both the Old and New Testaments.

The prophet Joel, speaking of the coming days, God will pour out his Spirit on all flesh: *"Your sons* and daughters *shall prophesy... even on the male and female servants I will pour out my Spirit,"* which we later see fulfilled in the book of Acts (Joel 2:28–29, 2:17–18, 21:9, emphasis added). In Luke's Gospel, we are told of how the prophetess Anna, who lived her whole life in the temple, spoke of God to those waiting for his coming redemption (Luke 2:36–38). And in 1 Corinthians, Paul gives detailed instructions about how women are to adorn themselves *when* they prophesy as the Church gathers to worship God (1 Cor. 11:2ff).

Women Encouraged to Teach and Lead

Also, and in several instances, gifted women are encouraged to fully use their gifts in the Church to teach and lead. This is where egalitarians have a strong point in contrast to more strict forms of complementarianism. Read within the full context of Scripture, passages like 1 Timothy 2:12–13 and 1 Corinthians 14:33–34 simply cannot mean women are restricted at all times from speaking in a church setting. Furthermore, to interpret such passages in such a narrow way is to promote an environment in which injustices toward women can easily occur, through the stifling and diminishing of their God-given gifts.

Examples are there in the Bible of women using their teaching gifts to instruct others in the ways of Christ. The more obvious passages include those where older women are encouraged to teach younger women and all women are encouraged to instruct children. The young pastor and protégé of Paul, Timothy, for example, had known the Scriptures from infancy because of the faithful teaching of his mother and grandmother (Titus 2:3–5, 2 Tim. 3:5, 2 Tim. 1:5).

The Bible reveals that even in ancient times, Christian women exercising their teaching gifts not just with other women and children, but also when men are present and where men become their pupils. Their teaching was done both by example and with speech. The "wife of noble character" of Proverbs gains praise from her husband, her family, and at the city gates for her example of godly living. We might say that her life itself is a sermon that "preaches" to those who know her. While much of her attention is directed toward her family as wife and mother, it is by no means *solely* directed there. In fact, she is also an industrious, successful businesswoman, and salesperson (Prov. 31:10–31).

There are also examples in Scripture of women giving testimony to the Gospel and exhorting others in public gatherings. The Samaritan woman at the well, after encountering Jesus Christ, goes back to her town and tells everyone—men and women included—about the man who told her everything that she ever did. Similarly, it was women that God chose to be the first eyewitnesses—the "apostles to the apostles"—of the resurrection of Christ (John 4:39–42, Luke 24:10).

Beyond these examples, Scripture also speaks of women proclaiming and teaching biblical doctrine when men are present. After God rescues the nation of Israel from the hand of Pharaoh and Egypt, Miriam the prophetess and other women declare a song of deliverance over the entire community, leading them all in worship. Likewise, after being told she was carrying God's Son in her womb, the virgin Mary composed and sang a theologically rich song that not only became part of Scripture, but that is preached from pulpits all over the world during Advent season. There is also Priscilla, who joined her husband, Aquila, in teaching biblical doctrine to Apollos—one of the early church's greatest preachers—to help him preach the Word of God more accurately (Exod. 15:19–21, Ps. 68: 24–25, Luke 1:46–55, Acts 18:24–26). Clearly, according to Scripture, there are many contexts in which women are free to exercise their teaching gifts. This is indisputable.

Many women in Scripture are presented as remarkable leaders as well. Deborah served as a judge of Israel, and Junia is said to have been *"well known to the apostles"* (Judg. 4, Rom. 16:7).

There are many other similar examples in Scripture that affirm the notion of women teaching and leading. This being undeniably true, if anyone is tempted to accuse egalitarians of playing fast and loose with Scripture, she or he should stop and reconsider.

Stuck in the Middle?

Too Egalitarian for Some Complementarians

As a complementarian who also sympathizes with much of what thoughtful, biblically serious egalitarianism has offered in the realm of scholarship, I have sometimes been accused of holding to a low view of Scripture by some of my complementarian sisters and brothers. The occasional critique has come as a result of my belief that the role of deacon in the Church should be open to women. I have personally become convinced of this view—along with scholars and pastors such as John Calvin, Benjamin Warfield, C. E. B. Cranfield, James Montgomery Boice, Philip Ryken, and Tim Keller to name a few—based on Romans 13:1, which identifies a woman named Phoebe as a *diakonon*. In our English Bibles, this Greek word is sometimes translated "servant," and other times "deacon." Personally, I have come to embrace the latter translation because *diakonon* is the same word that Paul uses when he describes the formal role of deacon in the Church. Additionally, and whereas the Greek word in the Bible for "elder" or "overseer" is a masculine word, *diakonon* is a gender-neutral and therefore (in my view) gender-inclusive one. Therefore, it seems to me that even complementarians can support women serving in the role of deacon in the Church (1 Tim. 3:8).

Once, when publicly explaining my beliefs on the subject, I was accused by a complementarian friend in the crowd for playing fast and loose with the biblical text. "You are completely discounting the fact that all seven of the deacons named in the book of Acts were men," the man argued (Acts 6:1–7). "What's more," he continued, "I'm concerned that you are basing an entire doctrine on just one single *obscure* verse of the Bible that's tucked away at the end of one of Paul's letters."

In what I hope was a respectful tone, I responded with a counter-point. To me, it seemed odd that someone who claimed to have a high view of Scripture would hold me in suspicion for basing my beliefs on one single verse of Scripture. For if we hold the Bible in high esteem, it seems that we will therefore treat *all* of Scripture as being *"breathed out by God and profitable for teaching, for reproof, for correction, and for training in righteousness"* (2 Tim. 3:16). Furthermore, it seems that we will treat *none* of Scripture as if it is "obscure" and therefore irrelevant to our beliefs and practices. If Paul, under the inspiration of the Holy Spirit, said that Phoebe was a deacon, then I feel compelled—not because of a low view of Scripture but because of a high one—to conclude that Phoebe served *as a deacon* in her church, and therefore other qualified women should be able to serve as deacons in their churches also.

Too Complementarian for Some Egalitarians

Similarly, there are others on the egalitarian side of the debate who have expressed dismay over those who lean toward complementarian teaching regarding a husband's leadership or "headship" in marriage, as well as the belief that preaching and positions of authority in the Church—for reasons that only God knows—have been assigned to qualified men.

When Tim Keller was selected by Princeton Theological Seminary to receive the inaugural Kuyper Prize named after the influential twentieth-century theologian Abraham Kuyper, an uprising occurred among Princeton students who asserted that Keller did not deserve this award. The reasons given by the protesting students were largely centered around Keller's complementarian belief that God has assigned the roles of preaching, pastoring, and eldering in the Church to qualified men. The student protest was so strong and outspoken that it caused the Princeton authorities to rescind the award from Keller, and to instead present it to a more "qualified" candidate—that is, to a candidate that is solidly egalitarian. Ironically, had these same standards been applied to Abraham Kuyper himself, then Kuyper, like Keller, would have been disqualified from receiving the award that bears his name.[5] Indeed, these are emotional and sometimes costly concerns for so many of us, regardless of which views we hold.

As Complementarians See It...

While unpopular in some circles, especially in a time when conversations around gender have become deeply sensitive and painful, most complementarians would give one, and only one, reason why they hold to the views that they do. Not all complementarians are out to grab or preserve male authority and patriarchy. In fact, most are not. Most, like their egalitarian sisters and brothers who hold the Scriptures in high esteem, see themselves as men and women who are *under* authority. They, too believe, as Luther once said, that on every matter about which the Bible speaks, the conscience must remain at all times captive to the Word of God (and, as the case may be, to one's own well-studied interpretation of the Word of God)—and that to go against conscience is neither right nor safe. Most well-studied complementarians, just like their well-studied egalitarian brothers and sisters, are seeking to be faithful to the whole Scripture, the whole time. Specifically, and along these lines, complementarians believe that the following (and sometimes controversial) statements from Paul were not written to apply only to Paul's unique, first-century, and Middle Eastern context, but to every time and context, specifically in regard to life in the local church.

Paul wrote: *I do not permit a woman to teach or to exercise authority over a man; rather, she is to remain quiet. For Adam was formed first, then Eve"* (1 Tim. 2:12–13); and, *"As in all the congregations of the saints, women should remain silent in the churches. They are not allowed to speak, but must be in submission, as the Law says"* (1 Cor. 14:33–34).

On the one hand—as most egalitarians would agree—it is a grievous error to dismiss these (or any) biblical texts as mere cultural artifacts. On the other hand—as most complementarians would agree—it is also a grievous error to interpret these passages while turning a blind eye to the broader context of the *whole* Scripture, and in a fashion that can limit women from pursuing God's gifts and calling fully.

We must allow Scripture to act as its own chief interpreter. And with this principle in mind, based on the biblical teaching already mentioned that affirms women exercising gifts of teaching and leadership in multiple contexts and in multiple ways, these words that were written by Paul in 1 Timothy and 1 Corinthians simply *cannot* mean that it is *never* appropriate for women to teach or lead in any way, shape, or form in the local church. Rather, there seems to be a certain *type* of teaching and leading in the Church, which, according to a complementarian understanding, God has assigned specifically to qualified men.

In the beliefs and practices of most complementarians, this means the following:

On Male Leadership in the Church and Home

Complementarians understand the word "authority" in 1 Timothy

2:12 (from the Greek word, *authentein*) as referring to the roles of formal governing and a more formal teaching that carries the authority of the governing office—namely, formal "eldering" and preaching in the gathered church—as assigned by God only to qualified men. This belief is based not on the norms of Paul's first-century, Middle Eastern culture where women were held in lower esteem than men, but rather for another, more enduring reason given by Paul: "... *for Adam was formed first, then Eve*" (1 Tim. 2:12–13).

By appealing to God's original creation as the basis for his argument, complementarians believe that Paul was putting forth this teaching not only for his own time and context, but for every time and context, including our current one. Additionally, complementarians see it as significant that all twelve of Jesus' disciples and all of the biblical apostles and pastors were men, and so were all known authors of the books of Scripture. Church elders who had spouses were to be "the husband of one wife." Biblical passages providing instruction about the office of elder or overseer—the Greek words for which are masculine—always appear to be written with men in view (1 Tim. 3:1–7, Titus 1:5–9).

Secondarily—but also significantly in support of the complementarian view—although women served as deacons from the earliest days of church history, there are no known examples of women serving as pastors or elders for the first three centuries of church history.

Along similar lines, complementarian views regarding husbands and wives are influenced by the account of God creating Eve in Genesis 2:18, where it is said that she will be Adam's "helper" (Hebrew, *ezer*). Likewise, complementarians look to Paul's teaching about husbands and wives, again appealing to God's creation design for men and women, as presented in these words from Ephesians 5:22–33:

> *Wives, submit to your own husbands, as to the Lord. For the husband is the head of the wife even as Christ is the head of the church, his body, and is himself its Savior. Now as the church submits to Christ, so also wives should submit in everything to their husbands. Husbands, love your wives, as Christ loved the church and gave himself up for her, that he might sanctify her, having cleansed her by the washing of water with the word, so that he might present the church to himself in splendor, without spot or wrinkle or any such thing, that she might be holy and without blemish. In the same way husbands should love their wives as their own bodies. He who loves his wife loves himself. For no*

one ever hated his own flesh, but nourishes and cherishes it, just as
Christ does the church, because we are members of his body. "Therefore,
a man shall leave his father and mother and hold fast to his wife, and the
two shall become one flesh." This mystery is profound, and I am saying
that it refers to Christ and the church. However, let each one of you love
his wife as himself, and let the wife see that she respects her husband.

The Meaning of Biblical Words Like "Helper" and "Submit"

Based on passages like the ones above, egalitarians and complementarians must contend faithfully with the biblical idea that wives are "helpers" to their husbands. In Genesis, it says, *"The Lord God said, 'It is not good that the man should be alone; I will make him a* helper *fit for him"* (Gen. 2:18). The meaning of words such as this one can sometimes get lost in translation from age to age and from culture to culture. In the modern West, for example, calling wives "helpers" to their husbands can sound diminishing, if not flat-out condescending—that is, until we understand the meaning of the word in its original context. In biblical Hebrew, and especially in the Old Testament, the word *ezer* or *helper* is also a word frequently used in reference to God. God is the helper to Israel, the helper to the fatherless, and King David's helper and deliverer (Deut. 33:29, Ps. 10:14, 70:5). In addition to these, there are eighteen other similar uses of the word in the Old Testament.

If you have ever seen the movie *My Big Fat Greek Wedding*, you may remember the scene where the matriarch of the family says that while the husband may be the head of the household, the wife is the neck, and the neck turns the head. This funny line is actually not far off from the biblical meaning of the term. A wife is a "helper" to her husband in that she *complements* or *adds to and completes* him, by bringing into his life a host of strengths that he would otherwise lack apart from her.

Similarly, the statement from Paul that *"wives should submit to their husbands in everything"* also comes to us from within a context. Wives are also told that wives must submit to their husbands not as if he were the Lord, but *as to* the Lord. This assumes that Christian husbands, in turn, are loving their wives as Christ loved the Church—cherishing her, honoring her, loving her, and deferring to her wants and needs and hopes and dreams regularly. In their book *The Meaning of Marriage*, Tim and Kathy Keller speak of a husband's "headship" in marriage as a sort of "tie-breaking authority"—which should only come into play after a husband and wife have worked tirelessly to come to a consensus *together* on this or that decision. And on the rare occasions in which this becomes the case, unless a husband's Scripture-informed conscience says otherwise, he should think of his God-given "tie-breaking authority" as a means by which to *lay down his life* for her, versus asserting his will to get his own way—because as Paul says in the passage above, headship in the home is a form of servant leadership, and a means of imitating Christ.

Whether a person is a complementarian or an egalitarian, it is hard to imagine how any wife would object to being "led" by a husband who —as Christ also does for us—is consistently laying down his own preferences, desires, and will, in order to serve *her*. Perhaps this is what Paul envisioned for husbands when he wrote the verse directly preceding this teaching, in which he tells husbands to "submit" *to one another* out of reverence for Christ (Eph. 5:21).

Where Do We Go from Here?

Many honest, biblically faithful complementarians and egalitarians will agree that there will be wrestling and tension for anyone who seeks to follow the *whole* Christ and the *whole* Scripture on this particular issue. If we land on the complementarian side of things, we will be thought of by many of our fellow complementarians as compromised by virtue of being too "egalitarian-friendly," and some of our egalitarian friends will think we are either culturally regressive or biblically incorrect in our views. Likewise, if we land on the egalitarian side of things, we will be thought of by many of our fellow egalitarians as compromised by virtue of being too "complementarian-friendly," and some of our complementarian friends will think we are capitulating to culture and therefore compromised.

I would like to humbly submit that in my opinion, this should not be an issue over which brothers and sisters in Christ divide over or pass judgment upon each other about. I would wish to remind the reader and myself that love, according to Scripture, *"believes all things."* That is to say, love gives the benefit of the doubt to those on the other side of an issue, especially when valid points can be made from Scripture on either side.

Ideally, a faithful complementarian should be able to worship and serve Jesus alongside a faithful egalitarian, and vice versa. Likewise, a faithful egalitarian should be made to feel at home at a church led by a faithful complementarian leadership, and vice versa.

One recent conversation I was part of makes the point, in which the wife of an associate pastor in an egalitarian church said, "Most of the time, my husband and I lean in the complementarian direction. That being said, our egalitarian church and its leadership have welcomed us with open arms. We feel zero shame or pressure or a sense of being regarded as 'lesser than' because of our minority views. We feel that our interpretations of Scripture around gender are respected, our right to have them esteemed, and our gifts utilized, and our contribution celebrated."

Similarly, I can think of no better example to end with than Katherine Leary Alsdorf, an egalitarian Christian woman who served for many years under the leadership of Tim Keller, a complementarian pastor in New York City. Katherine, who was the founding executive director of Redeemer's Center for Faith and Work, wrote the following about her experience working with Tim, and in reference to the occasion when Princeton rescinded the Kuyper Award from her former pastor and colleague:

> Like some of the women who have objected and instigated the withdrawal of this award by Princeton Theological Seminary, I do not share Tim's complementarian views. However, I am deeply saddened by the tone of these objections, more so by the final effect.
>
> Tim and many others have come to their position about the roles of women in the church (and marriage) based on Biblical study and deep reflection. I chose to submit to that view during my many years at Redeemer because of the way God was at work in the lives and work of the congregation. I use the term "submit" intentionally. There are many things I have and will "submit" to in order to live out the life to which God has called me.
>
> I have worked at a PCUSA church in which women, even when ordained, were marginalized more than those at Redeemer. I have worked in aerospace and tech (notoriously challenging environments for women), because the work I was called to do was worth it. We ask

our fellow Christ-followers to go out into every sphere of this world, regardless of how hard it might be, to do the work that Christ has equipped us to do so that He may be glorified. Tim has lived out for me, and many others, how to live with Biblical integrity, humility, and generosity, even on—especially on—issues where we disagree.[6]

May God give grace to us all, that we may follow Katherine and Tim's example of being able to love and serve together, even across our differences. Even more, may God give us a willingness—even an eagerness—to open our hearts to the merits of "the other person's view" on these important matters.

This chapter is adapted from chapter six "Him or Her?" in *Jesus Outside the Lines* (Tyndale House Publishers). Used with permission.

1. Rachel Held Evans, A Year in Biblical Womanhood (Nashville: Thomas Nelson, 2012), 255.
2. Rachel Held Evans, "The Absurd Legalism of Gender Roles, Exhibit D: 'Biblical' Manipulation," March 11, 2016, https://rachelheldevans.com/blog/absurd-legalism-gender-roles-submission-piper.
3. Beth Moore, "A Letter to My Brothers," The LPM Blog, March 3, 2018, https://blog.lproof.org/2018/05/a-letter-to-my-brothers.html.
4. Kathleen Nielson, "To My Egalitarian Friends," The Gospel Coalition, August 15, 2012, https://www.thegospelcoalition.org/article/to-my-egalitarian-friends/.
5. Jeff Chu, "Princeton seminarians were outraged over Tim Keller. Here's Keller's point I wanted my peers to hear," Religion News Service, April 12, 2017, https://www.washingtonpost.com/news/acts-of-faith/wp/2017/04/12/princeton-seminarians-were-outraged-over-tim-keller-heres-kellers-point-i-wanted-my-peers-to-hear/?noredirect=on&utm_term=.2c461ea49dcf.
6. Katherine Alsdorf, "Tim Keller Hired Women in Leadership," A Journey Through NYC Religions, March 29, 2017, https://www.nycreligion.info/oped-tim-keller-put-charge-train-men-women-leadership/.

WONDER WOMEN WONDERING
DOUG SERVEN

Doug Serven is a pastor at City Presbyterian Church in Oklahoma City. Doug graduated from the University of Missouri (BJ), Covenant Theological Seminary (MDiv), and the University of Oklahoma (OU) (MPW). He started the Reformed University Fellowship chapter at OU in 2001 and served there ten years. He is the author of Twenty Someone, The Organized Pastor, *and other books. He is studying history in the PhD program at OU. Doug enjoys eurogames, IPAs, the St. Louis Cardinals, OU football, and Thunder basketball. He is married to Julie, and they have four children.*

~

I am born of a woman. Her name is Donna. She's an inspiration, a scholar, a teacher, a prayer warrior, a nurse, an administrator. Her mother's name was Irene. My father's mother's name was Uldene, but we called her Grandma Deanie. I have aunts. I have a sister whom I love. I have nieces. Perhaps I might have granddaughters someday (yikes).

I am married to a woman. Her name is Julie. She's the best person I know. She is faithful, fun, passionate, beautiful, so smart, and an incredible leader.

I have two daughters whom I adore—Ruth and Anna. Ruth is my firstborn, and Anna is the last of four. I have a daughter-in-law, Mady.

They are incredible, and I hope everyone gets the chance to meet and know them. They're amazing young women.

All of us have women and girls in our lives. I'm not unique in that regard. I'm naming them to make it personal. I have in mind the women and girls in my church, all different, all so valuable, all making their way in this life of faith together.

As a campus minister for Reformed University Fellowship (RUF) from 2001 to 2011 (and in parachurch ministries before that), and as a pastor at City Presbyterian Church, I have had the privilege to minister to hundreds or thousands of women. I've had amazing women staff while I served in RUF and now as a pastor at City Pres. They make things go. They're 100 percent devoted to the Gospel of Jesus, our mission as a church to serve people, and for the most part in our denomination, the Presbyterian Church in America (PCA).

For the most part—we have conversations sometimes. We talk about the PCA. It's a topic over coffee or beer or lunch or watching baseball, or studying the Bible or between services.

Let me be clear: None of them are asking to be ordained as pastors and elders. If you're in the PCA for one month, you know that's a nonstarter, a no-go. They've all done their research, and they know we're an extremely conservative denomination, and we won't budge on some things. They're not asking about being pastors or elders. There are places to go if that issue is that important to them.

But they wonder.

They wonder whether the PCA really is for women and girls of all types. They're not sure—when they look around and read up and start to investigate—whether this denomination can really and truly invest in their giftedness and callings. They're not sure whether they can speak up. They're confused about how to navigate a space where people are accusing them of things they do not believe or want or follow. Will they be welcome if they work away from home? Can they attend a presbytery meeting if they'd like to? Will they be listened to by the pastors and session if they'd like to have a meeting, or are they a threat? Is there a place besides the nursery for them to serve? Will they be deemed unimportant if they're unmarried?

My female RUF interns, Brittany and Natalie, have wondered about their futures in the Church. They're incredibly gifted women. They've served the Church, raised money to reach students for Christ, moved to a new state, and studied in a rigorous program. They were not ordained ministers, nor did they seek to be. They were essential, ministering co-laborers to the mission we had for students at the University of Oklahoma. They did it all. They didn't preach on Wednesday nights in Dale Hall Room 103, and they didn't ask to.

They've gone to seminary because they love Jesus and his Church. They knew they wouldn't be pastors, and they never expressed that they wanted to. They love being women, and they love serving Christ. And they wonder about their place in the PCA.

My students at RUF and parishioners at City Pres have wondered. Where do they fit in the PCA? If a woman has accounting gifts or pastoral gifts, or administrative gifts, or teaching gifts, where and how will she serve in the Church? Will she be able to teach or read the Bible or sing songs or help with the finance team? Is this about giftedness or about gender? Again—I haven't heard them ask to be pastors. They would leave the PCA if that's what they wanted. They know there are options in other places. I haven't had many conversations with women inside of our church where they're wondering about being pastors and elders.

Instead, they're asking where they might fit in the body of Christ to be most useful and effective. It's an honest question. There are many churches in the PCA where they wouldn't fit in much at all. Roles are squeezed down and minimized to the safest and least. And while they understand that's a choice for some churches, they're afraid that may be more common than uncommon. This isn't some sort of revolution. It's a question, sometimes with tears.

My daughters have asked. They're insightful, informed, and committed. They've helped with both an RUF and a church plant. They're not on the periphery. They're considered crazy people by their friends. They *love* the Church. They're not asking to be pastors. They get the PCA. And they ask, "Can I make a place here? Will I fit here? Could I invite my female friends here?" These aren't rebellious questions. They're earnest, honest ones.

At our PCA General Assembly in 2016, RUF Campus Minister Rev. Kevin Twit spoke this at the microphone:

> And if you don't think that we have issues surrounding women's roles in the Church, you are not listening, or you are only talking to yourself. Because I talk to your daughters, and they've got all kinds of questions. And while we've said some clear things about what they can't do, there

are myriad questions about what they can do. And with the lack of specific, clear instruction, they are shrinking back rather than serving in places that God would have them serve. And I, for one, think that's a travesty. And all we are asking for is to talk about it, to study the issue.[1]

He was referring to a strong backlash about accepting a nonbinding study report on women's issues and ministry in the PCA. There are some who feel threatened by *even talking about* women in the Church. They feel like it's all been settled. That we're cracking the door to the slippery slope of liberalism if we allow a study report to get into the books. That we're ceding our church to the prevailing winds of culture, trying to be cool instead of biblical. I heard these criticisms of the study committee. They were spoken in public at the microphone. They were written up in blogs, sounding the warning cry of liberalism.

They were also spoken in "private" in Facebook groups, deriding the study committee, predicting doom, chiding Kevin and those who spoke like him and voted like he did.

Women were watching that too. They follow these discussions and debates, and they know erecting a study committee doesn't solve things. The tone of fear and worry about such matters isn't lost on them.

I think Kevin was and is right with his remarks. Others think he's wrong. It perhaps depends on the women you're around in your church or in your city. No one woman speaks for all females. There's not a unified voice. I hate to be master of the obvious, but they have different opinions.

It's possible that you have strained out dissenting voices so that you don't hear them. The PCA is a strange, small place. It could be true that you've made it even stranger and smaller. It could be true, I suppose, that I have hidden Marxist tendencies, or that I'm a liberal pastor who needs to leave the PCA, or that I have secret agendas (none of which are true).

Here's what I hear when I listen to the women I'm around, especially those inside our church:

- We want to be taken seriously, listened to, and understood.
- We want you to include us as much as possible. If there's a way to include us, please try.
- You need us. We want to serve. Don't push us out.

- We sometimes feel like second-class citizens. I know you're good-hearted about this, and you're not always doing it on purpose, but it feels like we're less important than you are.
- Give us as much to do as you can. Work on this. We need your help.
- We love what you have, but when we look around, it hurts us.
- We don't know what to do. We don't have seats at the table when you make decisions that affect the whole Church, and we're 50 percent of it.
- We are smart. We're scholars. We're teachers. We're not asking to be pastors or elders. But don't relegate us to the nursery and the Women's Committee.
- You don't understand. This denomination is dominated by educated, Southern, White men. We want this to change. We can help.
- We like to attend meetings too. When you cull us out, we are hurt by that.
- Your policies and rules are historic, but they may not be best. We'd like to talk about that.

I hear other, more extreme comments as well. That the PCA is not good for women. That the PCA is against women. I know none of us want that. I know my church has not been perfect for anyone, including women. We make mistakes.

We can make mistakes, and we can ask for forgiveness. We can hold the Bible, our standards, and our Book of Church Order, and care for women—all at the same time. We can go as far, as far we can, and that's not the same as capitulating to cultural winds. We can give each other grace and peace without sniping at each other if we come to different conclusions regarding debatable issues.

None of us do this perfectly. We're all somewhat trapped by our culture and our understandings. We're trying to work out what following Jesus means in our minds and bodies, in our time and place, in our churches and families. We're going to make mistakes!

We're also going to need to press into how much we can do to help *anyone*. It's not, How safe we can be. It's, How far can we go? How much can we do?

If we draw the boundaries too narrowly, in too small spaces with culturally bound gender roles, then we'll hurt the women and girls in our churches. We need to open up as far as we can go biblically. We can't clamp down.

Wendy Alsup has an important book, aptly named, *Is the Bible Good for Women?* The answer is a resounding "Yes!" But we know the Bible and the Church have been used against women and girls for a long time, and they still get misused by many today. Women and girls aren't sure whether Christianity is good for women. They're not positive about the Church. They're asking important questions, and they have been for a long time.

We need women teachers and professors. We need women leading worship and reading Scripture. We need women taking up the offering and leading finance teams. We need women present at presbytery meetings, session meetings, and diaconal meetings. We need women serving the Church in every possible way, using their gifts and talents as freely and widely as they can. Not just for their sakes. For all of us.

---

1. Said on the floor of PCA General Assembly in 2016. Comments made at GA are not notated or entered into the minutes. The recording can be found here: https://livestream.com/accounts/8521918/PCAGA2016

RESPECT IS MORE THAN WORDS
MARK LAUTERBACH

Mark Lauterbach is a pastor, soon to reach forty years in ministry. After his undergraduate degree at Princeton University, he completed an MDiv and ThM at Western Seminary, and a DMin at Trinity Evangelical Divinity School. His partner and companion, best friend, and fellow soldier is Rondi. Together they have raised three children and served six churches in Oregon, California, and Arizona. He also trains pastors in Serbia and Brazil, and is a Certified Conciliator. In his spare time he likes hiking with Rondi, reading, listening to jazz, playing golf, and traveling.

~

Let me start with some of my story. I am new to the Presbyterian Church in America (PCA), but not to ministry. I have been a pastor since 1981. For my entire ministry life, I have stood firm on God's order of creation—he made two sexes, equal, but with distinct roles in family and church. I have not read anything that would make me change my understanding of Scripture.

Throughout those years, I have discussed gender roles in the Church. Those discussions were not theoretical, they were about and with people I knew. They were about women in the churches I served. They were about their sincere questions about what they might do. You see, this is not just a PCA issue.

During those years I knew godly men and women who differed in how Scripture applies. There were brothers and sisters of good conscience, trying to be faithful to God with their use of Scripture. Sadly, I have also seen exegetical sleight of hand, twisting Scripture to support what it does not say.

I have witnessed humble disagreement among the faithful. And I have seen sinful strife and arguments. Sometimes the sinful responses included caricatures of the other side and its motives. Sometimes there was fear-mongering by appeal to a "slippery slope." (For Reformed folks this is ironic. I remember the Catholic church's certainty that the Reformation doctrine of *sola fide* would be a slippery slope to sin. Clearly they were wrong. Slippery slopes are often irrelevant.) Sometimes the sin was simple self-righteousness—assertions that one's position is more consistent, truer to the Gospel, or more careful than the view of others.

Over the years, what stood out most often was this: Many competent and godly women, with much to offer the Church, would receive a simple "No!" as the final answer to their questions. They wondered what they could do. They offered suggestions. In response, the door was shut. Period. End of discussion. Yet, in the wake of these abrupt "no's" I saw women respond with godliness to such poor leadership.

These debates have shaped me—the humble and sinful responses, the godliness of many pastors and my sisters in Christ. God has forged in me a conviction. I want to be a pastor who nurtures the women in my church. I want to find ways to say yes that are true to God's Word. My duty is to be more than a naysayer. Or, to put it another way, I do not want to be a passive-aggressive pastor.

What do I mean by that? Passive-aggressive people love to say no, but they do not provide anything positive to replace the no. Saying no does not nourish and cherish. Christian growth is No and Yes. Sanctification is putting off and putting on. Shepherding care is No and Yes. I am called to represent Jesus, the faithful husband of his people. He does not lead simply by negation. He nourishes and cherishes his Church. I believe we are called to practice God's order for gender roles in the Church, but not in the negative mood.

That's why I am writing—to encourage pastors and elders to grow in godly nurturing leadership. Godly leadership nurtures. Godly leadership honors our members, including women. Honor means esteem for the women of the Church. Godly leadership is more than a call to "keep women in bounds." I am convinced that pastors who look like Jesus nourish and cherish the women of the Church.

My experience is this: the problem is rarely about roles. Most of the difficulties I have had (or have observed with others) with women in the Church have not been resolved by clarifying roles. They have been resolved by my repenting of my male hubris and disrespect for women.

God is sanctifying me. Jesus died to make us holy. That holiness shows up in our official debates about our sisters in Christ. It shows up in *how* we speak of the issues and how we address the women asking questions. Jesus did not die to bring us into conformity with Robert's Rules. I have not been to many General Assemblies or presbyteries, but I have heard enough "points of order" during these discussions to last a lifetime. I value Robert's Rules, but sometimes I want to stand at the mic and say, "Point of sanctification." I think God is far more concerned with that than Robert's Rules.

The Big Question

Here is a fact: God has given strong and competent women to his Church. He has placed them with their gifts in the local bodies of Christ. The question elders face is not: "How do we keep them in line?" but "How do we see them come to the fullest fruitfulness within the boundaries of Scripture?" and "How can I honor and respect them for the complementary role and perspective they bring into the life of a local congregation, however my church may define that?"

I like to ask questions. So, pastors and elders, let me ask you a few big questions and a few smaller ones. Here is my first. God asks and wants every pastor or elder to answer this question: What difference would it make if I took women out of your church? Think about that. Think hard about that.

If you cannot even think about it, that is a problem. If you do not see the loss of women as an immense loss, you do not value women. That means you have a sanctification problem. By loss I do not mean you won't have children's workers. By loss I mean no longer having the perspectives and gifts and skills women bring to the local congregation.

Call for Respect

Here is another: Do you respect the women of your church, and do you honor them as the Lord honors them? I grew up in a family where my dad often told stories or jokes that were dishonoring to women. "It's not that married men live longer, it just seems longer" is the one that sticks in my memory. There were many more. Perhaps it was the World War II generation, but no one winced when he said these things. Not even the women. Not even my mom.

Maybe they all knew it was in good fun. But it seems wrong that this form of deprecation was acceptable in public settings. There was a subtle contempt for women as women. I have been around the country enough to know that there is a "good old boys" perspective on women that is much like my dad's. It is usually voiced only between men, and only with men who share the same "It's OK, dear, you're a woman, you can't help it" attitude.

I came into the Christian life under that influence. But God began to tear it down. The primary means he used was Scripture in relationship with my sisters in Christ. I became a Christian at the end of high school. Then I attended Princeton University. There I encountered highly gifted, motivated, intelligent sisters in Christ. In terms of raw ability, most of them could run circles around most of the pastors I know. But they loved the Word of God. They wanted to honor the roles God gave them. These mature women encouraged their brothers, who were usually less mature, to be godly men. Scripture changed how I saw—including how I saw women. That became especially meaningful when I met my wife-to-be.

Out of that group of friends in Christ, God introduced me to Rondi. I knew that God's Word spoke to my role as a future husband and to the qualities that make for a healthy marriage in Christ. I knew my former way of thinking was filled with lies and sin. So, I set myself to think God's thoughts.

I read lots of books. I studied Scripture. Back in those early days of feminism, I saw that roles were clear. But I discovered more than roles. I discovered my wife-to-be was and is an image-bearer. She will one day be crowned with glory and honor in Christ. She was to be my complement, the other half of the jigsaw puzzle that makes me complete—and I was the other half of hers. I saw that marriage was about companionship and partnership. Gender roles were unto union and unity.

Within the roles God has given, I determined she would always know my deepest respect. I determined I would never demean her with jokes, the way my dad did with my mom. I was so convinced of this, I told my dad he could not tell any jokes that deprecated women during his toast at our rehearsal dinner. I also began to see my calling as cherishing my wife into the fullest expression of her gifts and personality. Marriage was a lab. She became the one God used to teach me how to show deep honor while living out God's appointed marital gender roles.

Along the way, I discovered my male pride. What did that look like? I acted like I did not *need her*—that my life was fine without her. She sensed it and asked me about it. Today I think, "Not need her?" I would now say I cannot imagine life without her wisdom, counsel, courage, initiative, maturity—and dancing.

That disrespect showed up elsewhere. I often took her for granted. With the arrival of kids, she took up the role of house manager and stay-at-home mom. But I acted like my work was the real work and her calling was less significant. At the end of a day in which she had washed, cleaned, shopped, nursed, changed diapers, disciplined, all without a break—I arrived home complaining about how hard I toiled and how I needed a rest! I watched TV while she bathed the kids, put them to bed, and folded the laundry. I was clueless.

I could go on. My wife was the real-time, real-person means of God to teach me about women, roles, and my own sanctification. All of this carried over into the church.

So, church leaders, men, do you respect the women of the Church? Do you, if married, respect your wife? I do not mean appreciate them for their domesticity either. Let's be more specific: Do you see that there are women in your church who could do your job better than you do?

Yes, we have gender roles in the Church. But as far as I can see—as it is with my wife, so it is in the Church—women are often more competent, mature, and courageous than I or other men are. In fact, I have concluded that had not God established gender roles, the Church would at times be better served by women being elders and pastors.

I know men who think women are incompetent, by virtue of their two X chromosomes. I know men who think they are tougher and have more endurance in the face of difficulty. Brothers, I have watched moms for years—in the face of a 103-degree fever, surrounded by three children under three, who worked eighteen-hour days around the house for seven days straight—while husbands complained about head colds.

A few years ago, we had a young man in our church who passed BUD/S training and became a Navy Seal. He passed "hell week" while many of his classmates did not. Hell week is five and a half days with four hours of sleep a night and twenty hours of nonstop work. He was impressed with himself, until I told him I would put any mother of three children under the age of five up against him any time, and he would lose. I believe I am correct.

Let me ask another question: Do you take women for granted? I believe if you removed the women from the Church for a month, most churches would collapse into chaos, be filled with dirt, and be condemned as a health hazard. Their bulletins would be filled with typos. Their nurseries closed. And the care of people by phone calls and visits and emails—the fabric of community—would degenerate by 80 percent. Do you take the women of your church for granted?

Another question: Do you pursue the wisdom of godly women in your Church? When was the last time you or your session said, "Hold it. We need the godly perspective of some of our women on this issue?" Can you name ten situations where that would be the right thing to do? Let me prime the pump for you:

- Would you make any change in church life that affects the moms of the church without discussing it with them?
- Would you evaluate the quality of your communication to the church without asking perspective from women?
- Would you, without counsel from women, make plans to improve preaching or public prayer?
- Or plan on bringing better shepherding care, or more effective diaconal ministry?
- Would you discuss needs to be addressed in discipleship without asking godly women to weigh in?

Maybe your response to these questions is: "Women can't be elders." I said nothing about women being elders. You entirely miss the point. The point is your attitude. The point is your dishonor to those whom God has honored and given to your church. The point is your sanctification. If you think that all wisdom is wrapped up in the session, you are in error. Sessions have made many mistakes because they did not get the counsel of godly women.

We are to see our sisters as image-bearers, worthy of honor, and as fellow-heirs of the grace of life. God created male and female. God invested them with gifts and a perspective that is distinct when compared to men. We are to treasure them and avail ourselves of their counsel and gifts.

One more question about respect: Do you trust God's Spirit in the women of your church? That may need some explanation.

Our sisters in Christ have the same justification, the same union with Christ, the same indwelling Spirit, the same adoption, the same Word of God. Do I treat them as believers in Christ who, by the planting of a new heart, want to please God? Or do I treat them with suspicion?

When I was in seminary, our trustees decided to offer a modified version of the MDiv to women. Their reasoning was simple: Why would we not give to women the same original languages, exegetical skills, and training in systematic theology that we give to men? Don't they want to be faithful to God's word, just as men do? Are we afraid they may reach different conclusions just because they are women? Do we think they are less to be trusted than men are?

That reasoning was groundbreaking for me. God sanctified my respect for women. That reasoning also flushed out the male arrogance in me and in others. I listened as other students protested the decision. Their attitudes toward women sounded like parents dealing with rebellious teenagers who were always trying to break the rules or come as close as possible to doing so. In other words, they were suspicious. Let me say this clearly: That is ungodly. Either hold yourself under the same suspicion or trust God to work in both men and women. That someone is female is not reasonable grounds for distrust by elders.

When we, as pastors, focus our attention on keeping women in their place, perhaps we are treating them with suspicion—treating our sisters who have the same Spirit, the same regeneration, the same standing before God in Christ as less trustworthy than men. Really?

My experience is that the vast majority of women in the churches where I have served have been more cautious about stepping over the line than I have. But they have also seen through my male pride, and that is very difficult.

Leadership Is More Than "No"

That brings me to another big question: Do you seek to nourish and cherish the women in your church to the fullest expression of their gifts and godliness in Christ, and do you advocate for them? The greatest service I can do for my wife, and the mother of our children, is to cultivate her in the fullness of her person. That means her personality, her gifts, her intelligence. She is not her role. She is a woman fulfilling a role. I want her to be a thriving woman in the role.

Anyone can say no, but I want to find ways to say yes. How am I saying yes? How am I cultivating the women of the church? If I have women in the church who are theologically minded, I should work to enrich their education, pass articles and books on to them, and ask them for their evaluation of my teaching. If I have women in the church who are administrative, and can lead teams, I should put them in places where they can lead and organize. I should ask their counsel on how we can be better led and organized. If I have women in the church who are exceptional at counseling or conflict conciliation, I should seek to equip them and deploy them with their gifts.

I could go on. But I must ask, pastors and elders, do you even know the gifts of the women of your church? Can you identify ways to cultivate them? And deploy them? And to do so within the boundaries of Scripture as your session understands them?

If you have seen the movie *Hidden Figures*, you know about the example of a male, White leader (Al Harrison). He paved the way for a Black, female math whiz (Katherine Johnson) to be effective. When Katherine Johnson is found delinquent in her work, she explains it to Al Harrison. She notes that due to "coloreds only" restrooms, her trips to use the restroom require a long walk. She cannot do her job because so much of her time goes into keeping the rules of segregation. Al Harrison's response? In short, he takes a crowbar to the "coloreds only" sign. He makes a way for her to do her work without prejudice. He, a man, is the blocking tackle for a woman to run her race more fruitfully.

Al Harrison needed to listen to her. He never would have reached the right conclusion without asking her perspective. Al Harrison is what pastors and elders should be for women—sponsors, barrier removers, and cultivators. We must ask and listen. We alone can take a crowbar to rules that go beyond Scripture. That means consciously cultivating the women in the Church. That means paving the way for their service, within the boundaries of Scripture. That means a change of demeanor from "keeper of the boundaries" to "nourisher of women and opportunities."

Do We Pave the Way?

One of the most effective leaders in our church was the woman who led our children's ministry. She brought order to chaos, excellence to sloppiness, and high morale to indifference. We simply trained her and coached her and let her go to it. We used to say she could run a small country. She showed it in leading the largest ministry in the church.

I have seen a session ask a woman to lead a building committee. The outcome was as good as I have ever seen for any building committee. Another session asked a woman to head up a search committee. She was the most experienced and gifted person in the church at evaluations of personnel and processes for doing a search. We most honor women by knowing their character, their gifts, their skills—and calling them to roles appropriate to them. They should hear us say, "This role has your name on it."

I served on the board of an international mission agency with 700 missionary families on the field in twenty-six countries. The board had been a male-only group for decades, but they decided we needed godly women on the board. We needed their perspective on so many issues. I remember the board meeting where I met Janet (not her real name). She was new to the board. At breakfast the first day, I asked her how she became part of the board. She told me she had been invited three times, but had said no the first two times.

I was curious, "What made you change your mind?"

She said, "Let me tell you the story. Three years ago, the regional director for the mission called me up to ask if I would serve on the board. When I asked him 'Why me?,' he said, 'Janet, we are looking for women to be on the board.' So I told him no."

"Two years ago, he tried again. I asked the same question. This time he said, 'We have women in our churches who love missions. You are one of them. We need women on our board.' I told him no again. I must have discouraged him, because it was just a few month ago he called and asked again. I said, 'Bill, I have asked you why you want me each time. Why do you want *me*?' This time, he said, 'Well, I have been thinking about that. I spoke with a few other leaders in the mission about this. Yes, we need women on the board, but not just any woman. We want a woman with character, serving in her church in missions, giving to missions, with proven contribution to her church in influencing the church for missions. You have been doing exactly that in your church for ten years. You are unique. That's why we need you.' I told him yes."

Do you see the difference? It is not an honor to women in our churches to treat them as a "class"—no, we treat them as individuals, with awareness of their gifts and character.

Pastors and elders, are you aware of the gifts of the individual women in your church? Or do you think only about the men? Here is a quiz: If I called you to ask for the name of three people in your church with leadership gifts, to serve on a nonchurch board (maybe at the local YMCA), would you know the women of your church well enough to name the ones who are gifted to lead? Or would you only know the names of men?

The Upside-Down Kingdom

Here is my last big question: Have we allied ourselves with the dark rulers of the age in our view of power and authority? May not this debate be founded on both sides being caught up in a false model of significance?

No temptation has overcome me except as is common to all men and women in Christ. At the core of temptation is a perspective on power and influence. Right next to it is a view of self-fulfillment through my works and my position.

We serve a Lord who turned things upside-down. He came not be served, but to serve. He did not cultivate himself. He did not take thought of himself, so he might serve us. He did not worry about whether he was doing anything of significance. He certainly did not seem to give his energy to keeping people in line. No, he served others. He said the greatest in his kingdom were servants.

God sees significance and influence so very differently from the world system led by the evil one. In God's kingdom the one who serves the most is the greatest. Pastors and elders, do you serve the most? Or do you strut? Do you esteem people for their true greatness? Or do you honor those who are publicly successful? Are you impressed and aspire to larger churches and higher salaries? Or do you seek to be the servant of all?

Are all your thoughts about your authority and position or are they about doing everything you can to see your people come to their fullest maturity as men and women? Are you a naysayer? Or do you cultivate?

Do you bring out the best in others? Do you esteem the gifts of others, including women, as greater than your own? If you do not live by Jesus' definition of true greatness, why would you expect the women of the church to do so?

Do you put to death the idol of significance? Do you respect your fellow elders enough to call them to humility and service? Do you respect women in the church enough to help them with an idolatry of significance?

My wife is a highly gifted, intelligent, well-educated woman. For forty years, she has faced the temptation to seek her significance according to this present evil age. She wanted to be Secretary of State. That is why she attended Princeton and majored in Russian. But the arrival of our firstborn upended all that. She embraced being a mom but lived with that haunting voice that told her that her life was a waste.

That's not feminism whispering in her ear. That is the same Satan who moved Peter to reject the path of humiliation for our Savior. But I face the same temptation as a man. I do not help her when I bow to the same lies. If my response to her was, "Wait 'til the kids are gone, then you can do something significant," I am joining forces with the evil one. Or if I say to her, "Let's get a nanny, so you are free to do important things," I am on the dark side. Or if my response to her was, "Only men get to do significant things in the church," I am also an ally of the devil.

But if I say to her, "He who is the servant of all is the greatest. Let me take care of our children for a day so you can get undistracted time to read and pray"—then I am both encouraging true godliness and modeling true significance. I want to remind my wife that God will determine who had the greatest significance. And it may not be husbands, nor pastors and ruling elders.

The women of our churches face this shaming whisper. They wonder whether their lives in the Church have significance. We do not help them by simply keeping them in their swim lanes. We help them by examples of humble service and reminders of the true greatness of Christ's kingdom.

Pastor, have you worked in the nursery or taught the children? Have any of your ruling elders? If not, why not? If the Kingdom of God is made up of such as these, why are you not caring for them? Or is that women's work? Beneath you? We help them by honoring those who serve invisibly and being less impressed with those seemingly important. We help them by refusing to worship an idol of significance.

Men and women of the PCA, are you pursuing significance in all the places it is not to be found? The greatest act of redemptive history was the most ignominious—Jesus' obedience unto the death of the cross. But God saw that differently than the world.

Leaders of the PCA, are you grasping for influence and significance anywhere else but following the crucified, the servant of servants? This whole debate would be well served by all of us walking our Savior's path of self-forgetfulness. He did the lowliest task, washing our feet, not seeking his own glory but our good. He esteemed others of greater importance than himself. Have we done the same?

TREAT WOMEN AS MOTHERS AND SISTERS

GREGORY R. PERRY

A Vision of Covenantal Intimacy and Practical Interdependency in God's Household

Greg Perry serves as Vice President of Strategic Projects at Third Millennium Ministries in Orlando, Florida, and Professor of New Testament and Congregational Studies at the Missional Training Center in Phoenix, Arizona. Ordained as a pastor in 1991, Greg taught at Covenant Theological Seminary for fourteen years. He has attended far too many Presbyterian schools and holds a PhD in New Testament from Union Theological Seminary in Virginia. Greg is married to Darlene, and he likes her company in a kayak on Southern rivers, at live music venues, seafood restaurants, and spring training baseball games.

∾

In his podcast series *Ask Pastor John,* John Piper answered a question from a seminary student who shares his complementarian conviction that only qualified men are called to the office of pastor or elder. The student wondered, "Should women be hired as seminary professors?" Piper answered in the negative.[1] I do not question his motives, nor do I believe he intended to harm his sisters and mothers. Nevertheless, as a seminary faculty member and pastor who shares Piper's commitment to the authority of Scripture, as well as his view of gender complementarity in the intimate relationships of marriage and church, I must respectfully, but clearly, disagree. We need female and male faculty and ministry leaders working together in our seminaries and colleges, on our agency boards and ministry committees, and in our local congregations, because it is a robustly biblical, complementarian, and mutually edifying relational practice.

A Biblical Exercise

We need male and female faculty and ministry leaders working together because it is a biblical exercise of the Holy Spirit's gifts for the edification of the body of Christ. Piper drew attention to the text of 1 Timothy 2:12, which recognizes the responsibility of church elders for authoritative teaching in our corporate worship. But the pastor is much more than a preacher, and 60 percent of those who hear him preach are women.[2] Indeed, according to Paul, the larger job of pastors or elders is to see to it that all church members are equipped for the work of ministry (Eph. 4:11–16), a shared task that requires all kinds of gifts, joints and ligaments working together, and many more tools than the important tool of preaching. Paul makes it plain, in Romans 12, 1 Corinthians 11–14, and Ephesians 4, that the gifts of the Holy Spirit, including *speaking gifts* like teaching, evangelism, prophesying, tongues and their interpretation, and *leadership gifts* like administration, discernment, and wisdom are not restricted with reference to gender, and are given for the edification of the whole body of Christ.

In the wake of multilingual, transgenerational, interclass, male and female prophesying at Pentecost (Acts 2:17–18), Paul calls every church member to seek the gift of prophecy (1 Cor. 14:1, 3) and describes women and men who exercise that gift in corporate worship (1 Cor. 11:4–16, 14:26–32). Moreover, he encourages every member of the congregation to *"instruct one another"* (cf. Rom. 15:14, Col. 3:16). Indeed, the edifying effects of instruction from women and men together is depicted dramatically in Acts 18:24–28, where *"Priscilla and Aquila... explained the way of God more accurately"* to Apollos. Paul mentions them again along with *"Phoebe, a deacon of the church at*

Cenchreae," who carried Paul's letter to represent him and his teachings to ethnically mixed congregations in Rome (Rom. 16:1–4).

Indeed, Phoebe's and Paul's co-laboring relationship embodied the interdependent social ethic the apostle articulates in Romans 12–15.[3] Though a Gentile woman, Phoebe accepted (Rom. 14:1, 15:7, 16:2) and helped Paul, a Jewish man who described her not as "unclean" or "common" (Rom. 14:14) but as "our sister" (Rom. 16:1). Though a woman of means, who could have obligated many as clients in the Roman patronage system, Phoebe acted instead as a "sister" by giving freely. Even if, in some unusual case, a first-century Jewish man had benefited financially or socially from a Gentile "patroness," he never would have called her his "sister." By accepting Phoebe and giving her "whatever help" she needed (Rom. 16:2), the Roman Christians would not only start off well with her brother, Paul, they would demonstrate their awareness that "Christ's Body" had family business throughout the so-called "Roman" world.

I have had the privilege of serving on several faculties that remain committed to the authority of Scripture, to complementarian expressions of authority in the home and church, and to training Spirit-gifted men and women for many roles in Christ's body for God's world mission. These faculties are careful not to assume the unique supervisory role of local elders for their students. They recognize the limits of their teaching and discipleship authority in three important ways: 1) faculty members are required to be members in good standing of a local church or presbytery in submission to their elders; 2) members signs a statement of agreement with and submission to the doctrinal standards of their church, standards adopted and supervised by their elders at every level of their church courts; and 3) members do not administer membership vows or the sacraments, nor exercise church discipline in their role as faculty. Nevertheless, the unique role of elders is also limited. So, in the same way, elders must recognize the biblical limits and edifying purpose of their authority in the Church.

Scripture does not recognize a general authority of men over women. Rather, as we examine further below, it describes a particular authority and responsibility given to husbands in relation to their wives, to parents in relation to their children, and to elders in relation to the members of a congregation. The modus operandi for exercising this particular authority is sacrificial love, and its primary purpose is edifying and equipping others, not self-protection.

To extend the particular authority of elders by analogy not only transgresses its biblical limits, it violates its purpose to equip others by assigning tasks to fellow-elders which are not unique to their responsibility, tasks that could and often should be done by other members of Christ's body. Indeed, Piper built his argument on an analogy between the pastoral office and the role of a seminary professor. He reasons, "If it is unbiblical to have women as pastors, how can it be biblical to have women who function in a formal teaching and mentoring capacities to train and fit pastors for the very calling from which the mentors themselves are excluded?"[4]

As we have seen, however, Paul did not restrict teaching to preachers nor mentoring to pastors. Indeed, Paul not only looked to the example of *"a father with his children [who] exhorted... encouraged... and charged [them] to walk in a manner worthy of God"* (1 Thess. 2:11–12); he also compared his apostolic oversight of the Thessalonian church to *"a nursing mother taking care of her own children"* (1 Thess. 2:7).

Pastors and elders need more than male mentors and examples to shape their ministries. Indeed, in his farewell letter, Paul charged Timothy to *"continue in what you have learned and have firmly believed, knowing those from whom you have learned it and how from childhood you have been acquainted with the sacred writings"* (2 Tim. 3:14–15). The relative pronoun is plural because Timothy not only learned from Paul, he learned from his *mother*, Eunice, and *grandmother*, Lois, whom Paul mentions explicitly in 2 Timothy 1:5. Not only in his childhood, but in his Church at Ephesus, Timothy was to honor older women as *mothers* (1 Tim. 5:2), seeking their prayers, counsel and wisdom, not despising their gifts or prophecies (1 Thess. 5:19–21).

An elder is not formed by males only, for males only, but by many Spirit-gifted teachers, prophets, and servants, whether *fathers or mothers, brothers or sisters* in the faith, because he must learn to relate and work well with each of them. After all, pastors are called to be examples of following Christ for all Christians. Remarkably, the character qualifications of elders (1 Tim. 3:1–7, Titus 1:6–8) are required also of all Christians (Rom. 12:9–21, Eph. 4:17–5:21, Col. 3:5–17).

Interdependency by Design

We need male and female faculty and ministry leaders working together because it reflects God's design of covenantal interdependency for leadership in the households of home and church. One of the New Testament courses I teach consistently includes the Pastoral Epistles. As the appointed dates approach for our study of 1 Timothy 2–3, I remind students to invite their spouses into their preparatory studies and to our class discussions, which I often co-lead with female colleagues.

Students arrive, having translated the text from the Greek New Testament and articulated exegetical questions arising from Paul's vocabulary, syntax, social and literary contexts. After our somewhat nerdy, geeked-out discussion of text and context, I often ask, "How many of you are parents?" After a show of hands, a follow-up question, "Who among you has ever tried to establish a parenting policy in your home without prior consultation and agreement with your spouse?" Often, someone shares the unique challenges and joys of being a single parent. Occasionally, a male student states that he has done so as "the head of the household." Our class discussions of texts in their contexts consistently reveal that isolated, noncomplementarian policy-making does not resonate with Paul's metaphor of head-body interdependency, nor does it serve our inter-gendered partnership to form redeemed image-bearers.

"Do we, as elders, sometimes operate like single dads?" Do not misunderstand me, most single parents I know are making courageous sacrifices to nurture and lead their children, but those in our class discussions have said plainly they cannot be both Mom and Dad. Moreover, they are grateful for the additional support they and their children receive from *mothers and fathers, brothers and sisters* in the family of God.

If the images of Christ and his bride, head-body interdependency, and household management are primary metaphors Paul deployed to teach servant leadership in the Church, would we not be better equipped to fulfill our supervisory role if we operate in high consultation with Spirit-gifted women as we do in our immediate families? Would not we fulfill our charge more effectively *"to equip the saints for the work of ministry"* if we were more relationally connected to ministries that disciple women, youth, and children as we are with our own families? Indeed, we would bless and edify our ministry teams, committees, and agency boards, if we used our oversight authority to fulfill our equipping aim by consulting with, nominating, and appointing women and men who are members in good standing, gifted by God's Spirit, and prepared well by life experience and training to guide and support their specific work.

Healthy Patterns

We need male and female faculty and ministry leaders working together to support healthy patterns of covenantal interdependency between men and women, and to correct malformed patterns that undermine the Spirit's gifts, which resource our shared mission of forming disciples. Writing to Timothy and the church at Ephesus, Paul described a familial pattern to guide pure, yet intimate, relationships in the Church between women and men. He explicitly marked gender and age, instructing Timothy not to "rebuke an older man, but encourage him like a *father*. Treat younger men as *brothers*, older women as *mothers*, and younger women as *sisters* in complete purity" (1 Tim. 5:1–2, emphasis mine).

Why is this level of intimacy and interdependency called for? Because redeemed image-bearers are being formed by the grace of God in the covenantal bonds of Christian families and congregations. Indeed, this is the hopeful conclusion of Paul's recollection of Adam's and Eve's tragic story. The narrative sequence of 1 Timothy 2:13–15 echoes Genesis 2–3 in relation to the men and women of the Ephesian church. Adam was formed first, then Eve, who was deceived, but "*she* will be saved through childbearing, if *they* continue in faith, love, and holiness with self-control" (1 Tim. 2:15). The shift from the third person singular to plural is significant. "*She*... if *they*" marks the shared purpose and destiny of men and women in the family of God. *She* is united to Adam to form *they*. *They* conceive and disciple image-bearers "*in the discipline and instruction of the Lord*" (Eph. 6:4).

Ironically, Artemis, the local deity of Ephesus, was the goddess who was said to protect women in childbirth, while some of the "myths" (1 Tim. 1:4, 2 Tim. 4:4) circulating in Ephesian streets celebrated her celibacy, discouraging marriage and sexual intimacy in marriage. Paul countered with a different, truer story about men and women: "*In the Lord, woman is not independent of man nor man of woman; for as woman was made from man, so man is now born of woman. And all things are from God*" (1 Cor. 11:11–12).

This story is embodied in Christian households and the household of God. Salvation is more than mere rescue from childbirth, it is the redemption of all of life through *"one mediator between God and humankind, the man Christ Jesus, who gave himself as a ransom for all"* (1 Tim. 2:5–6). But this redemption, this restoration of image-bearing through the shared tasks of discipleship happens together, intimately, and interdependently. *"She* (and he) will be saved, if *they* continue in faith."

Sadly, some, in the name of complementarianism, segregate and isolate women and their ministries.[5] This is not treating women as mothers and sisters, whom we cherish, honor, trust, advocate for and co-labor with in the Gospel.

Do we seek the wisdom and leading of the Holy Spirit in the gifts given to our sisters and mothers by including them on our shepherding and service teams, on our worship and missions teams, on our faculties, church committees, and agency boards? Elders have the responsibility to oversee and the empowering purpose "to equip the saints for the work of ministry" (Eph. 4:12). Are we co-laboring alongside our mothers and sisters in the household of God, or do we work in structural and practical isolation from them? Our Lord modeled the role of a shepherd as one who was among us as a servant (cf. Matt. 20:20–28, Mark 10:35–45, Luke 22:24–27, John 13:1–17, Phil. 2:1–11).

A few brief examples will suffice to demonstrate the formative power of women and men ministering apart and together, for ill and for good, respectively. In several churches, I have had the privilege of training small group leaders and elders, mercy team members, and deacons together. The session and diaconate of these congregations structured their ministries through small groups (which were geographically organized) and ministry teams (which were organized by tasks). Both types of groups were supervised by elders and deacons, who met with small group and ministry team leaders (men and women) quarterly in a Leadership Community. Many elders and deacons were involved directly in at least one type of group, though they also supervised leaders of other groups. Moreover, they communicated regularly as shepherding and service needs emerged.

In this type of relational leadership structure, Spirit-gifted, nonordained men and women are much freer to exercise their *charismata*, including gifts of teaching and administrative leadership. Because the oversight of elders is visible through their direct involvement and regular teaching, gifted women and men can teach or lead in small groups or ministry teams, because everyone knows they are not the overseers.

Moreover, elders who work closely with gifted nonordained men and women have a better chance of rescuing those who are threatened or abused, as well as those who wander or fall. However, those who keep their mothers and sisters at arm's length foster a culture in which abusers and false teachers can flourish. Without intimate, pure, brotherly and fatherly relations that listen to, learn from, edify and, advocate for our sisters and mothers, the trust necessary for vulnerable truth-telling cannot bear the fruit of justice and repentance.

In the same way that sanctioning discipline has a much better chance of working in the context of loving parents whose unity is palpable and whose history with their children is one of nurturing discipline, the sanctioning discipline of elders has a much better chance of success in the lives of church members who are being nourished by familial bonds with fathers and mothers in leadership.

While there are countless variables in the lives of church members that determine whether or not they might participate in a pastoral process to restore them (Gal. 6:1), the reasons for nonparticipation that I have heard most often are "I don't know them and they don't know me" or "I will be the only woman in the room." Is it not fatherly and wise to structure our nurturing and sanctioning discipline as families, so the interdependency of the men and women who lead the household as small group and ministry team leaders is evident to every family member? Happily, I know a few stories of redirection, restoration, and rescue because elders, alongside female and male co-laborers, shepherded and served their flock together.

Co-Laborers and Co-Heirs

The human mission of image-bearing and the Church's mission of discipling all nations in a renewal of image-bearing is a mission we cannot do alone as men or women, ethnic groups or generations, or as one relatively small denomination. According to Scripture, intercultural, transgenerational disciple-making is a family business, a shared task that requires intimate and interdependent relationships between Spirit-gifted fathers and mothers, brothers and sisters.

In the same way that God designed men and women to conceive and disciple their children together within the bond of marriage vows, he has designed men and women to disciple the nations within the bond of membership vows. We need male and female faculties, agency boards, and ministry team leaders co-laboring under the oversight of highly engaged, collaborative elders to form healthy familial patterns of truth-telling, justice, repentance, and faith, if we are to clearly articulate the Gospel in our words, deeds, and relationships.

In his own remarkable take on the household codes that were a common feature of Roman social ethics, the apostle Peter wrote, *"husbands live with your wives according to knowledge as with a weaker vessel by showing honor to the woman who is also a co-heir of the grace of life, so that your prayers may not be hindered"* (1 Pet. 3:7). Typically, honor, praise or social recognition was owed to social superiors who had acted generously as benefactors to their clients or for the public at large.

Like Paul, Peter acknowledged that all those who are called to share in Christ's sufferings will also share in his glory (cf. Rom. 8:17, 1 Pet. 4:13), *"an inheritance that is imperishable, undefiled and unfading"* (1 Pet. 1:4). They understood that each of us have received gifts for sharing with the other (cf. Rom. 12:4-8, 1 Pet. 4:8-11). They understood that the meaning of "co" is *with*—consulting *with*, walking *with*, parenting *with*, and discipling *with* until we receive our family inheritance together.

---

1. John Piper, "Is There a Place for Female Seminary Professors?," January 22, 2018, in *Ask Pastor John*, produced by Desiring God, podcast, https://www.desiringgod.org/interviews/is-there-a-place-for-female-professors-at-seminary.
2. See "Attendance at Religious Services among Evangelical Protestants by Gender," Pew Research Center, 2014.
3. A detailed, exegetical argument for this translation of Romans 16:1 is provided by Gregory R. Perry, "Phoebe of Cenchreae and 'Women' of Ephesus: 'Deacons' in the Earliest Churches," Presbyterion 36, no. 1 (Spring 2010): 9–36. On the representative and interpretive role of letter-carriers in Paul's day, see Allan Chapple, "Getting Romans to the Right Romans: Phoebe and the Delivery of Paul's Letter," Tyndale Bulletin 62.2 (2011): 195–214.
4. See note 1 above.
5. Please read Aimee Byrd's constructive critique in *No Little Women: Equipping All Women in the Household of God* (Phillipsburg, NJ: P&R Publishing, 2016).